ROUTLEDGE LIBRARY EDITIONS:
PHILOSOPHY OF TIME

Volume 1

TIME AND ITS IMPORTANCE IN MODERN THOUGHT

TIME AND ITS IMPORTANCE IN MODERN THOUGHT

M. F. CLEUGH

LONDON AND NEW YORK

First published in 1937 by Methuen

This edition first published in 2019
by Routledge
2 Park Square, Milton Park, Abingdon, Oxon OX14 4RN

and by Routledge
52 Vanderbilt Avenue, New York, NY 10017

Routledge is an imprint of the Taylor & Francis Group, an informa business

© 1937 M. F. Cleugh

All rights reserved. No part of this book may be reprinted or reproduced or utilised in any form or by any electronic, mechanical, or other means, now known or hereafter invented, including photocopying and recording, or in any information storage or retrieval system, without permission in writing from the publishers.

Trademark notice: Product or corporate names may be trademarks or registered trademarks, and are used only for identification and explanation without intent to infringe.

British Library Cataloguing in Publication Data
A catalogue record for this book is available from the British Library

ISBN: 978-1-138-39397-4 (Set)
ISBN: 978-0-429-40127-5 (Set) (ebk)
ISBN: 978-1-138-39398-1 (Volume 1) (hbk)
ISBN: 978-1-138-39403-2 (Volume 1) (pbk)
ISBN: 978-0-429-40125-1 (Volume 1) (ebk)

Publisher's Note
The publisher has gone to great lengths to ensure the quality of this reprint but points out that some imperfections in the original copies may be apparent.

Disclaimer
The publisher has made every effort to trace copyright holders and would welcome correspondence from those they have been unable to trace.

TIME

AND ITS IMPORTANCE IN MODERN THOUGHT

by

M. F. CLEUGH

with a Foreword by
L. SUSAN STEBBING

NEW YORK / RUSSELL & RUSSELL

REPRINTED FROM A COPY IN THE COLLECTIONS OF
THE BROOKLYN PUBLIC LIBRARY

FIRST PUBLISHED IN 1937 BY METHUEN & CO. LTD.
REISSUED, 1970, BY RUSSELL & RUSSELL
A DIVISION OF ATHENEUM PUBLISHERS, INC.
BY ARRANGEMENT WITH METHUEN & CO. LTD., LONDON
L. C. CATALOG CARD NO: 71-102479
PRINTED IN THE UNITED STATES OF AMERICA

TO
E. A. M.
With Love

FOREWORD

THERE is a time for everything and the present moment is opportune for writing a book about Time. Bergson, Alexander, McTaggart, and Dunne have given us something fresh to think about and to take us farther than St. Augustine deemed possible. And the end is not yet. Those whose interest is mainly in physics are inclined to perplex us with paradoxes and to put us off with a mere t. The plain man may have been led to suppose that Einstein has somehow turned our workaday world into a looking-glass world, but somehow or other the Lewis Carroll-like glamour eludes him. It is well that we should be reminded of the poets and not forget the philosophers and psychologists. They also have something worth while to say. One main value of Miss Cleugh's book lies in the comprehensiveness of its outlook. It will provoke some people—that is all to the good; it will instruct others—that, perhaps, is better; it will amuse those who are not too tightly wedded to their own mode of philosophy to be able to take themselves unseriously.

Someone may say: 'But there really is no problem of Time. We make problems for ourselves by asking the wrong questions. All that we have to do is to take into account the context in which our remarks about time [and, by the way, be sure to spell it with a small t] occur.' There is much truth in this comment. To clear our minds of rubbish is well. Still, there remains something to be said. To begin with, it is by no means easy to ask the right questions, and no little perspicuity is needed even to discover that the wrong question has been asked. To continue, it is well not to forget that 'the context' is sometimes a whole philosophical system, as witness the remarkable cases of Bergson and of Alexander. To end with, the plain man cannot help but be puzzled and must not be treated in the cavalier manner of our imaginary objector. So, after all, we can reply to him that it is well that Miss Cleugh should have striven to winnow the significance to be discerned in the 'great philosophers' with whom she deals, instead of dismissing them as poets, drugged themselves and drugging us with emotive language masquerading as philosophical terminology; it is useful for us to be provided with a fresh treatment of those very fashionable topics—prediction, becoming, and reality. I, at least, have found much profit in the reading, notwithstanding some measure of disagreement with her views.

L. SUSAN STEBBING

NOTE

I AM glad to have this opportunity of thanking those who have helped and encouraged me in the writing of this book.

The work, which was written as a thesis for the Ph.D. degree of London University, was made possible by the award of studentships by the Council of Bedford College and the Senate of London University, to whom I express my sincere thanks.

I am indebted to Mr. M. Black and to my father for help in the chapter on Physics, and to Miss T. M. Hudson, B.A., and Miss V. J. Willis, B.A., for assistance with proof-reading.

I am also indebted to Mr. J. W. Dunne and to Messrs. Faber and Faber for permission to reproduce certain diagrams from Mr. Dunne's *Experiment with Time* and *The Serial Universe*.

But above all I have to thank Professor L. S. Stebbing, to whom I owe more than I can say, and whose constant kindness has been an inspiration throughout.

WHITTINGTON,　　　　　　　　　　　　　　　　　　M. C.
23. 7. 37

CONTENTS

CHAPTER		PAGE
	INTRODUCTION	1

PART I
ANALYSIS

I.	PSYCHOLOGY	15
II.	PHYSICS	38
III.	LOGIC	72
IV.	METAPHYSICS—KANT	86
V.	METAPHYSICS—BERGSON	109
VI.	METAPHYSICS—ALEXANDER	128
VII.	METAPHYSICS—McTAGGART	148
VIII.	METAPHYSICS—DUNNE	166

PART II
SYNTHESIS

IX.	PREDICTION	191
X.	IRREVERSIBILITY	210
XI.	"BECOMING"	231
XII.	CONTINGENCY	252
XIII.	REALITY	274
	BIBLIOGRAPHY	295
	INDEX	303

INTRODUCTION

ONE cannot read much metaphysics, either of this age or of any other, without finding frequent references to "the problem of time". At first sight this may seem rather absurd. For what can be more familiar than time? Everyone, however young, unthinking, or impatient of "metaphysical moonshine", has immediate experience of temporal succession: nearly everybody in this enlightened and civilized land can "tell the time" and inform us that an hour has elapsed; and even the most unreflective of these have a dim suspicion that this elapse is in some queer way final, that the past hour will 'never' return, but that it will remain 'for ever' in a kind of wastepaper basket called The Past, along with all the other hours that have ever been, and all the other events that have ever happened 'in' them. The transitoriness of human experience has been an all-too-abiding (we are sometimes tempted to think) theme in literature from very earliest times.

"There is no remembrance of the wise more than of the fool for ever; seeing that which now is in the days to come shall all be forgotten."

"As soon as thou scatterest them, they are even as a sleep, and fade away suddenly like the grass. . . . Though a man be so strong that he come to fourscore years, yet his end is but labour and sorrow, so soon passeth it away and we are gone."

> "Gather ye rosebuds while ye may,
> Old time is still a-flying,
> And that same flower that smiles to-day
> To-morrow will be dying."

> "Golden lads and girls all must,
> As chimney sweepers, come to dust."

"I came like water, and like wind I go."

> "Even such is Time, that takes in trust,
> Our youth, our joys, our all we have,
> And pays us but with earth and dust,
> Who in the dark and silent grave
> When we have wandered all our ways,
> Shuts up the corners of our days."

But it is needless to quote further, since even without the aid of literature we can all recognize the complacent knowledge of and familiarity (even to the point of contempt when an unwary metaphysician dares to hint that that knowledge is "riddled with contradictions") with the notion of time. How, then, can what is so blatantly obvious to common sense be a centre of perplexity in metaphysics? The reason is, that metaphysical explanation is of a different order from the 'explanation' which satisfies the practical man. He is satisfied if he can link up the phenomena to be explained with his everyday experiences: his standard is familiarity. From his point of view, then, temporal succession is not even thought of as *needing* explanation, for it is so absurdly familiar—an unseparated and perhaps inseparable ingredient of all our experience. But the metaphysician has no such practical aim: he desires merely to understand, and this desire is constantly frustrated by those elements of our experience which are temporal. It is now generally agreed that what is logically prior may be, psychologically, far from obvious, while, on the other hand, what is 'given' to experience may be, logically, of an almost unmanageable complexity. Such would seem to be the case with time. Familiar though the notion is to us, as soon as we attempt to penetrate beneath the surface we become, in Berkeley's picturesque phrase, "lost and embrangled in inextricable difficulties".[1] The common-sense view simply will not stand logical analysis.

What do we mean by 'elapsed'? To say that an hour has elapsed simply presupposes the notion of time: it is a mere re-statement of one of the characteristics of time that is most in need of explanation, its "passing away". To say that it has elapsed means only that it has gone, but how or why or where, we are none the wiser, and the mere invention of a new word does not clear the issue.[2] Every-

---

[1] *Principles of Human Knowledge*, § 98.

[2] I do not mean to suggest that common sense considers that this *is* an explanation: the point is, that common sense takes the notion for granted, without stopping to inquire into its complexity, and whether it *needs* an explanation—as it does.

body would agree that the use of tense in a statement is temporal and that there would be no sense in using tense expressions in a timeless world. To say, then, that the past is what *will* not return, is, to put it mildly, unintelligible; and the position is not improved, rather the reverse, if we substitute for 'not', 'never', since 'never' has itself temporal connections.

"The Past" is a curious entity, with characteristics that are more than curious—downright contradictory. Although changeless (see Omar Khayyám) and uncompromisingly closed to our repentance (see almost any moral tale), it yet has a peculiar habit of growing. Now, the wastepaper basket is fuller than it was a century ago: a century hence it will be still fuller. This is an obviously unsatisfactory conception. In the first place, we are liable, in unguarded moments, to say that it does change, in that it is continually growing; and this, if it is not to be contradictory to the original view that the past does not change, requires a thorough examination of the ways in which 'change' is used, to see whether the contradiction is more than verbal—and this implies metaphysics. Secondly, there is an implied contradiction in that The Past does not stay put, but continually encroaches on The Present and The Future. What *is* now Past was once Present; what *is* Future *will be* Present. It is obvious that a reference to time is not yet eliminated; and even more obvious that a logical explanation, so far from lying on the surface, recedes farther and farther away the more we probe. Thirdly, the wastepaper-basket conception is unsatisfactory in that it treats the Past as an abstract and separately existing container just waiting for cast-off events to be popped into it. But as it is also considered to have some hand itself in the process by which events become cast off (Chronos devouring his children), we may be excused a little bewilderment.

Apart from the incompatibility of these two views in the case of the past, the container view of Time in general is open to the further objection that it is an undesirable bolstering-up of 'Time' into a substantialized 'thing in itself' (symbolized by capital letters), whereas time is never given apart from experience. Such bolstering-up (or, as it is somewhat grandiloquently called, "the hypostatization of time") is very common, and we shall often meet it. Past, Present and Future, considered as entities apart from events, are decided abstractions. Really, the plain man is becoming quite metaphysical! And bad metaphysics it is, too, to say that events are 'in' time, and to imply that they are in time in a sense analogous to that in which a chair is 'in' a room. Such a view, for the plain man, is a curious one, since it is one which is certainly not given by experience, but is a double abstraction from it. We experience events: from these, we infer temporal succession stretching from the remote past to the remote future. So far, so good; but when we proceed to make a second inference, that this temporal succession, or, as we now prefer to call it, Time, is something which exists so that events are contained in Time (with the probable consequence that we look upon Time as something having an independent existence), we are doing something that has not the slightest justification in experience. It may or may not be justified on other grounds: the view of time as a kind of abstract metronome that would go on ticking even if there were nothing else in the world, may be a good or a bad one. I think that it is a bad one; but the point here is that it is essentially metaphysical.

The last criticism I wish to make about the common-sense view of time concerns its conception of the status of Past and Future. Common sense is very exercised on this matter, and certainly it is a difficult one—and not improved by the hypostatizing tendencies of common sense. There is an obvious difference in our attitude to the past and to the future. Without going into the controversy, which is anyway far removed from the sphere of the plain man, of whether or not we have direct memory of past events, nobody would deny that we have knowledge of past events in a sense in which we have not knowledge of future events. Secondly, the present is, evidently, in a privileged position, since it is only the present that is open to our activity. Thirdly, we think of our activities now as influencing the future, but not as influencing (though possibly influenced *by*) the past, which is looked upon as unchanging in that sense. (These facts are very important, and will need to be considered in detail later, but here we are only concerned with the plain man's account of them.) It is here than the plain man becomes openly and unashamedly metaphysical. His account is positively spattered with 'real' and 'exists' and 'unreal', and the ontological argument claims many victims. On the one hand, only the present 'is', that is 'exists', that is 'is real': by parity of reasoning, the past and the future, which are not now, do not exist, and so cannot be 'real'. On the other hand, there is something solid and substantial about a (suitably hypostatized) Past and Future: they stretch backwards and forwards, if not to infinity, at least as near as does not matter. Whereas the Present is merely a tenuous, dimensionless limit between these satisfying blocks—and it does not even 'stay put'. How, then, can *it* be 'real'?

And to complicate matters still further, the decision is not even between an unreal past and future and a real present, and a real past and future and an unreal present, for the past and the future are, as we have seen, not on the same cognitive level. This is the last straw: the plain man does not stop to consider whether past and future could have, *ontologically*, the same status, even though there are obvious cognitive differences between them, but, with his admirable practical and moral bias, he concentrates on the fact that activity is confined to the present, and influences only the future, and drags joyfully in the question of free will—which is hardly calculated to elucidate the discussion.

Augustine, in his *Confessions*,[1] said: "What is time? Who can simply and briefly explain it? ... Yet what is more familiar and well known in conversation than time? ... What, then, is time?—if nobody asks me, I know; but if I try to explain it to one who asks me, I do not know."

After the foregoing attempts to extract a coherent meaning out of the common-sense views of time, the statement that the problem of time is one of the hardest with which the philosopher has to deal, may no longer elicit contemptuous jeers from the plain man. Augustine's remark is only too true. Though we manage to get along in practical life with such notions of time as we have, we find it extraordinarily difficult, if not impossible, to give a coherent account of them. I do not mean to suggest that common sense is to be blamed for this—to do so would be to judge it by standards which it does not recognize, and as long as it is adequate for practical concerns, that is sufficient for it. But my point has been that metaphysical discussion of the problem of time cannot be called otiose, and more, that a metaphysical background is presupposed by many common-sense conceptions. The philosopher is a plain man half his time, and the plain man often asks questions

[1] XI, 14.

which are essentially metaphysical. Metaphysical questions as to the nature of time are by no means purely academic.

Granted, then, that time is a question with which metaphysics is rightly concerned, is it a sufficiently important one to justify metaphysics in dealing with it? It is important in proportion to its difficulty, and it lies at the centre of some of the most difficult problems in philosophy, which cannot be answered, if at all, until we have first got a satisfactory conception of time. The importance of time in metaphysics is more fully realized at present than ever before, and, as Alexander says, the most characteristic feature of the thought of the last twenty-five years is the discovery of time.[1] This does not mean, of course, that nobody until the last few years had speculated about time—on the contrary, the essential problem of the relation between temporal flux and eternal abidingness, between Being and Becoming, is fully recognized as far back as the Vedas, and, in Greek philosophy, by Heraclitus and Parmenides. What is meant is that the present age is more *consciously* aware of the difficulties and importance of time, as the following quotations will show: "No question has been more neglected by philosophers than that of time, yet all agree in declaring it vital."[2] "The key of the greatest philosophical problems is there."[3] "To realize the importance of time as such is the gate of wisdom."[4] And finally, even from the idealistic side, comes the admission that the problem of time "is the ultimate crux of speculation".[5]

Time is important, then, because, though apparently a simple 'given' in experience, it involves a great number of difficult questions. Some of these, as we saw, appeared as soon as we even began to scratch the surface of common-sense notions: others appear at more sophisticated levels. Some apply to characters which are specifically temporal: others are only incidental, in that their difficulty is equally felt in other questions. Some, again, are essential difficulties, which any satisfactory theory of time must attempt to answer: others are irrelevant to the metaphysical question of the *nature* of time. Others rest upon logical confusions, such as ambiguous language and fallacies of substantialization,

[1] *Spinoza and Time*, p. 1.
[2] Bergson, *Durée et Simultanéité*, pp. vii and viii.   [3] *Ibid.*
[4] Alexander, *Space, Time, and Deity*, I, p. 36 note.
[5] Bosanquet, *Meeting of Extremes*, p. 125.

upon insufficiently grounded psychological generalizations, and lastly, and worst of all, upon the indiscriminate and ambiguous use in different contexts of 'real' and 'unreal'. A statement of the various difficulties is sufficient at present: they will need to be analysed in detail later.

It is generally agreed that time and change are closely connected with each other, whether or not a relation of implication holds between them. Change is a difficult, and, as many have believed from Parmenides down to Hegel and Bradley, a self-contradictory notion. To say "A has the property x" is obviously contradictory to "A has not x": to put the two together and say "A has x and then A has not x" is in itself unintelligible. How can it be that two contradictory statements are asserted together? To answer that there is no contradiction in the statement as a whole because A has *changed* in the meantime, is, I submit, the mere addition of a new word for a notion which must remain for ever inexplicable to pure logic. If such are the disreputable associates of time, the adherent of logic may well despair of satisfaction.

The second difficulty is the task of reconciling time considered as a sum of discrete 'nows', with time considered as a homogeneous continuum. Zeno's paradoxes illustrated this difficulty, and according to him, the two views were incompatible. There can be no doubt that the cleavage he remarked upon has persisted up to the present, and, in E. A. Burtt's words, "The scientific notion of time has almost entirely lost touch with duration as immediately experienced. Until a closer relation is regained, it is probable that science will never reach a very satisfactory description of time".[1]

Thirdly, it may be objected that time is 'subjective'. An hour, as measured by a clock, may seem long to one observer and short to another, as Shakespeare long ago pointed out. What is more, an interval that is 'filled' with events seems short in passing and long in retrospect: thus an hour on a walk in the hills soon goes, whereas the next hour, spent in waiting on a country platform with the knowledge that the earlier train can only have been missed by a few minutes, is intolerably long. But, in memory, the hour spent in walking becomes much longer than the hour of waiting. What, then, can be 'time', since it appears different to different observers, and to the same observer at different 'times'?

[1] *Metaphysical Foundations of Modern Science*, p. 262.

But even (so-called) 'objective' time is not free from difficulty. Time is measured by means of motion; but motion presupposes the notion of time: how can we explain away the circularity?

Again, is there an absolute time, as Newton held, or is what we call 'time' only a name for relations between events? If the latter, is there an infinite number of time-series? Following on from this come new questions that the theory of relativity has introduced. What exactly can be meant by the statement that a certain velocity, the velocity of light, is critical in such a way that the ordinary addition and subtraction of relative velocities no longer holds? and what is its effect on the conception of time as relative?

Has time a beginning and an end? and what is its connection with eternity? Is there any sense in the theory that after a certain number of years, no matter how great, 'the same' collocations of events, down to the tiniest detail, will recur?

To come from this cosmic grandeur to the difficulties of to-day, how can we explain the 'passing' of time? At present I am writing *this* sentence x, but five minutes ago I was writing quite a different sentence y, and five minutes hence it will be no longer true to say, "I am *now* writing x." Put differently, we cannot distinguish between past, present and future in such a way that the distinction will 'always' remain. On the contrary, what was present becomes past, and what is future will be present. Given three events, A, B, C, I can say that A is past, B present, and C future, and in so doing I have sufficiently distinguished them—for the present. But there *was* a time when A was present, and B and C both future: and there *will be* a time when A and B are both past and C is present. How, then, can I distinguish between A, B, and C, since none of them possesses the characteristic of presentness by divine right? As Broad put it, we must distinguish between changes *of* time and changes *in* time: we cannot analyse the former in terms of the latter, since time would then need another time to change in, and so on *ad infinitum*. Or, more forcibly, past, present and future are incompatible characteristics. Yet every event has them all.

Can we, or can we not, get out of this difficulty by saying that these characteristics are not incompatible, because every event has them *at different times*? If we did, we should still have to explain what we meant by 'at different times', and it has been denied (by

McTaggart) that we can avoid an infinite regress, except by vicious circularity.

Again, the difficulty arises about the relation between time and events. Is time something that could go on even if there were no events: or is it merely an abstraction, and a vicious one at that, from events, or is there a middle way between these two opposed conceptions? Supposing we were to deny that time could exist *in vacuo*, the problem still remains whether there would be time in a mindless universe.

As has already been said, there is an essential difference in our cognitive relations to past and future. Is it, or is it not, valid to infer from this that they have a different *ontological* status?

Lastly, perhaps the most obvious thing about time as given in experience, and the characteristic which makes it unlike anything else, is its irreversibility. Is this an accident, or is it inherent in the nature of time? and, secondly, if it is inherent, how do we propose to explain it? Certainly not by logic, for the laws of logic have no cognizance of irreversible process, but how else?

Such are some of the difficulties which have accumulated in the course of time, and which any metaphysical theory of time must either explain or explain away. Should the list seem too short, it can be indefinitely increased by the addition of causality, free will, determinism, since the most difficult aspects of these are those into which the consideration of time enters.

Confronted by all these difficulties, what is to be done? One very simple and obvious way out, and one which has been popular with idealists of all ages—Parmenides, Plato, Spinoza, Hegel, Bradley and McTaggart—is to say that time is riddled through and through with contradictions, and hence cannot be real. The major premise of the argument is that the Real (note the capital) cannot be self-contradictory, or possess contradictory characters. It is a summary solution of the difficulty, and one for which there is much justification. Nobody who has contemplated the awe-inspiring accumulation of problems given above can be out of sympathy with it. But *merely* to say that because time is self-contradictory it must be appearance only, is, so far from solving the problems, not even an answer to them. It is doubtless interesting to know that time is not real, but only apparent, but it is not sufficient. The denial of reality to time avoids the main problem, for you have still to explain the *appearance* of time. McTaggart is almost alone among idealists in realizing this.

I do not mean to suggest that the idealist has not, at first sight at any rate, a good case for rejecting time from a Reality in which no contradictions remain, nor that he does not frequently make very important remarks about time—such, for instance, as are contained in the *Timaeus*. But I cannot see that we get much farther in understanding the nature of time—though possibly, in understanding the nature of Reality, since we now know the negative fact that temporal experience is not a part of reality,[1] when we say that time is not real. Real or not real, the facts of temporal experience remain, and any satisfactory metaphysics of time must take account of them.[2]

Moreover, 'real' is a very ambiguous word, and its presence in any discussion, at least in the early stages, is more likely to be a source of confusion than a help. We may, and probably shall, have finally to make up our minds whether time has any meaning apart from our experience: whether it is merely a condition of our experience, of all possible experience, or has a separate and independent subsistence of its own. This is a very important question, and to each of these alternatives corresponds a possible meaning of 'real', but it is not a question with which to begin. Again, we saw in our discussion of common-sense notions that in one sense the present is more 'real' than the past and future, while in another sense they are more 'real' than the present. Or, to take an example from another field, the plain man usually says that what he can see, hear, touch is 'real'. But then Descartes tells him that secondary qualities are 'unreal' and that only extension is 'real'. After which, along comes Berkeley and shows that primary qualities are on the same footing as secondary ones, and so they are all condemned as not belonging to Reality. Evidently, then, 'real' is used in a variety of different senses. Granted that considerations of 'reality'

---

[1] I agree that in so far as the aim of idealist metaphysicians is to apprehend the Real, it is not fair to criticize them for having failed to elucidate the nature of something which to them is appearance: my point is, that for a metaphysical theory of *time*, it is not sufficient to dismiss time as mere appearance, without discussing how it is that the appearance arises.

[2] "Calling a thing an illusion doesn't free us from the responsibility of accounting for how an eternal, static system could produce the illusion or appearance" (Boodin, *Time and Reality*, p. 65).

must in the end be brought in, and that this is ultimately an indefinable notion: yet it seems advisable not to introduce it too soon, or to define it when we do. (This is not a contradiction, for though 'reality', as ultimate, is indefinable, there are plenty of loose usages which would be all the better for being defined.)

My last objection to the indiscriminate use of 'real' is that it is exceedingly emotive—as is shown by the customary appellation of appearance as 'mere'. Granted that the distinction between what appears to be and what really is, is for many purposes a useful one, it is also dangerous, since it is liable to lead to an absolute dichotomy in which what appears is opposed to what is. Hence the undesirable and unverifiable assumption that whatever is given —'appears' in that sense—is also 'appearance', as opposed to reality.

To say, then, of time that it is 'not ultimately real' in itself explains nothing: what we have to do is first to analyse the concept of time, and only secondly to discuss wherein is its place in the Ultimate Scheme of Things. It may be that at the end we shall agree that fundamentally time is only an appearance, a phenomenon, an imperfect copy, a 'moving image' of a changeless Being; but to start from this point is not to have rendered unnecessary an analysis of time, rather is it to have begged the question.

To this analysis, then, we must now proceed, after briefly indicating the scope of what follows. Before we can hope to analyse the genuine metaphysical problems that have been raised, it is first necessary to consider the various other aspects—psychological, physical, logical—from which time has been discussed. It will be shown that a treatment from these points of view is not enough, and that metaphysical considerations are always presupposed. Some, but by no means all, of the possible metaphysical positions will then be discussed, and an attempt made to evaluate them. Finally, the second part will contain an attempt to co-ordinate the conclusions reached in the first part.

PART I

CHAPTER I

PSYCHOLOGY

I

IT is by now a truism that what is immediately given in experience—is psychologically simple, in that it is familiar—is not necessarily, nor even usually, logically and epistemologically simple. Whether we follow William James and say that to the very young child the world is a blooming buzzing confusion, or whether we hold that the child's world is logically simpler and that the complexities are only gradually introduced by criss-crossing and irrational associations, there is at least general agreement that by the time we become adult our world is exceedingly complex. And (since, fortunately or unfortunately, we do not normally indulge in psychological introspections at a tender age), it is from this complexity that psychology must start.

In any psychological analysis we are faced with three main difficulties in addition to those peculiar to the subject-matter (in this case, time as it is given in experience).

The first is that we are seeking to express the familiar, but logically complex, in terms of the unfamiliar, which is yet logically simpler. The psychologist, dealing with sense-perception, does not rest satisfied with my description of what I see when I look up—a garden, fields, trees, two houses, seen through a window—although my recognition of them is immediate. Instead, he tells me that my seeing these *as* houses, etc., is not original, but requires interpretation: what I 'see' is an irregular pattern of different colours, to which, with the help of past experience, I attribute a meaning. On reflection, I may agree. But he goes further—he talks of processes of which I am, and must be, unconscious: he distinguishes between 'sensation' and 'perception' and talks about pure sensation, which no one ever has after the first moment of his life if then. Although logically simpler than our perceptions of 'objects', the clearly defined concepts which he uses are much less familiar.

The second difficulty follows on from this. It is that the psychologist seeks to express explicitly what is held implicitly. The very familiarity of the experiences with which he deals hampers him, since familiarity begets lack of interest and the tendency to 'take for granted' which is fatal to enquiry. He is forced to begin by making divisions and distinctions, such as 'emotion', 'conation', 'sensation'. (These divisions, if taken too seriously, are themselves a source of stumbling, for they lead to the fallacies of a too atomistic conception.) At first he gets on well. Some of the 'elements' which he chooses are easy to separate from the rest; but sooner or later he finds himself handicapped by the interconnections of the various elements that he uses, and by the complacent familiarity which precludes their unravelling. Importance and ease of explicit statement are almost in inverse variation, for the more important an element is, the more it becomes tangled up and interwoven with others. To use a dubious metaphor, which, however, is harmless if not taken too seriously, a thread which comes out easily is of little importance. This difficulty is of special application in the case of time, which is essentially a form of the connectivity of experience and so can hardly be expected to be easily unravelled.

The third difficulty concerns the 'irrational' accretions to experience from half-forgotten associations, modifications of past events, and the like. How far are we to admit this irrationality? On the one hand, we must distinguish the real core from non-essential and subjective wrappings: on the other, we must remember the opposite danger of peeling the onion until there is next to nothing left, and of whittling down the rich and varied content of experience to a tenuous 'rational' element. For it is a characteristic of experience that it is not static, but is modified by, and constructed out of, past events: however irrational some of these modifications may appear, we should be gravely at fault if we ignored them altogether and began with some abstract propriety.

How is time given in experience? Think of the temporal notions which we use so glibly—past, present, future, the irreversibility of time, the flight of time, eternity. What psychological basis have they?

The present, the immediately given, the whole of present experience (note the verbal circularity) needs no introduction. We know that it includes different sense-impressions[1]—of sight and hearing and touch and internal sensations—and also emotions, such as anger or fear, although not all may be consciously perceived. "We are constantly receiving innumerable impressions from things without us and from the varying states of our internal organs. . . . Suppose that I am reading a book by the light of a candle standing immediately beside me on the table. The object with which my mind is occupied at that moment is the topic treated of in the book: my mind is occupied with this object under the spatial aspect in which it is presented by the sentence I am following with my eyes. I take no notice of the lines on the opposite page, or of other lines on the same page, or of the margin of the page, or of the candle flame, as such, or of the surface of the table, or of the clothes in contact with my skin, or of the clock which is ticking behind me. Yet all these things are producing impressions on my senses, so as to affect my consciousness in specific ways."[2]

But this complex whole of experience also includes something else, of extreme importance for the present topic—it also includes the perception of movement, not merely the perception that a change in the visual (or tactual) pattern *has* occurred, but that it *is* occurring.[3] Birds fly across the garden: the sycamores move in the wind: a dead leaf floats gently down: my hand moves over the paper. For the psychological present (in Wildon Carr's phrase, the moment of experience: or in William James's phrase, the specious present) is not an extensionless, photographic glimpse of the

[1] "Dans une masse absolument homogène rien ne pourrait donner naissance à l'idée de temps: la durée ne commence qu'avec une certaine variété d'effets" (Guyau, *Génèse de l'Idée de Temps*, p. 20).

[2] Stout, *Manual of Psychology*, 4th edition, p. 162.

[3] "The bare fact of the existence of change is in itself irrelevant to the problem of time-perception. The essential point is that the transition involves a peculiar immediate experience which we may call the experience of transience. When we are in the darkness and the electric light is suddenly turned on, it is quite an inadequate account of what has taken place in us merely to say that first we have darkness sensation and that immediately following this we have light sensation. It must be added that the transition itself from the one to the other is experienced in a peculiar way" (Stout, op. cit., p. 496. Compare also p. 132). (The first sentence does not mean, of course, that change is irrelevant to *time*—but that *a change having occurred* cannot give us any clue to time-*perception*. For this we need further the consciousness of a change *as occurring*.)

world 'at an instant'. That this is not so is shown by the fact that we can actually *see* changes occurring *within* one moment of experience. But all change takes 'time': therefore, the moment of experience must last for a finite 'time'.[1] Using the more sophisticated conception of time as a line—whether this is legitimate will be discussed later—the moment of experience is not a mere durationless point: it is a finite length of the line, however small. The durationless point—the source of many antinomies concerning continuity—is an abstraction: it corresponds to nothing in experience. As Wildon Carr puts it: "The moment of experience has no distinction of past and present, but it has distinction of before and after."[2]

The second point, elucidated by James, is that the content of consciousness is not constant throughout the specious present: there is a maximum intensity, between two minima at beginning and end. The specious present is: "no knife-edge, but a saddle-back, with a certain breadth of its own on which we sit perched and from which we look in two directions into time. The unit of composition of our perception of time is a *duration*, with a bow and a stern, as it were—a rearward and a forward-looking end".[3]

Lastly, in admitting that change can take place within the specious present, we are in effect admitting that we can have *direct* consciousness of something which is no longer happening, that is, of the immediate past. If I am conscious of 'X moving from A to B' within one moment of experience, it follows that I am conscious of 'X's being at A' when X is no longer at A, that is, when 'X's being at A' is *past*.[4] This is of the very last importance in the genesis of our conception of the past, since it provides the basis of our knowledge *not only* of an event E (X's being at A) as being past, but *also*

[1] I need hardly draw attention to the different use of the word 'time' here. Whether such a use is justified in elucidating the primary *origin* of our notions of time must be discussed later.

[2] Wildon Carr, *A Theory of Monads*, p. 133. The whole of the chapter is relevant.

[3] James, *Principles of Psychology*, Vol. I, p. 609. See also, Hodgson's discussion in the first volume of the *Metaphysic of Experience*, and Strong's article on "Consciousness and Time" in the *Psychological Review*, 1896 (American).

[4] But, as Fouillée insists: "La succession dans la pensée n'est pas par elle-même la pensée de la succession" (*Psychologie des Idées-Forces*, p. 94).

of its *being present and then becoming past*. Expressed differently, the specious present contains both immediate perception and immediate memory; more than that, in its welding of the two it shows also how the configuration at one instant is related to the configuration of a previous instant, and provides the ultimate basis of the mysterious way in which the present (as we say) becomes the past.

(This account of the moment of experience is a sketchy and inadequate one. It is not treated in detail, because, on the one hand, what we immediately experience can best be studied by each for himself: on the other hand, the work of James and Wildon Carr has made any attempt here at exhaustive analysis unnecessary.)

Beyond the wavering indications of the specious present, 'past' and 'future' originate from extrapolation. "The distinction between past, present and future can be apprehended only in a rudimentary way at the perceptual level. But there is, even at this level, what we may call a 'not-yet' consciousness and a 'no-more' consciousness. The 'not-yet' consciousness is contained in the prospective attitude of attention—in the pre-adaptation for what is to come—which it involves. This 'not-yet' consciousness is emphasized when conation is delayed or obstructed. . . . The 'no-more' consciousness emerges most distinctly when conation is abruptly disappointed or frustrated."[1] Let us deal with the past first. Suppose that I am listening to somebody who says to me: "Mathematics is the science in which we do not know what we are talking about, nor whether what we say is true." It is a convention of the English language that words shall be arranged in a certain order, and a change in order may involve change of meaning (compare 'Is mathematics?' and 'Mathematics is'). The word 'is' precedes the word 'the': hence when my informant says 'the', his saying of 'is' is already in the past. But we have seen that the specious present may be extended to cover two sensations that are not simultaneous,[2] such as 'is' and 'the'. 'Is' fades into the past: our moment of experience now includes 'the' and 'science'[3]; and so on. Thus there is a continual

[1] Stout, op. cit., p. 499.
[2] Not only in the strict mathematical sense. I would also agree to that from introspection.
[3] Strictly, of course, the specious present would include more than two words, spoken quickly. A better example is that of James: "If the present thought is of *ABCDEFG*, the next one will be of *BCDEFGH*, and the

linking together of words within the sentence into subordinate and ever-changing groups. It is this grouping which helps to make memory possible—though it does not ensure that we should, *in fact*, have memory of what we hear.[1] By this unexplained phenomenon which we conveniently call 'memory', we remember that 'is' *was once* conjoined in a specious present with 'the', while 'the' and 'science' are now included in one specious present. That is the *basis* of the process: in practice, of course, memory is much more immediate than that, making its integrations directly from the elements which sensation affords, and not necessarily by way of the prior integrations of the specious present. But that the phenomena of memory cannot be reduced to the extended influence of a number of specious presents does not mean that they must be considered as fundamentally dissimilar. It may be, on the contrary, that the specious present contains what is essentially a direct and immediate act of memory—a special case of the general integrator. From which would arise the interesting question as to the precise distinction to be drawn between perception and memory[2] (especially in cases such as the oft-quoted one of Mozart, where the specious present is abnormally great). This, however, is speculation; what is certain is that by memory we are enabled to extrapolate, and to 'add on' to what is actually given to us in present experience. From this point, the development into a fully-fledged concept one after that of *CDEFGHI*—the lingerings of the past dropping successively away, and the incomings of the future making up the loss. These lingerings of old objects, these incomings of new, are the germs of memory and expectation, the retrospective and the prospective sense of time" (James, op. cit., p. 606). The length of the specious present seems to be connected with the span of apprehension.

[1] That we should *remember* what is past can, I think, not be explained by any extension of the theory of the specious present. It remains ultimate and irreducible—a miracle, as far as the specious present is concerned. For, that past and present should be linked together in the specious present, does not explain the further, and quite distinct, fact that the past can be remembered when it is also 'past' to the specious present.

[2] As the Critical Realists point out, in memory the object known cannot be identified with the idea of it which the subject has before his mind when he remembers. We must also bear in mind that point on which James insisted (op. cit., pp. 627–31), that the feeling of past time is a *present* feeling. It would be injudicious to draw too sharp a line between perception and memory. For a general discussion of memory, compare Pierre Janet's *Evolution de la Mémoire*.

'The Past'—boasting a capital letter and of dubious metaphysical status—is easy to trace. I will not trace it, but will add only two more remarks. The first is, that we must beware of over-hypostatizing 'memory', of turning it into a 'faculty' with an occult 'power', however important it may seem. Secondly, memory is not necessarily confined to conscious processes, though for the sake of simplicity I have spoken as if it were. Theories of 'traces' postulate that an organism can retain effects without being aware of it: then, too, there are theories such as Butler's of 'race-memory'.[1]

With regard to the future, that is an extrapolation based ultimately on the immediate intuition of process, of continual becoming *within* the moment of experience itself, and proximately on an analogy with the past. The past is the sum-total of all the 'immediately-givens' that have been: the future is the sum-total of all that will be.[2] Of course the analogy is not exact: we have, through memory, if not a direct, at the very least a reasonably exact knowledge of the past, which is altogether lacking in the case of the future. Consequently the future usually occupies a subordinate place in psychology, even as compared with the past (it is at least possible to introspect our memories!). The exceptions are those psychologies that lay the chief emphasis on conation, and on the *end* to be achieved, rather than on the *action* by which it is brought about.[3] On the other hand, the psychologist may very well seek to explain, for instance, instinct, by throwing the emphasis back on the past with theories of race-memory, instead of on the future object of the complicated set of actions.

[1] See Butler, *Life and Habit*; Ward, *Psychological Principles*.
[2] I apologize for the language: there is no cure for it short of metaphysics.
[3] Stout says (op. cit., pp. 415–16): "In early stages of mental development, owing to the dominance of direct practical interest, the mind is preoccupied with continuation into the future rather than into the past. Such reference to the future seems involved even in the most rudimentary forms of the attention-process as indicated by the behaviour of animals and children. Even the most primitive attention is essentially prospective: it is a waiting or watching, a being on the alert for what is to come. The given situation has for it a transitional character: it is not something which merely is, but something which is to be. Only on this condition is there a possibility of apprehending it as alterable or of wanting it altered in however vague a way. In other words, the reference to the future must be as primitive as conative consciousness." For the opposite view of the psychological priority of the past, see Sturt, *The Psychology of Time*, p. 44.

Past, present and future. We begin with the present, the immediately given: from it, we infer and construct the past and the future. But I am now going to make what is perilously near a contradiction: at any rate it is a paradox. It is, that the present, in the temporal sense of present, the *'now'*, is not prior in consciousness to past and future. On the contrary, we are rarely directly conscious of the present *as* present, *except* in contrasting it with past and future. An example may make this clearer. Most of us live our lives in a routine: not necessarily a particularly circumscribed one, but nevertheless what we are doing on a certain weekday evening, say Tuesday, in practice varies within certain limits only. I may stay at home and read, or play bridge, or write letters, or I may go to visit friends, or to a theatre, or to a meeting: there are fifty different things that I may do. But, it being an evening in the middle of the week, I am unlikely to be anywhere more than fifty miles away from home, and this unlikelihood increases with the distance.

Now suppose that my holidays have just begun, and that I am a hundred miles from home. The place need not be unfamiliar: I may know it from week-end visits. But there is a sense of strangeness, of getting away from habitual routine, of pleasant insecurity. We all know the feeling—a kind of perpetual exclamation: "How funny that I should be here *now*!" and I am suggesting that part of its strangeness is due, not only to the break in routine, but also to its consequence, the unusual conscious emphasis on the present, instead of its being implicit and unconscious.

Another example, to show the queer instability of the present in consciousness. We have looked forward to—or, alternatively, dreaded—something for some time. We know quite a lot about it —the day and the hour, the approximate time it will last, the train we must catch to get there in time, and so on. Once in the train, it is difficult to realize that this *is* the outing to which we have so looked forward. Nothing very exciting is happening: yet every minute that passes is taking away something of the splendid whole. It is the feeling of a child at 7 p.m. on its birthday, with the knowledge that there is only another hour left before bedtime, and that to-morrow will be like any other day. We may feel curiously flat, and disappointed. Or we may be puzzled at the disappearance into a tenuous 'now' of what had been so long expected, and with a shock of surprise—amounting almost to terror sometimes—we realize that what we call 'now' is to us an unknown, masquerading in a guise of easy convention and everyday familiarity. (From this shock may come *metaphysical* speculations as to the nature of time)—but the point I am trying to make here is a psychological one. We know less of the present than we do of past and future, and we do not[1] think of what is present (that is, given to consciousness) as being present (that is, temporally present) except by contrasting it with our habitual routine—the past, or our expectations—the future. I can only appeal to your introspections, whether you have, in fact, that feeling of instability and unfamiliarity in such circumstances as I have sketched. If so, I would suggest that the instability is due to the strain involved in considering explicitly what is normally unconsidered.

To solve the apparent contradiction (that we start from 'the present', and yet that it is derived), I wish to distinguish, provisionally, between 'present' as meaning 'spatially present' (or, more satisfactorily, because not imposing unnecessary spatial limits, 'given to immediate experience') and 'present' as meaning 'temporally present'. I will call the former 'the given' and the latter 'the now'.[2] (It must be emphasized that this distinction is only provisional, and cannot be made absolute. Obviously the 'now' is only regarding the 'given' in its temporal aspect, and the 'given' is what is given *now*.) But I submit that it is a valid distinction none the less. It is perfectly consistent to hold that we must start from the given, and that it is psychologically prior to all constructions which may be based upon it, and yet to hold also that we are very rarely conscious of it *in its temporal aspect* except in contrast to the constructions past and future.

I would add, also, that to say of the 'now' that it rarely enters explicit consciousness is not to belittle its logical, if not psychological, importance. We began by saying that what is most familiar is not necessarily on that account also logically prior: so in denying to the 'now' the psychological priority which is usually

[1] Except by a conscious intellectual effort (as when we are engaged in metaphysical speculations).
[2] Compare also the remark of Ward: "The primary meaning of present is 'here' rather than 'now' " (op. cit., p. 212).

accorded to it, we have said nothing at all to prejudice the question of its logical importance.

The psychological basis of our belief in the 'flight' of time and the 'irreversibility' of time is not far to seek: it is to be found ultimately in the moment of experience, with its transition from present to past. Ward holds that "it depends (1) upon the continuous sinking of the primary memory-images on the one side, and the continuous rising of the ordinary images on the other side, of that member of a series of percepts then repeating which is actual at the moment: and (2) on the prevenient adjustments of attention, to which such words as 'expect', 'await', 'anticipate', all testify by their etymology. These conditions in turn will be found to depend upon all that is implied in the formation of the memory-train and upon that recurrence of like series of impressions which we attribute to the 'uniformity of nature' ".[1]

For immediate experience, the important direction is from present to past—we think of the present receding into the past, rather than of the past growing on, and swallowing up, the present. Consequently the sophistication of the primitive intuition of process into a definite concept of 'Time' in which the present 'moves along' from past to future involves also a change of emphasis: and any theory as to the development of the concept must take account of this. I would suggest that the key to the change is to be found in the distinction that is early made between 'self' and what is not 'self':[2] we attribute to ourselves the emphasis on 'presentness-becoming-past', at the same time admitting that, objectively, the alternative way of regarding it may be more fundamental. This point has been very well brought out by E. A. Burtt in an article entitled "Real and Abstract Evolution", which was published in the *Proceedings of the Sixth International Congress of Philosophy*. He says:[3] ". . . Empirically the past always emerges out of the present rather than the present out of the past. . . . The world as empirically revealed always begins in the present, and remains within it while expanding into the past and the future. This may sound startlingly paradoxical—the opposing view would, however, be much more startling if it were not so fully ingrained in our

---

[1] Ward, op. cit., p. 211.
[2] For an account of this, see Stout, op. cit. (Book III, Part II, chapters i and ii; and Book IV, chapter v). [3] Loc. cit., p. 172.

thought-habits that we never dream of questioning it. . . . Appeal to fact on such a matter may be unconventional and embarrassing, yet I beg of you to consider whether the world as actually revealed to any of you began in a remote past with Space-Time or electrons, or whether these things did not emerge after the world had gone through many adventures and assumed many shapes. . . . Real evolution, that is, evolution as empirically discovered, is not a movement from past through present to future (such a process is itself an emergent abstraction from the course of real evolution), it is evolution from the present into both past and future. The world always takes shape from the present outwards. It expands into the past as knowledge of the past is needed to satisfy present desires: it expands into the future as grasp of recurrent regularities permits anticipation, prediction, and intelligent purpose."[1] But whether we state the passage of time with the emphasis on the recession of a given event from the future through the present to the more and more remote past, or with the emphasis on 'the present' moving along continually into the future, in either case we are considering the resultant movement as unidirectional. (This will be seen if we slide two rulers, the inch edge of one representing events, the centimetre edge of the other representing the past-present-future series, along each other. Whether we slide ruler R along ruler S or vice versa, makes no difference to the direction of the process.)[2] Unidirectionality is an empirical necessity: constituted as we are, it is a brute fact, which cannot be gainsaid, that the process of which we are immediately aware in the moment of experience is not ('cannot' be is another matter, outside psychology) reversible.

Eternity, the notion of an endless abiding, of an escape from the flux of time, adds point and contrast to the former notions. It may be suggested that it originates from that contrast, or from the conceptual extension to infinity of an immobilized instant[3]—itself an abstraction; but the widespread use of this concept at an early

[1] Compare also Guyau's remark: "L'avenir n'est pas *ce que vient vers nous*, mais *ce vers quoi nous allons*" (*Génèse de l'Idée de Temps*, p. 33).

[2] Of course, both the language and the analogy are open to criticism. But, at this level, that cannot be helped. See also McTaggart, *Nature of Existence*, II, p. 10 n.

[3] Cf. Eriksen, *Consciousness, Life, and the Fourth Dimension*, p. 140.

era would seem to show that it is not merely a sophistication based on temporal notions, but an original tendency of our nature. In Parmenides' view: "what is, is uncreated and indivisible; for it is complete, immovable, and without end. Nor was it ever, nor will it be: for now *it is*, all at once, a continuous one".[1] Plato, too, in a celebrated passage,[2] tells how God "devised the making of a moving likeness of everlastingness". But psychologists, as distinct from philosophers, have for the most part found little to say about eternity, preferring to concentrate on more immediate manifestations.

The foregoing pages are an attempt to sketch, very briefly, the experiential basis on which the temporal notions which we use so light-heartedly are founded.[3] It is evident that there is a considerable gap between them. But before we go on to the points of difference, there is a second aspect of time, considered from the point of view of experience, which needs discussion. This concerns subjective measures of duration.

II

We may define duration, as it is used in this chapter, as being the temporal extension of an event or events in the experience of a subject. Thus, though I am not immediately aware of successive events within a specious present as taking time (the knowledge that they must do so is a later addition, the result of inference, and of sophistication of what we mean by 'momentary events'), I *am* aware that longer events, such as hearing the complete sentence: "Mathematics is the science where nobody knows what he is talking about, nor whether what he says is true", have some temporal extension. As Stout puts it: "When we are listening to a sound, our experience is different at the end of one minute from what it is at the end of two minutes, although the sound itself may not have altered in quality. This experience is unique in kind, and it certainly does not consist in having the parts of the sound-sensation, as they successively occur, spread out before us in a sort of duration-line or duration-block."[4]

Probably the awareness of events as 'taking time' is at first implicit: it only becomes explicit if we have other reasons to con-

[1] Burnet, *Early Greek Philosophy*, p. 174. [2] *Timaeus*, 37c.
[3] Reference may also be made to the good discussion in Gunn's *Problem of Time*, pp. 376–95. [4] Stout, op. cit., p. 501.

cern ourselves with time-lapse, for instance, sensations of hunger, feelings of boredom occasioned by a too long speech, or definite attempts at introspection. Nevertheless there is no question that with the progress of civilization the notion of time-lapse becomes very important. What is more, we are not merely aware of the fact that an event E 'takes time': we can to a certain extent correlate and compare it with another event F in respect of the 'length' of time it occupies. Our standard for such comparison is a purely subjective one, and is probably connected with the feelings and ideas which the events evoke in us, as has been recognized since the time of Locke. "We have no perception of duration but by considering the train of ideas that take their turns in our understandings."[1] It is by now a truism, however, that our subjective estimates of duration do not agree, and that what is objectively[2] 'the same' interval may appear of different duration to different observers, and to the same observer at different times. Shakespeare gave classic expression to this when he said: "Time travels in divers paces with divers persons. I'll tell you who Time ambles withal, who Time trots withal, who Time gallops withal, and who he stands still withal."[3] What is more noteworthy than the mere statement of subjective differences in estimation is, that he attempted to give reasons *why* the condemned man should find time pass more quickly than the lover. In recent times, this and connected problems have received considerable attention from psychologists, and much work has been done, the results of which may be briefly summarized here.

Without in any way pre-judging the metaphysical question of whether time is anything in itself apart from events, it is exceedingly useful to distinguish between empty and filled periods of time—as long as we remember that 'empty time' is only relatively empty. For the accuracy[4] with which time intervals can be estimated varies with the content of experience during that interval. It is at first

[1] Locke, *Essay*, Book II, chapter xiv, section 4.
[2] What is meant by the 'objective measurement of duration', and the evolution of a common standard out of the varying estimates of different people is not dealt with until the next chapter, as also the notion of 'accuracy'. For the present I rely on the familiarity of these notions.
[3] *As You Like It*, III. 2. 1. 326.
[4] Accuracy, that is, as measured 'publicly' by clocks—a subject that will be dealt with in the next chapter.

sight paradoxical that the more we deliberately set ourselves to note the passage of time, the harder it is to estimate. We all know how long a minute can be if we watch the finger of a stop-watch going round. It is, in practice, impossible to note 'the passage of time' for long. In spite of ourselves, our minds wander: we feel bored: it is with an effort that we re-concentrate: our attention slackens again: we find ourselves counting the ticks.[1] It is an evidently artificial procedure: consequently most experiments on time-estimation have dealt, rightly, with filled intervals. Those who adhere to the Bergsonian view of consciousness have an added reason for this. Professor Edgell, for example, says: ". . . for psychology, Duration belongs only to the dynamic view of Consciousness—Consciousness viewed as a stream, as a Life of connected processes. To predicate duration of an isolated sensation is . . . unthinkable. . . . It is the metaphysical standpoint which makes us predicate time of the element which we are avowedly considering in the abstract. . . . It is in the Dynamic view of Consciousness that the explanation for the phenomena of over- and under-estimation should be sought."[2]

Several factors appear to influence accuracy of estimation: as usual, fatigue, interest, practice, and individual differences play their part. More peculiarly relevant to the subject of time-estimation, though, is the way in which the interval is filled[3]—whether with one relatively unchanging event or with successive well-marked changes.

Changes which take place too rapidly, or on no apparent plan (like the groupings of a kaleidoscope), soon induce fatigue: on the other hand, too slow a procedure results in boredom. Apart from the disturbing effects of fatigue, an interval in which there are many ideas passes quickly: but it is long in retrospect.[4] The child who is taken for a treat to the theatre finds something new and exciting each minute—the journey to the town, the marvellous trams, the crowds and shops and traffic, the importance of having a real grown-

[1] Compare James, op. cit., p. 626.
[2] *American Journal of Psychology*, 1903, p. 434.
[3] Stern says: "Der Optimalwert ist in hohem Masse abhängig von dem Inhalt des Bewusstseins" (*Zeitschrift für Psychologie*, 1897, p. 343).
[4] This statement, generally accepted, is questioned by Miss Sturt (*Psychology of Time*, p. 102).

up lunch, the thrill of getting seated, the tuning-up of the orchestra, the rising of the curtain—and it all passes much too quickly. But afterwards, going home, it seems incredible that so much could have happened in one day, and 'this morning' seems ages ago. On the other hand, where the succession of ideas is slow, the time drags; but when we look back on it we have little to remember it by, and so it is foreshortened, just as, in looking along a flat, straight road, we notice the landmark at the end, and tend to under-estimate the intervening distance.

We must distinguish, then, between events in their passing, and in retrospect, and between dull and eventful periods: and we must also remember that further complications may be introduced by their affective tone (painful, or boring, or unsettling, or annoying). In general, it may be said, that wherever our attention is explicitly called to the passage of time—the "Oh! that this were over" of boredom or pain, the "What a long time the train is!" of impatience, the *"Carpe diem"* of an enjoyment oppressed by transience—there we have an approximation to the conditions of empty time, and consequent aberrations of judgment.[1] It seems a paradox to say that when we are explicitly noting the passing of time we are more likely to make mistakes than at other times, but I think that it is so. Looking up after an interval spent in writing, I have a pretty good idea how long it is since I last looked at my watch; but I have never yet succeeded in boiling an egg properly without some kind of clock. In some experiments on this point I found that "tell me when you think x minutes are up" gave poorer results than "how long is it since so and so happened?" The distinction may seem a fine one, but I would tentatively suggest, if properly substantiated experiments prove it valid, that it may be related to Bergson's distinction between time passed and time passing. When it has passed we may estimate the lapse of time: but we fail utterly with time in its passage.

But apart from all these factors affecting the accuracy of our estimation of time-intervals, there still remain considerable varia-

[1] Compare the passage in Meredith's *Vittoria* where Wilfrid and Rinaldo Guidascarpi are released from imprisonment in a dungeon: "A thunder was rolled in his ears when he heard of the flight of two months at a bound. Two big months! He would have guessed, at farthest, two weeks" (Memorial Edition, Vol. II, p. 382).

tions, which are generally accounted for by the hypothesis that certain intervals, other things being equal, favour accurate estimation. Many experiments, mainly by German psychologists, have shown that this best interval, or "optimum time" as it is usually called, is about ·75 seconds, though different people vary to some extent. Shorter intervals than this tend to be over-estimated, longer ones to be under-estimated.[1] It is also asserted, in support of the conception of an 'optimum time', that the accuracy of estimation shows a certain periodicity, and fluctuates with the multiples of the optimum time.

For reasons which will be given in the next chapter, I am rather sceptical about the value of this type of experiment, as there is a suspicion of circularity about it. But if it is regarded merely as a basis for a physiological theory of time-estimation, there is no harm in it. The position may be expressed here shortly as follows: All measurement depends ultimately on a direct perception of equality and inequality. Hence it should not be a matter of wonder and self-congratulation, as it is, to too many psychologists, when they 'discover' an interval that can be 'estimated' 'with great accuracy'. But that our primitive perception of equality is based upon physiological rhythms, such as breathing,[2] is a different matter, and one which, if substantiated, would be important. This topic, of the importance of rhythm, will be returned to later on, when other aspects of our apprehension of time have been considered.

Other experimenters[3] have attempted to ascertain the duration

[1] Original articles on this subject by Wundt, Kollert, Estel, Mehner, Schumann, and others are to be found in the *Zeitschrift für Psychologie* and Wundt's *Philosophische Studien*. An excellent historical account, and an attempt to render the results of different experimenters consistent, is to be found in Münsterberg's *Beiträge zur Experimentellen Psychologie*. See also Vierordt, *Der Zeitsinn*, and Stevens (*Mind*, 1886), the latter of whom reaches results in conflict with most of the others.

[2] See Münsterberg, op. cit., for this view, and Fouillée's criticisms of it in the second volume of his *Psychologie des Idées-Forces*. It has been suggested to me that such rhythms vary considerably during the daytime (with exertion, excitement, and so on), but are much more regular when we are asleep, so that our appreciation of time-intervals as measured by physiological movements should be more accurate during trances and sleep than when we are awake. If this is so, it might help to account for some of the paradoxes of extraordinarily accurate perception mentioned later.

[3] Such as Stern, loc. cit.; Strong (*Mind*, 1926).

of the specious present, and its variations under abnormal conditions, such as in dreams, drug-taking, and moments of excitement. De Quincey, in his *Opium Eater*, tells how everything for him took place slowly (so that one idea was spread over several specious presents): "Space swelled, and was amplified to an extent of unutterable infinity. This, however, did not disturb me so much as the vast expansion of time; I sometimes seemed to have lived for seventy to a hundred years in one night; nay, sometimes had feelings representative of a millennium passed in that time, or, however, of a duration far beyond the limits of any human experience."[1] Mr. Morley Roberts tells of the experiences of a man shortly before a serious operation: "His mind was many-coloured, rapid in motion, magical. Stimuli played upon him from without and within, and he answered with inconceivable rapidity. He thought not of one thing at a time, but of all things at once. The complexes of his life and character interpenetrated each other. They were like nets laid on nets: they were infinitely reticulated. In the time he took to move one step he seemed to have time for eternal thought. Time in his processes was slackening. . . . He heard his own physician speak: 'Hullo, Waring!' He had known Heathcote for many years. But Waring found it difficult to answer. It seemed to him that he had not opened his mouth for a very long time."[2]

On the other hand, Miss Sturt quotes the example of a soldier, to whom a day passed like half an hour:[3] and there are also the stories of drowning people whose whole lives passed before them in a minute, and of Mozart, who 'heard' his music all at once, and of dreamers who go through long and complicated adventures in a few seconds. What would their specious present be, compared with De Quincey's or 'Mr. Waring's'? Stern, in the article quoted earlier, rightly insists that the specious present has nothing to do with the duration of a presentation, and he criticizes James for equating these. But little is known beyond this negative criticism, and beyond the general belief that the specious present is connected with the succession of ideas in our minds. Hence anything which retards this succession, such as a boring occupation, means that one idea is, so to speak, 'spread over' many specious presents, and time passes abnormally slowly.

[1] Edited Saintsbury (Constable, 1927), pp. 114–15.
[2] *Time and Thomas Waring*, pp. 16–17.   [3] Op. cit., p. 90.

There would seem to be two main factors influencing our apprehension of time, which have not always been sufficiently distinguished. I think that in their distinction is to be found an explanation of some of the paradoxes of time-perception.

First there is the importance of tempo, and this is connected with the phenomena of optimum time, and the rhythms of physiological processes. Recently, the important experiments described by Lecomte du Noüy[1] suggest that reparation of injured tissues is also relevant here.

On the other hand, there is the succession of ideas in our minds. In normal life, these two are connected; thus a quick succession of ideas and an attempt to translate them into actions that are physiologically too rapid for us, lead to fatigue, and ultimately to a breakdown. But under certain conditions they may be dissociated. In sleep, we are not under the necessity of translating our thoughts into actions: a succession which, if we had to *do* it, would be much too rapid, causes us no inconvenience.[2] What would take two hours *to do* may occur in a dream of a few minutes' duration, and if we are told how long our dream 'really was', we are frankly incredulous—*because we judge the dream by the standards of ordinary life*. On the other hand, when all our attention is actively engaged on what we are doing—as in Miss Sturt's example of a soldier—we have 'no time to think', and one idea only occupies our minds, so that (if we judge by our thought-content and not by what we have done) the time seems shorter than it really is. If the soldier afterwards thought of all that he had *done*, the time would seem longer. Normally our thoughts and actions keep pace more or less, so that it does not matter which we go by in our estimation—we shall get the same result in either case. It is only when the two become dissociated that we get different estimates according to which we use, and hence paradoxes. (Of course, not all abnormal estimations can be explained like this. The drug which De Quincey took affected *both* his thoughts and his acts: both were

[1] In his book *Biological Time*.

[2] "The speed of thought" is a familiar phrase. When our attention is called to it (which is not often) we are amazed how many thoughts come in a short interval of time. A cyclist sees danger: he swerves and brakes, but sees a crash to be inevitable: *after* he has done everything he can do, and *before* the crash comes (an interval of perhaps two seconds), many ideas pass through his mind.

slowed down, so that whichever way he regarded it, time was lengthened.)

Lastly, it has been suggested[1] that, granted the hypothesis of an ideal 'tempo' which is most satisfactory to us, there is no need to maintain that this tempo is the same for all living creatures, but that it may vary between different species. So that, as James puts it,[2] commenting on a similar suggestion of Von Baer's: "Suppose we were able, within the length of a second, to note 10,000 events distinctly, instead of barely 10, as now: if our life were then destined to hold the same number of impressions it might be 1,000 times as short. We should live less than a month, and personally know nothing of the change of seasons. If born in winter, we should believe in summer as we now believe in the heats of the Carboniferous era. The motions of organic beings would be so slow to our senses as to be inferred, not seen. The sun would stand still in the sky, the moon be almost free from change, and so on. But now reverse the hypothesis and suppose a being to get only one-thousandth part of the sensations that we get in a given time, and consequently to live a thousand times as long. Winters and summers will be to him like quarters of an hour. Mushrooms and the swifter-growing plants will shoot into being so rapidly as to appear instantaneous creations; annual shrubs will rise and fall from the earth like restlessly boiling water-springs: the motions of animals will be invisible as are to us the movements of bullets and cannon-balls; the sun will scour through the sky like a meteor, leaving a fiery trail behind him."

It might be possible to extend the suggestion, and to hold that the tempo may vary also in the same individual at different times of his life, and under different bodily conditions: and that would allow for the anomaly first pointed out by Paul Janet,[3] that to

[1] By Herbert Spencer. See *Principles of Psychology*, section 91.
[2] Op. cit., p. 369. I have been unable to check the reference to Von Baer.
[3] *Revue philosophique*, Vol. III. Janet's own explanation, that a year represents to a child a much longer time in proportion to the rest of its life than it does to an adult, has not been generally accepted. For alternative explanations, see also James, op. cit., p. 625; Sturt, op. cit., p. 103; Romanes, *Mind*, 1878, p. 289; Pierre Janet, *Evolution de la Mémoire*, p. 515; and Guyau, op. cit., p. 110. The recent work of du Noüy (op. cit., pp. 158 ff.) seems, however, the most important, as being based on experiment and not merely on theory.

the child a year is longer than it is to an adult, and also for the agreed fact that when we feel particularly alert, we can stand a rapid succession of events that would usually tire us. But it could only be regarded as an *explanation* in the very vague sense that the general hypothesis of ideal tempos applies: it is no particular explanation of the *special* problem of Janet, and for this a more definite reason is required. Nevertheless it is well to note that this hypothesis applies here as well as in the more often quoted case of the difference in normal length of life of different species.

But besides being vague and needing substantiation, the theory of tempos fails to explain the power that some people possess of waking at set times, the apparent development of a time-sense in children,[1] and above all the extraordinary feats of hypnotized and mediumistic subjects, which have been reported by medical psychologists.[2] These feats are well-authenticated, and in some cases the circumstances were such as to make "calculation and watching the clock" impossible. As Mitchell rightly pointed out, *calculation* and *appreciation* of time are quite distinct, and we cannot assume the latter unless we have excluded the former. It would almost seem that there is some obscure and imperfectly understood way of estimating time-intervals, distinct from ordinary methods[3] and in this connection those theories (such as Von Cyon's)[4] which hold that we have a definite time-sense, are interesting. It is, however, difficult to see why it has taken us so long to discover that we have a direct apprehension of time, and also such theories are open to the objection that they raise metaphysical difficulties about the

[1] See Miss Sturt, op. cit., chapter lv, who considers that young children have a very sketchy sense of time. For the opposite view, see James, op. cit., Vol. I, p. 631.

[2] See Bramwell, *Hypnotism*, and T. W. Mitchell, *Medical Psychology and Scientific Research*, chapter i. These deal with abnormally accurate estimations of time-lapse. Also Osty, *Supernormal Faculties in Man*, and Flammarion, *Before Death*. These deal with unexplained examples of what is popularly known as 'second sight', including examples of predictions. False recognition of events as having happened before is dealt with by Bergson, *Mind Energy*, chapter v; Pierre Janet, op. cit., XIV; and Wohlgemuth, *Mind*, 1924 (with bibliography).

[3] A good discussion is to be found in Bramwell, op. cit., p. 402 et seq., containing criticisms of the explanations brought forward by Beaunis, Delbœuf, and Gurney.

[4] E. von Cyon, *L'Oreille*, and C. Vierordt, *Der Zeitsinn*.

relation of time and events. A great deal of work still remains to be done on these topics before any definite conclusions can be reached, and any psychological treatment of time for many years to come must inevitably be left in an unfinished and unsatisfactory state.

III

The 'time' of experience has one great drawback in a gregarious world. It is private, and varies with the subject. The conventionalizing of duration is inevitable if we are to live peaceably with our fellows, to prevent unnecessary disputes and uncertainties and waste of time. Eddington expressed this neatly in his imaginary meeting between the Astronomer-Royal and M. Bergson. "I rather think that the philosopher would have had the best of the verbal argument. After showing that the Astronomer-Royal's idea of time was quite nonsensical, Professor Bergson would probably end the discussion by looking at his watch and rushing off to catch a train which was starting by the Astronomer-Royal's time."[1]

We shall be concerned with this turning of time into a public services company in the next chapter: here we need only remark that a proper study of time must of necessity go beyond the limits of psychology, at the behests of practical utility. And from the point of view of theoretical consistency, too, the need is no less pressing, for by now the logician has many complaints, and with good reason. He points out the inadequacy of the suggested 'premises' to warrant all that is drawn from them: he scornfully exposes the vagueness and lack of precision in the terms used, and the blatantly circular procedure by which temporal terms such as 'transition', 'priority', and 'past', are used throughout, even in elucidating concepts on which they themselves depend. He says in effect—granted the difficulties with which you have to deal, and especially the difficulty of dealing explicitly and in isolation with such an important concept as time—granted that it is almost impossible not to presuppose time somewhere: I still think that you should have made a better job of it than you have done. You attempt to give an exposition of the development of temporal notions: starting from the admitted complexity and sophistication of these notions as they

[1] *Nature of the Physical World*, p. 36.

are in civilized adults, you postulate original unexplained miracles such as 'memory' and the 'moment of experience' on which you base the rest. That does not matter so much: what does matter is that in your so-called exposition of 'the rest' you use them indiscriminately to explain each other, and you constantly refer back to everyday experience. This reference, to a much greater degree of sophistication that you profess to allow, is invalid.

The psychologist, on the other hand, pleads extremity, and urges that a genetic explanation is bound to be in terms of the highest level. Now whether we admit the claim of the logician (and the metaphysician, with appropriate changes of detail) to set the psychologist's house in order, or whether we accept the psychologist's excuse, and leave his competence unquestioned, one thing emerges definitely.

It is that we cannot ultimately remain satisfied with a purely psychological account of time. Too many questions have been raised that are unanswerable by psychology for that—such questions, for example, as—Is irreversibility *essential* to time, or only empirically connected with it? Is there any sense in talking about 'only empirically', and thus implying that time may be something apart from experience? Is there any way of judging between different time-series, and saying that one person's estimations are 'more accurate' than another's? (Although psychology uses the notion of accuracy, it nowhere explains it except in terms of notions which themselves presuppose it.)

In short, psychology stops just where things begin to become interesting: its account glosses over the distinction between accredited entities and bogus entities (such as 'the' Past), and it provides no criterion by which such may be judged: it is too inclined to adopt circular procedures. Now these may, or may not, be unavoidable for psychology; we are not concerned here to judge psychology, but to discuss 'time'. And if we can go farther outside of psychology, we will.

The plain man, in the contempt born of over-familiarity with temporal flux, with a bad grace referred us to psychology. But although it cannot be too strongly emphasized that our findings must be in agreement with the immediate experience on which ultimately all our notions of time are based, psychology alone is not enough.

PSYCHOLOGY

Resulting from practical considerations, there is the development of the conception of a measurable, conventional, standardized time-interval in physics. With this we shall next be concerned. On the theoretical side, an excursion into logic and metaphysics is now inevitable.

CHAPTER II

PHYSICS

I

ALTHOUGH our experience of time is the ultimate datum from which we must of necessity begin, it is open to certain obvious objections in practical life. It is private and subjective: my estimation of the duration of two intervals may not agree with yours, and I have no way of showing you that mine is the better. This is very inconvenient if we wish accurately to communicate the length of a certain interval: hence the need of finding an 'objective' means of measuring intervals, one that shall be independent of our individual eccentricities.

It is important to notice that by 'objective' here is meant originally, not necessarily "accurate" (as we of a highly sophisticated generation would use the word), but fixed in the sense that it is common to all. Let us suppose a very powerful primitive king who succeeded in imposing on his subjects his own private reckoning of time. This would be an advance on the former state, in that all would agree, perforce, in the estimation of a given interval. But such a system could not prove satisfactory in the comparing of *different* intervals: and this is the chief thing. For, as Weber pertinently pointed out in his brilliant article "The Reality of Time and the Autonomy of History"[1], when we consider the measurable aspect of time (that is, time as rate of change), it is not sufficient that there should be discontinuous units—such, for example, as our primitive king would call a single event—but also two more conditions are necessary. The first is that these discontinuous units should be equal to each other: the second is that the repetition of "the same time" should be possible.

The first section of this chapter will be taken up with discussing how these conditions are realized in the measurement

[1] *Monist*, 1927.

of time: but first some remarks must be made on measurement in general.¹

All measurement, of whatever kind, depends on the use of a standard unit. *What* this unit is, is logically indifferent: the important point is that it shall be constant. Let us take the measurement of length, as this is the simplest case. I may measure a piece of cloth with my outstretched finger-tips, and say that it is five hands' breadths long. But you, doing the same, say it is only four and a half. Evidently, if neither of us has made a mistake, your hands are bigger than mine. We can quickly check this. You find a piece of wood the exact length of your hand and say, "*This* is what I call a hand's breadth: this cloth is four and a half hands' breadths long." Then *either* I can reject your definition (if I am foolish), which will mean that both of us will have to correct each other's estimates, with other, and probably different again, corrections for third parties, *or* I can agree to use your convention. Others agree, too, until finally we have a whole community meaning the same thing by 'hands' breadth' or 'ell' or 'metre' or whatever we call it.

This is all very familiar: and its explicit statement may seem childish. But its very familiarity may blind us to the postulates on which all measurement is implicitly based—postulates which, though they may be unquestioned, are not on that account unquestionable. And, when they are brought into the light, we often find it hard to rationalize them fully—perhaps because they are so fundamental. Here they are:

(1) *Transitivity and Additivity*. "Things which are equal to the same thing are equal to one another." If one object is twice as long (or as heavy) as my standard unit, and another is four times as long as the standard: the former is exactly half the latter. (But, of course, the plain man does not appeal to the generalization in Euclid's best manner: he appeals to *his* cloth and *his* standard. If they did not, *in fact*, tally, there would be no theory of measurement.² The appeal to sense-experience is all-important.)

(2) The material of which my standard is made, and the length

¹ See also Ritchie, *Scientific Method*, chapter v; Westaway, *Scientific Method*, chapter xxiv, Campbell, *What is Physics?* chapter vi; Stebbing, *A Modern Introduction to Logic*, XVIII, section 5.

² Though there could still be mathematics.

of it, are logically indifferent. I suit my own convenience, and use a flexible tape-measure on some occasions and on others a hard piece of wood. Then, too, we may make our measurements in 'inches' or 'yards' or 'miles': we would not measure the distance between two towns with an inch-tape. *But*, we are bound to show which unit we are using: it is useless to say, "This is 36" without saying 36 *what*. Convention plays an essential part in measurement, and it is just *because* there is no divine right in the units which we choose, that we have to make clear which one we are using on a given occasion.

(3) But we have to be assured that our standard of length or weight or whatever it is remains constant. A yard-stick that was twice as long on Monday as it was on Tuesday would be useless. Consequently, though, as was said above, the exact material of our standard is strictly irrelevant, in practice we do not choose a standard that is liable to stretch, contract, or be sensibly altered by changes of temperature.[1] Also, we are bound to assume that our yard-stick when carried about in space remains of a constant length.

(4) But—and here is the crux of the question—what is meant by "remains constant"? How do we *know* that it is constant? If we doubted the reliability of one particular stick, we would measure it against another to see whether it coincided or not. But we cannot do that here—it is the whole process which is in question. There is an inevitable begging of the question in measurement, which is partially masked by the familiarity of the operation. *How* do I know that this is constant? Not, in the last resort, by more measurement: ultimately the only answer I can give (which the plain man would have given long ago) is—Because I do. We have a primitive and direct perception of equality, and it is on this that the whole of our measurement is based. I *see* that these two pieces of wood sensibly coincide: I *feel* that the weight in my right hand is slightly greater than the weight in my left. Psychologists talk of 'optical illusions', such as the converging lines which are shown by measurement to be "really" the "same" length: but though measurement,

---

[1] It is beside the point to object here that all physical bodies are affected by temperature. Such a generalization can only be reached after many measurements have been taken. This is measurement highly sophisticated and very delicate, but it *is* measurement, and cannot well be used as an argument against the first stages of the process on which it is itself based.

in its developed form, may be more accurate than our eyes and able to discover small differences imperceptible to the naked eye,[1] we must nevertheless remember that in the end measurement is only a gigantic circular structure wholly dependent for its validity upon the validity of our direct perception of equality and inequality.

(5) A familiar poser at present is—"Supposing, while you were asleep, *everything* in the world were increased to twice its present size, how would you find out?" You could not perceive the difference directly, since the retinas of your eyes would be twice the size they are now, and neither could you perceive it indirectly through measurement, since your yard-sticks would have increased too. The answer is, of course, that you would never find it out, *because everything would be in exactly the same proportions as before.*

There is a moral to this story. It is that measurement is concerned with relative *proportions*. Measurement does not tell you *the* length of this piece of cloth (if, indeed, "*the* length" has any meaning): what it tells you is "the length relatively to this tape-measure". When I say, "it is three yards long", I mean that its proportion to my standard is three to one, and I add the 'yards' so that I can remember which standard I am using. Common language is inclined to hypostatize (and, in practice, it is harmless enough to talk as if there "really are" such things as yards and feet and inches), but at bottom all we assert is a numerical correlation. Hence the introduction of measurement in science corresponds to the increasing use of mathematical methods.

We must now apply these general considerations to the special case of the measurement of intervals of *time*, though here the question is complicated by the essential character of time, which is its 'passing away'. Intervals of time cannot be placed side by side and directly compared in respect of their duration, because they do not both exist at the same time. (A more exact formulation of this sentence would reveal numerous difficulties—indeed, it is hardly too much to say that the whole of the metaphysical problem of time is involved—but here we need not raise them, relying on the fact, elsewhere a hindrance, that the passing away of time is instantly familiar, so that everyone knows *what* is meant, however difficult it be to formulate it accurately.)

Here again we have to rely on primitive perception and also

[1] For example, the marvellous feats of astronomy.

on what may be called primitive memory. Our experience is not atomic in the sense of consisting of momentary flashes, as has already been said. On the contrary, past and present are continuous, and the past can be *remembered*. This is tremendously important, since without it there would be no experience of time. Without going into the controversy whether or not we have direct memory of past events, it is not too much to say—and in support of this I can only appeal to your introspection—that with regard to certain very short intervals succeeding each other within the specious present, we have an immediate and primitive perception of equality and inequality comparable to that which we have in the case of two co-existent perceptions.[1] This primitive perception is "objective" in the sense that everyone's judgments do, as a matter of fact, agree. If we could not agree, we should have no way of comparing, objectively, two intervals separated in time. And it is strictly nonsense to ask of this primitive judgment, "Is it accurate?" for if it were not, we should have no means of knowing. "Accuracy" is not the test of it: rather is *it* the test of accuracy. Hence the faintly comic flavour when psychologists, after much research, assure us with great solemnity that there is an 'optimal time' which can be estimated with "surprising accuracy"! Of course there is!

Granted, then, that we have this direct judgment, the next thing is to erect, on the basis of it, a standard. Apart from accuracy, *what* standard we take is, of course, logically indifferent. For instance, we might have taken pulse-rate, or the beating of the heart, or breathing as our standard, except for the facts *directly observable* that when we are excited our breathing is quicker, and that there are slight individual variations in heart-beat, etc., with age, state of health, etc. And since it would involve a lot of trouble as to when a man is, and is not "excited", and which of several men is the most "normal", this standard is not generally used[2]

[1] Poincaré takes the opposite view when he says: "Nous n'avons pas l'intuition directe de l'égalité de deux intervalles de temps" (*La Valeur de la Science*, p. 38). Instead, he makes the ultimate basis of our measurement depend upon the *postulate* that astronomical phenomena are regular. I cannot think that this is so.

[2] But that is not to say that such physiological rhythms have not an essential part to play in the development in us of a sense of time. See previous chapter for references to those who would support this view.

PHYSICS

(though accurate for short intervals, as the celebrated tale about Galileo shows). The simplest way of getting a standard that shall be "public" and exclude individual variations is to choose natural phenomena. The recurrence of day and night is an obvious example. On a larger scale there are phases of the moon, seasons, and the important interval which we call a 'year'. Apart from the week of seven days, all the divisions of our calendar from a day upwards have their origin in cycles in nature. But it was soon discovered that those cycles had no common denominator, hence came ceaseless attempts at 'correcting' the calendar. It is very puzzling to children why a year should be made up of $365\frac{1}{4}$ days— why the quarter? Secondly, as regards the subdivision of the day, the Greeks divided the period of daylight into a fixed number of hours. But then the hours were longer in summer than in winter. We, on the contrary, keep the hours constant, so that in summer we have more than twelve hours' daylight, and in winter less.[1]

But it is obvious that in saying this, by no means the last word has been said upon the subject. *How* do we know that to the Greeks the hours were "longer in summer than in winter"? What do we mean by "keeping the hours of a constant length"? Evidently a reference to more than astronomical phenomena is required: otherwise it would be nonsense to say that one day is equal (or unequal, as the case may be) to another day. Put differently— the choice of astronomical phenomena as a standard has the advantage, like the primitive king in the example at the beginning of the chapter, of ruling out dissent as to the duration of a given interval. But it is important to see clearly that the second and more fundamental condition of measurement—that the units should be *equal*—is logically entirely independent of this. It might be the case that different astronomical intervals were not all of "the same length" (and it is, in fact, true, as the plain man asserts with the utmost confidence, that the night is shorter on June 21st than on December 21st). This apparently simple statement is, however, logically of a high degree of sophistication.[2]

---

[1] For fuller treatment, see Nilsson, "Primitive Time-Reckoning"; Nordmann, "The Tyranny of Time"; Shotwell, "The Discovery of Time" (*Journal of Philosophy*, 1915).

[2] And still more, Eddington's statement that the length of day is increasing gradually throughout the centuries.

What is it that leads us to suppose that we can attach a meaning to the statement that a summer's day "is longer" than a winter's one? Evidently only that we have some *other* standard by which we compare them: otherwise we could never ask ourselves the question, "Are the well-marked intervals that astronomy gives us all *equal* in length?" In other words, astronomical phenomena provide a means of correlating the 'private' estimations of individuals: they do not themselves provide a standard of accurate measurement. How else may time be measured? Firstly, by the simple devices of water or sand flowing through a funnel, or by the sun's shadow passing over a marked board; and, secondly, by clocks of various degrees of ingenious complexity. But the problem is the same in either case, and so it may well be taken on its simplest level. Grains of sand fall through an hour-glass. How do we know that they fall at the same "rate", so that one emptying of the hour-glass is equivalent to another? *Not*, obviously, because each "takes an hour", but because, if I watched closely enough, I should see that x grains fell through in a certain short interval, and that in *every* similar interval x grains fell through, and because you and and everybody else would agree with me on this point. Similarly, in the more complicated mechanisms that modern ingenuity has produced, the escapements are so adjusted that the rate of rotation of the flywheels is constant—that is, that the same number of teeth are engaged in equal intervals of time.[1] It is useless to think that in objectifying our standard of measuring intervals, we are eliminating the personal factor entirely: if we did, there would be no measurement at all, because the ultimate reference *must* be to direct perception of the equality of two intervals. It has often been said that the essential circularity involved in all measurement is greater when dealing with time than in dealing with anything else: we make our standard of measurement something that goes at a constant "rate" (revolutions of the minute hand of a clock, for instance), while on the other hand, all that we *mean* by rate is that a certain distance is covered in a *certain time*. The point has been very well put by Sigwart:[2] "If we define a uniform motion

---

[1] For detailed descriptions of the various types of mechanism, see Berthoud, *Histoire de la Mesure de Temps*; Gould, *The Marine Chronometer*; Cunynghame, *Time and Clocks*; Bolton, *Time-Measurement*.

[2] *Logic* (English translation), Vol. II, p. 240.

as one in which equal spaces are traversed in equal times, then in order to know it as such we must suppose that we are able to measure directly the equality of two periods of time. Thus all the means which we can employ for measuring time depend upon assumptions which can never be strictly proved: they depend ultimately upon the assumption that the rotation of the earth is constant in velocity,[1] and that the time between the culmination of a fixed star and another is, therefore, always the same: and, again, upon the assumptions that the oscillations of the pendulums regulating our clocks are isochronous. . . . Our conviction that in our clocks and our astronomical observations we really measure equal times depends ultimately upon nothing more than the agreement of those motions which various physical principles lead us to expect with those motions which we actually observe." The reference to time cannot be entirely eliminated, and there is an inevitable circularity. But it is not a vicious circle, I think. Granted that the notion of rate or velocity, which is used to measure duration, itself involves duration before it can be comprehended (that is, the notion of "duration" is logically prior to that of "velocity"), we can yet escape an endless relativity by the fact that our original judgment of the equality of two intervals is a *direct* one. Or, as Cunningham puts it in a slightly different way, "Metrical space and time are not independent and self-contained concepts, but are conditioned by the very phenomena which they are used to describe."[2] The measurement of time-intervals, like all measurement, is ultimately based on primitive perception.

The objective measurement of duration, or physical time, is therefore an abstraction from lived duration, but because of its greater (logical) simplicity, we often express the latter in terms of it. Thus we say, "*The same* interval may appear of different lengths to different observers, and to the same observer at different times."

This raises the last point about time-measurement—how it is

[1] Reasons have been given above for doubting whether the reference to astronomical phenomena *is* ultimate: but here the point is rather that *some* reference is required (whatever it may be), and that ultimately our measurement of time depends upon unproved assumptions.

[2] *The Principle of Relativity*, p. 217. Compare Balmes (*Fundamental Philosophy*, Book VII), who rightly pointed out that time is prior to the watch by which we undertake to measure it, and though it is measured by movement through space, it may yet be independent of movement.

that we can say, as we do, that "the same" interval is repeated, for this would obviously be nonsense if we had no "conventional duration". What can be meant by the "same interval" "at different times"? We have here the beginning of the crux of the whole question of physical time, since without the possibility of talking of "repetition" the other two conditions which Weber mentioned would go for nothing, and there could be no measurement of time. There is an interesting passage in Weyl, which shows how physics postulates repetition and how this is related to the possibility of constructing instruments for measurement: "If an isolated physical system reverts to exactly the same state as that in which it was at some earlier instant, the same succession of states will be repeated in time, and the whole series will constitute a cycle. This is a clock".[1] Hence physical time is doubly an abstraction: not only in that it abstracts from the different judgments of duration of individuals, but also in that it abstracts from the irrevocability and irreversibility of time. What is the wildest absurdity of dreams is merely altering the sign to the physicist. Take, for instance, the formula "$s = ut + \frac{1}{2}at^2$". What significance for ordinary life in time is there in the notion of "time" multiplied by "initial velocity", or (still less) in "time squared"? The 't' of physics is improperly called *time*: it should be *time-interval*. It is an abstraction from lived time, and in the process all that is distinctively temporal has been eliminated. Past, present, and future have gone: in their stead remains only the logical relation of before and after, expressed in terms of numbers. And this is the fundamental result; it is the great triumph of those who have sought to measure time that they have succeeded in overcoming the great obstacle of time as 'going on'. In abstracting from this, in refusing to consider diversities which, from their point of view, are irrelevant, and in concentrating on time as serial, as a homogeneous continuum, they have rendered the passage of time susceptible to mathematical treatment.[2] This is a loss, in that certain aspects are ignored, but it is also a great gain in that its clarity and simplicity make further develop-

[1] *Space, Time, and Matter* (English translation, p. 7).
[2] "Physics has no concern with the feeling of 'becoming' which we regard as inherently belonging to the nature of time, and it treats time merely as a symbol: but equally matter and all else in the physical world have been reduced to a shadowy symbolism" (Eddington, *Science and the Unseen World*, p. 22).

ment possible. For, as Cisar expressed it, "space" and "time" are insusceptible to measurement, and it is nonsense to talk of measuring *them*—what can be measured is *experience* with regard to its *order* in respect of space or time, and so physics is concerned with them as serial and ordered.[1]

"$s = ut + \tfrac{1}{2}at^2$." We should find it difficult to interpret this: but as long as we are concerned only with the manipulation of numbers and symbols, this formula may be of great utility. But how do we know it in the first place? it may be asked. It is certainly not self-evident, and it sounds perilously near nonsense, *in ordinary speech*, to talk of 'time squared'. But, as it occurs in the formula, we are not multiplying "time" by "time", but one number by another number, and these numbers happen to stand for units of time. They happen thus as the direct result of combining two equations, which granted the notions of velocity (involving distance and time), and acceleration (rate of change of velocity) are self-evident. (1) $v = u + at$. If the moving body goes every second 'a' f.p.s. faster than it did the preceding second, after t seconds it goes $a \times t$ f.p.s. faster than it did at first: hence the final velocity is the initial velocity *plus* the increase, which must be proportional to the time.

(2) $s = \dfrac{u + v}{2} \times t$. The distance travelled is equal to velocity (which in the case of a constantly accelerating body is the simple average of initial and final velocities) × time. It goes without saying, that when we say, "The answer is $\dfrac{u + v}{2} \times t$ ft." we do not mean that time, by some curious alchemy, is now expressed in *feet*. On the contrary, it is the *whole* which is expressed in feet: time has been eliminated and all that 't' stands for is a certain *number*. By parity of reasoning, when we combine the two equations, and obtain the far from self-evident "$s = ut + \tfrac{1}{2}at^2$", we are not squaring time or doing anything sensational: we are merely multiplying two numbers. The source of confusion is that 't' is not "time" but t *seconds*, that is, a number: and when 't' appears in an equation alone, the 'seconds' having disappeared (as they do, for instance, when "time" is multiplied by $\dfrac{\text{distance}}{\text{time}} = $ velocity),

[1] *Mind*, 1924.

it is just a number like any other number. That it originally stood for a time co-ordinate is neither here nor there, because time has been eliminated: just as it is neither here nor there whether the 44 feet that appear as 's' were originally measured over the floor of a boy's room, the course of a toy train, or along a railway embankment, the course of a real one. Hence we are at perfect liberty, as long as we confine ourselves to mathematics, to interpret our 't' as we please. We may make it stand on its head, or run backwards, or use in our equations t^2, t^{-1}, or $-t$, to our heart's content. *But*, when we start to interpret our results, the reckoning comes.[1] A schoolboy, given that a car is moving at 30 f.p.s. with a constant acceleration of 4 f.p.s., is asked to calculate how long it will take the car to go 368 feet. He substitutes correctly:
$368 = 30t + 2t^2$
∴ $t^2 + 15t - 184 = 0$.
Factorizing, $(t + 23)(t - 8) = 0$.
∴ Time taken is 8 seconds, or -23 seconds.

Now this is perfectly correct. But if the boy were to present this in an unexpurgated form he would be hardly likely to get full marks. The master would say that the boy was lacking in common sense to talk about a "minus time", even though such was a possible solution of the equation. From the point of view of the mathematician, it is quite illegitimate to allow only one of the roots of a quadratic and to discard the other: from the point of view of the plain man, it is obviously silly to talk of a negative number of seconds. Both are, from their point of view, right: the dispute is a real one and cannot be evaded. The question is not merely one of the interpretation of results: it goes deeper than that. Fundamentally, it is the question whether, and how far, the 't' of physics accurately represents 'time' as it is given in experience.[2] For physics 't' is little, if at all, differentiated from 's': that does not matter as long as they remain t and s, but does it when 't' is interpreted as time and 's' as space?

[1] Compare Merrill, "The t of Physics" (*Journal of Philosophy*, 1922, p. 240): "t, while created originally from our direct experience with real time, is subsequently handled in a way that has no relation to real time at all, since real time can't be increased or decreased by us, nor can it equal zero."

[2] See also Bridgman, *Logic of Modern Physics*, p. 63, commenting on the difficulty of applying mathematical results to the physical world.

These are metaphysical questions, and with them the physicist, and still less the pure mathematician, does not concern himself. But they are questions which must be faced. Put shortly, the crux of the matter is—Is the 't' which physics gives us, (*a*) a complete, (*b*) a legitimate, (*c*) a successful description, of time?[1]

The first question is quickly answered. It is not complete, and it is the pride of the physicist that it is not—that he has merely taken one aspect in which he is interested and developed it, sternly ruling out everything else as irrelevant to his purposes. The third question also is simple. The astonishing progress of the physical sciences and their achievements in the last three hundred years can leave little doubt as to the success of physics and to the utility of this, one of its main concepts.

But—and here comes in the difficult second question—is the physical concept 'time' a legitimate representation of that time which is a standing metaphysical problem? The hocus-pocus whereby the mathematical part of the physicist conveniently turns a blind eye while the common-sense part hastily wipes out half his results is very suspicious. We said above, carefully skating over the thin places, that "what is the wildest absurdity of dreams is merely altering the sign to the physicist". A fundamental feature of time as experienced is its irreversibility: is this really so, or is it merely an anthropomorphic prejudice, and is physics right in abstracting[2] from this?

This question, of course, raises a fundamental issue that will need very much more careful handling: here, where our main concern is the 't' of physics, we cannot hope to deal with it properly.

It must be reiterated that physicists have a perfect right to use what concepts they please: and criticism can only enter when one of these is labelled 'Time'. Then it is fair to ask whether those characteristics of Time which are neglected and even implicitly negated are not important. If they are, it is reasonable to hold that, however useful 't' may be for physics, its *complete* identification with Time

---

[1] Similar questions arise with regard to space. But there is no need to go into them here, as long as it is realized that the conflict, though perhaps most serious in, is not *confined* to time.

[2] Mr. M. Black points out that care must be taken in using the word 'abstraction'. t is not an abstraction from time in the sense that the notion of 'triangle' is an abstraction from particular triangles.

is fallacious. It is necessary—and it is a possible criticism of Bergson that he never properly realized this—to distinguish between legitimate abstraction and falsifying abstraction. The spatialization of time, against which Bergson protested, is not necessarily illegitimate. Where the irrevocability of time does not enter, we may profitably regard time as an interval, abstracted from its content, distinct from and yet comparable to space intervals, and capable of mathematical development. But it is when we forget that our spatialized representation is only an abstraction from temporal sequence, which is essentially alogical—as we may say, considering it only as "sequence" and forgetting the specifically "temporal" part—that we are liable to become confused. For if it is claimed, whether openly or by implication, that the characteristics of 't' give a finally satisfactory account of time, that claim is unfounded. This is not, of course, to say that the pliable, reversible 't' may not be very useful and important in its own sphere, but its sphere is not that of metaphysics. The excursions into metaphysical fancy of a scientist who has written a standard book on scientific method may be quoted here as an awful warning. "Space and time are so similar in character, that if space be termed the breadth, time may be termed the length, of the field of perception."[1] Worse still—"The irreversibility of natural processes is a purely *relative* conception. History goes backward or forward according to the relative motion of events and their observer. Conceive a demon, gifted with an immensely intensified acuteness of sight, so that he could watch from an immense distance the movements of the earth. Now suppose him to travel away from the earth with a velocity greater than the velocity of light. All natural processes and all history would be for him reversed. Men would enter life by death, grow young, and finally leave it by birth. Complex types of life would grow simpler, evolution would be reversed, and the earth, growing hotter and hotter, would again become nebulous. Shortly, by motion to or from the earth, our demon could go backward or forward in history, or with one speed—that of light—live in an eternal *now*."[2] One is tempted to remark that "Keep off the grass" is as applicable to scientists in metaphysics as the other way round!

[1] Karl Pearson, *Grammar of Science*, p. 181.
[2] Ibid., p. 394. For a similar idea, compare C. Flammarion's *Lumen*.

That 't' does not give the whole of time is implicitly admitted by every schoolboy who, secure in the knowledge that everyone will understand why, "cooks" his results to the extent of rejecting out of hand one of his answers—a sure indication that there are two, quite separate, standards to which he conforms, the laws of mathematics and the facts about time. (If he fails in one, it will almost certainly be the former!) That being so, it is strange that writers on physics should not, apparently, perceive any difference.

To sum up, the abstraction which physics makes from the events which make up the content of time is legitimate and useful for the purposes of physics: but, overridden, it may be fallacious. Apart from the ignoring of what is, at first sight at least, the most striking characteristic of time—its irreversibility—there is a second danger in that hypostatization is only too easy. The separation of time from events into something absolute, a bare continuum (like Newton's "absolute, true, and mathematical time" which "of itself, and from its own nature, flows equably without regard to anything external", and which is contrasted with "relative, apparent, and common time", that merely measures duration by means of motion,[1]) is a profitable breeding-ground for *metaphysical* fallacies.

It cannot be too often emphasized that physics is concerned with the measurement of time, rather than with the essentially metaphysical question as to its nature. Granted that no metaphysical theory can hope to survive which puts itself in needless opposition to facts established by physics, it yet remains true that in the last resort a purely physical description is insufficient, and sometimes fallacious, from the point of view of metaphysics. We must not believe that physical theories can ultimately solve the metaphysical problems that time raises, or that they have any *special* relevance to these problems.

II

Within the last fifty years the basic concepts of physics—among them time—have undergone a radical alteration. Certain fundamental assumptions, as we saw, are made in all measurement, and these assumptions are common to the simplest form of measurement and to their development into the highly complex, ingenious and delicate measurement which the modern physicist makes. Amid

[1] *Principia*, I, 6.

this sophistication, the underlying assumptions were thrust out of sight, and this did not greatly matter from the physicist's point of view—that of getting valid results—as long as the results were forthcoming. But a fundamental check, in the unexpected negative result of the Michelson-Morley experiment, meant that the optimistic *"laissez-faire"* policy could not continue indefinitely, and that a radical overhauling of these important assumptions, and of the basic concepts of physics—time, space, energy—would soon be necessary. The work of Lorentz, Minkowski, and above all, Einstein, was to accomplish this. Hence, in spite of the originality of the questions raised and answered by Einstein, it would be a mistake to suppose that his work can be treated in entire isolation from that of his predecessors: on the contrary, it was only made possible by the previous research of specialists. Relativity, at least as regards space and time (perhaps not so much with the brilliant electro-magnetic speculations of the Generalized Theory), is a stage in the historical development of these concepts rather than a dramatic surprise entirely unconnected with their former history.

This point, regarding the need of considering the doctrines of Relativity in their historical setting, has been emphasized, partly because it is apt to be overlooked, but chiefly because I do not propose to set out in detail the events which led up to the Special Theory of Relativity, since they have been many times recapitulated.[1] The brief reference to these events must not be taken to mean that this method of approach is unimportant.

The Michelson–Morley experiment (which Eddington calls the Prince of Denmark in the physicists' performance of *Hamlet*) was designed to measure accurately a certain time-interval. This time-interval, *which was confidently expected*, was the difference between the time taken by two light-signals to return to the point of origin. From this difference it was hoped to calculate v, the speed of the earth through the ether.[2] But no difference at all was observed,

---

[1] An especially good account of the historical development is to be found in Silberstein, *Theory of Relativity*. See also Cunningham, *Principle of Relativity*; Benedicks, *Space and Time*; Cassirer, *Einstein's Theory of Relativity*; and Langevin, *La Physique depuis vingt Ans*.

[2] In Maritain's pleasant phrase, "The ether, where the physicists used to put their blackest contradictions out to pasture" (*The Freedom of the Intellect*, p. 63).

though the experiment was carefully repeated many times to obviate possible counteracting conditions that might mask the expected effect. It should be noticed, too, that while slight inequalities, where equalities are expected, may be put down to experimental errors, this could not be done in the opposite case which is now in question, for it would be simply incredible that *every time* there should be equality instead of a varying degree of inequality. Hence the continual negative result of the Michelson–Morley experiment could not easily be explained away.

A makeshift was proposed in the celebrated Lorentz–Fitzgerald contraction. This said, in effect: We have reached a contradiction between our results and our calculations. The two times should be in the ratio to each other of $1 : \left(\dfrac{c^2 - v^2}{c^2}\right)^{\frac{1}{2}}$, but they are not,[1] (for whatever the unknown v may be—unless it is zero, in which case *cadit quæstio*—the ratio can never work out at unity). If we accept the result of the experiment as being accurate, there is only one way out. That is to assume that the light rays did not, after all, travel equal distances. They were *measured* as being equal? Nevertheless, that proves nothing: If we assume that *every* moving body contracts in the direction of its motion in the ratio $1 : \sqrt{\dfrac{c^2 - v^2}{c^2}}$, our instrument of measurement will itself contract, and the shrinkage cannot be detected. On the other hand, if we assume this contraction, it will explain the contradiction.

On the face of it, this is an arbitrary and an unsatisfactory explanation. In the first place, there is no obvious reason *why* we should assume that our measurements of time are accurate, and that our measurements of space are at fault, since the latter is much easier to measure. It seems paradoxical so radically to distrust space-measurement, and at the same time to insist on our accurate measurement of time, which is usually measured by motion in space. As Gunn expressed it: "The supposed contraction to which the Lorentz–Fitzgerald figures refer is a matter of perspective. The Lorentz–Fitzgerald equations merely interpret the Michelson–

[1] This result can easily be worked out for oneself, by using the familiar analogy of the swimmers across stream and down stream. If the distances are equal, the former swimmer *must* get back first.

Morley experiment if we define distances by the time it takes light to traverse them."[1] Secondly, this postulated contraction cannot be empirically confirmed. The velocity of light, c, is so enormous compared with speeds of moving objects on the earth, that with normal speeds the contraction is so small that it is impossible to detect. Whereas when we are dealing with supposedly high velocities, such as the velocity of the earth through space, the contraction should in theory be detectable, but unfortunately it cannot be detected, because we and everything we might measure with are moving with the earth, and therefore are presumably undergoing the same contraction. Hence the postulated shrinkage can neither be proved nor disproved, and for this reason it could not be more than a temporary makeshift.

Thirdly, the contraction, if there be one, is of a different kind from any known contraction, since it sets up no effects, such as strains and stresses, which contraction normally does: and, too, there is no apparent difference between different materials, for example, wood and glass, in their resistance to the contraction. It would seem that the contraction is not a *physical* contraction, but a methodological 'dodge' contrived to make the mathematical results tally. It is obviously only a makeshift.

But the importance of this suggested explanation was, that it went further afield than other more obvious explanations (such as that the ether-drift always managed exactly to nullify the expected effect), and raised a number of questions which are of capital importance.

The first concerns the nature of measurement. If, as we are told, objects "really are" a different length from what they are measured to be, we get what is a very undesirable distinction between the appearance and the unseeable reality, and one which is in the end fatal to science.

On the other hand, it does raise the very important question how far what is measured by physics corresponds to the concepts which physics has of the things which are supposed to be measured. In other words, the concepts 'space' and 'time' and so on, as at present used in physics, are admittedly different from the plain

[1] Op. cit., p. 205. On the other hand, see Whitehead's article, "Space, Time, and Relativity" (*Arist. Soc. Proc.*, 1915–16).

man's conception of them:[1] is it also the case that they are different from the measurable quantities with which the practising physicist is concerned? It would seem so. Hence the need for a clearer and stricter use of these concepts. Broad put the point concisely when he said, "The Lorentz–Fitzgerald contraction ceases to be a physical shortening, and becomes a question of units of measurement."[2]

Thirdly, the old controversy between supporters of relative and absolute motion is reopened, this time in connection with such questions as "What do we mean by '*the*' velocity of light?" "What do we mean by the velocity of the earth through space?"

Fourthly, the old physics took it for granted that we knew what we meant by saying that two light rays left or returned to a source O "at the same time".[3] Is this the case, or have we in physics, with an increasing sophistication in the concepts we use, to discard our primitive intuitive awareness of "simultaneity" and to make that sophisticated too?

The last two questions are the fundamental ones: the others, though sufficiently important, arise incidentally. It is in asking these questions, and in the originality of his answers to them, that Einstein's great advance, as far as physical time is concerned, consisted.

The rest of this section will be taken up with dealing with these two problems, of simultaneity (and hence temporal relations in general), and of the critical velocity of light, and with a third, more usually associated with the name of Minkowski, but a logical development of the theory of relativity—the question of the hyphenating of space and time. Such a procedure, of course, is not to be taken as implying that these three topics exhaust the bearing of the Theory of Relativity on time, nor that they are independent of each other: it is used merely for convenience of

[1] Though Eddington surprisingly says, "Perceptual space and time is the same as the measured space and time which is the subject-matter of natural geometry" (*Space, Time, and Relativity*, p. 15).

[2] "Euclid, Newton, and Einstein," *Hibbert Journal*, 1919–20, p. 439.

[3] As Whitehead expresses it: "The measurement of time-intervals is a detail compared to simultaneity. *A* may think a sermon long, and *B* may think it short, but at least they should both agree that it stopped when the clock hand pointed at the hour" ("Space, Time, and Relativity", *Proc. Arist. Soc.*, 1915–16, p. 118).

discussion, and it must at the outset be emphasized that 'time' is but one of the questions with which Einstein dealt, and that its exclusive consideration can give us only a very one-sided view of the importance of his work. Bearing this in mind, the discussion of particular points can begin.

The denial of simultaneity is so generally regarded as a consequence of the new doctrines in physics that it is often overlooked that the "simultaneity" which Einstein denies is only one specialized kind of simultaneity. Granted the assumptions which physics makes,[1] it can be shown that simultaneity is relative *in the sense that* it implicitly involves reference to a system, and that by changing from one arbitrarily chosen system to another we can upset our former definitions of simultaneity. Hence the conclusion that "absolute simultaneity" is as redundant and otiose a conception as "absolute time". But Einstein does not deny the possibility of an objective determination of simultaneity within a single system, and still less do his doctrines affect our *immediate* judgments of simultaneity. (This latter point will be returned to later.) It should be clearly realized that the doctrines of relative simultaneity and of the critical velocity of light are closely connected. "Simultaneity is relative" *means* "Under certain conditions, my judgments of simultaneity are (and must be) different from yours, and *there is no way of showing that mine is preferable*." What are those conditions? Simply that the systems of reference which you and I choose are in motion relatively to each other. As Einstein saw, once we hold the doctrine of relative motion (so that the train no longer "moves" while the station "stays still") we have no longer any grounds for saying—apart from practical convenience—that A's judgments of simultaneity are "better" than B's (where A is on the platform and B is in the train). As Einstein himself put it, "Certain sense perceptions of different individuals correspond to each other, while for other sense perceptions no such correspondence can be established. We are accustomed to regard as real those sense perceptions which are common to different individuals, and which therefore are in a measure impersonal. . . . The only justification for our concepts and system of concepts is that they serve to represent the complex of our experiences: beyond this they have

[1] Such as, that time can, for its purposes, be regarded as a measurable continuum, infinitely divisible, reversible, etc.

no legitimacy."[1] This may be granted. But it is a *further* point, and one which does not follow logically from it, but is based on the *practice* of physicists, that the physicist's judgment of simultaneity should be determined by the characteristics of light. These two separate points have been severally criticized.

Firstly, as regards the importance of light-signals. It is one thing to say that we cannot make judgments of simultaneity with regard to events at some distance from each other without the help of light-signals: it is quite another to *define* simultaneity as depending on light-signals. Mr. W. D. Ross, in his paper in a Symposium on "The Philosophical Aspect of the Theory of Relativity",[2] asserted that if Einstein had done the latter, his procedure would have been circular, but as it was, he was only seeking a *test* of simultaneity. On the other hand, according to Whitehead,[3] Einstein *was* attempting to define simultaneity by means of light-signals. If that is so, there is a suspicion of circularity about it, since the velocity of light is taken as finite and to measure it, judgments of simultaneity are required. As Reichenbach says, "Velocity can be measured only when simultaneity is already defined: hence simultaneity cannot be regulated by measurements of velocity."[4] But it could very well be replied that the procedure is not really circular, *if* the primitive judgment or simultaneity on which the measurement of the velocity of light is based is not the same as the simultaneity which in the final result is called "relative". And I think a very good case could be made out for saying that these are *not* the same.

The second point has been something of a "*cause célèbre*" in recent years. The protagonists have been such celebrated men as Bergson, Maritain, and Nordmann. Briefly, the two former have criticized Einstein on the ground that, after all, Einstein has not succeeded in his attempt to do away with a privileged system. They base their criticism on the celebrated analogy about the judgments of simultaneity made by a man in a very fast train and a man standing by the railway line. According to Einstein, these differ. According to his critics, Einstein has only shown that the

[1] *The Meaning of Relativity*, p. 2.   [2] *Mind*, 1920.
[3] *Principles of Natural Knowledge*. But see Broad's review of this book for remarks on this point (*Hibbert Journal*, 1910–20, p. 397).
[4] *Atom and Cosmos* (English translation), p. 58.

man on the ground would judge that the man in the train saw the two events at different times, not that the man in the train actually *did* see them at different times, which is the real point at issue. They claim that Einstein has no right to consider that A's judgments about B's perceptions agree with what B actually perceives; and that the mistaken identification is due to the fact that Einstein is still implicitly considering the judgment of the man on the ground to be the "correct" one. Nordmann, who acted as judge in the controversy, pointed out that the criticism of a particular *example* did not demolish Einstein's main contentions with regard to simultaneity, since these depended on mathematical premises, and not on a semi-popular exposition. He also showed that it was possible to re-state even the example in question so that the criticisms of Bergson and Maritain no longer applied. In all probability Nordmann's view is correct, and there is no need to enter into it more fully here.[1]

For physics, then, simultaneity is relative—in a sense that can be strictly defined, if necessary. That this is so does not mean any very great modification in practice, for it is only where great speeds and great accuracy are concerned that the old method does not give a sufficiently exact approximation. Eddington's aviator is not, as yet, in serious danger of competition.

The next question, and a very important one, is the effect that the new doctrines regarding simultaneity have on the plain man's unhesitating belief that two events just *are* simultaneous, and that there is an end of it. But if he is given a carefully graduated series of examples, beginning with the familiar "flash and bang" of a distant gun, going on to two guns between which he stands, and ending with full-blown Einstein and trains and light-signals, he will admit that it follows from these that simultaneity is, after all, relative. How is he to reconcile the two? The fundamental point is, I think, that the simultaneity with which Einstein deals is only a very distant cousin of the simultaneity with which the plain man

---

[1] See Einstein, *The Theory of Relativity* (especially Section 9); Bergson, *Durée et Simultanéité*, pp. 116–56; and Maritain, *Revue Universelle*, 1924 (not 1923, as Nordmann and, following him, Gunn, give).

Detailed accounts of the controversy are given by Nordmann, *The Tyranny of Time*, pp. 157–204, and by Gunn, op. cit., pp. 192–8, who agrees with Nordmann's summing up.

PHYSICS

and the metaphysician are concerned, just as the physical concept "t" is a very different thing from time as experienced and Time as the bane of the system-builder. Einstein's assertion that simultaneity is relative has no derogatory effect at all—except as the result of confusion—upon the *certainty* of the plain man that his judgments of simultaneity are true.[1] If the sceptical scientist says that this is "merely subjective" and that certainty is not knowledge, we may grant it, but assert that it does not matter—if it did, there could be no science.

"Simultaneity" is now a dangerously ambiguous word, standing for at least two quite different notions.[2] That they are different does not necessarily mean that one is a great improvement on the other. "Simultaneity" as it is now used in physics is a logical development of that aspect of time in which alone physics is interested—its measurable aspect. Consequently, there is both gain and loss—gain in that it is strictly delimited and plays its part in the perfected technique of physics—loss in that certain aspects are, necessarily, ignored.

The plain man is, justifiably, rather puzzled when he is told that events are not "really" simultaneous, however much the demonstration of the mathematician may have silenced him. He may wallow in an infinity of "here nows" and "absolute elsewheres" and he may acquiesce in talking of events that are "neither before nor after" each other: but when it comes to the point, however much he may agree in theory, there will be a mental reservation somewhere that "really" it must be either true or not true that two events "are" simultaneous, and that failing simultaneity, there must be some kind of temporal relation (before or after) holding between them—though to him and everyone else they seem to be in different causal series. In other words, the admission that two events are not causally related does not seem to him to entail

---

[1] Allowing, of course, for errors of observation in complicated cases. But I am referring once more to the primitive perception of two events as happening "at the same time". Compare Bergson, *Durée et Simultanéité*, pp. 116–17.

[2] There may be more. Gunn, for instance, distinguishes four senses (op. cit., p. 424). But the fundamental distinction is between these two. See also the clear and interesting remarks of Maritain in his essay on "The Mathematical Attenuation of Time" in the volume *The Freedom of the Intellect* (especially pp. 85 and 90–6).

that there can be no temporal relations holding between them. He is justified, in that the sense in which physics talks about events that are neither before nor after each other is a specialized one—rightly from its point of view, but liable to cause confusion if too cavalierly equated with what we ordinarily mean by before and after. For temporal relations, as treated in modern physics, are relational right enough—in their connecting of events lies their utility and importance—but they are scarcely "temporal", except in the specialized sense in which physics uses the word. We have seen this in the case of simultaneity, with which Einstein himself was specially concerned, but it holds good throughout. Physics never talks about "past" and "future": it is always "before-and-after", which is a logical relation used to connect events. Expressed differently, physics takes events in abstraction from their *happening*, and considers only the *order* of their happening: hence before and after is not strictly a temporal *relation*, though the elements which it relates are temporal. Thus Robb, who has made an interesting and important attempt to construct a geometry based on the before-and-after relation (rather than on the more usual spatial relations), finds no difficulty in fitting *space* into his geometry. "Spatial relations are to be regarded as a manifestation of the facts that the elements of time form a system in conical order: a conception which may be analysed in terms of the relations after and before."[1] Again, "If we call any element of the entire set an 'instant', any inertia line of the selected system a 'point', any acceleration plane of the selected system a 'straight line', and any rotation threefold of the selected system 'a plane': we can speak of succeeding instants at any given point, and have thus obtained a representation of the space and time of our experience in so far as their geometrical relations are concerned."[2] Since Robb is not a supporter of Einstein and has, indeed, criticized him (for overlooking the importance of the before and after series[3]), we may take it that this tendency to detemporalize time and temporal relations is not confined to the relativists, but is common to all physicists. The difference between the plain man and the physicist is well expressed by Eddington: "Those who suspect that Einstein's theory is playing unjustifiable tricks with time should realize that

[1] *A Theory of Time and Space*, p. 370.
[2] Op. cit., p. 367.   [3] See *Absolute Relations of Time and Space*.

it leaves entirely untouched that time succession of which we have intuitive knowledge, and confines itself to overhauling the artificial scheme of time which Römer first introduced into physics."[1] Relativity physics, then, in raising the question as to the precise significance which temporal relations such as simultaneity have *for it*, is not necessarily saying anything which is relevant for the metaphysician, still less is it laying down dicta to which metaphysics must conform. This is not, of course, intended as a criticism of physics. What can be criticized is the illegitimate passage from the results of physics to metaphysics. Bergson rightly points out that the 't' of physics is hardly distinguishable from space, that the concept of "simultaneity" is sophisticated and a long way removed from the experience of the plain man, and that physics confuses time as passing and time as passed, with disastrous results. But these are not valid criticisms against physical time, *unless* physical time is claimed to be a fair and complete representation of "Time". And this is very rarely seriously held, except by implication, when it is most dangerous.

The second topic to be discussed concerns the notion of the velocity of light as critical. The Restricted Theory of Relativity depends in great part upon the assumption that light, unlike anything else, has a velocity which is independent of the motion of its source, so that the ordinary addition and subtraction of velocities no longer holds good. It has been made a subject of criticism that in the Generalized Theory this assumption is cast aside, and that the Generalized Theory apparently rests on postulates contrary to those of the Restricted Theory. But it is not that they are in *contradiction* so much as that the General Theory includes what was only incompletely synthesized in the Special Theory. The criticism rests on a wrong conception of what "the critical velocity of light" *means*.

It is usual to say that the velocity of light is finite, and that it is 186,000 miles per second. Such an enormous velocity, *empirically*, differs from infinity not at all: no one, it is safe to affirm, has ever directly observed that light "takes a finite time" (however small) to travel a certain distance. But very minute and exact experiments have established *indirectly* that light takes a finite time to travel. (Secondarily, and more weakly, it may be urged

[1] *The Theory of Relativity and its Influence on Scientific Thought*, p. 18.

that the time-lag between "flash" and "bang" shows that sound has a finite velocity, and from that an analogy may be made to the case of light: or a metaphysical view may be taken that all events —including the propagation of light—must "take time".) Evidently only the first argument is of much value—nevertheless I think that it is often supplemented in practice by vaguely formulated metaphysical assumptions.

On the other hand is the insistence of the Restricted Theory that the velocity of light has a peculiarity that, otherwise, characterizes only infinite wholes. This characteristic is, that the ordinary rules of kinematics do not apply to it. This is tantamount to saying that, *in one sense*, we might as well call the velocity of light infinite and have done with it.

If we *define* time-intervals, as Nordmann did,[1] in terms of the velocity of light (admittedly a highly Pickwickian definition), we cannot but admit in the end that time is merely a function of light. In other words, time measured *exclusively* by light-signals is bound to lead to the notion of the velocity of light as *peculiar*, and distinct from other velocities, simply because there is no way of giving meaning to the question "*How long* does it take light to traverse this given finite distance?" It is because we have a dual conception of time, because we do not *only* think of time in terms of its measurement by light-signals, that we can attach meaning to this question: otherwise it would be silly to say either that light "took time" or that it did not 'take time', since the notion of time would have no application. Einstein saw that the natural result of the physicist's conception of time as an interval measured by light-signals was that light must be considered as exempt from ordinary considerations, such as the addition and subtraction of relative velocities. The point is liable to be obscured by the retention[2] of the finite figure for the velocity of light: there seems no more magic in the number 186,000 (especially as it is not a round number!) than in any other. And of course there isn't: the magic lies in the simple fact that we have started by *assuming* its constancy (as we must, if it is to be our standard). Poincaré, writing before Einstein's work was published, puts the point clearly: "Il a commencé par

---

[1] "A second is the time which light takes to cover 186,000 miles in empty space and far from any strong gravitational field" (*Einstein and the Universe*, p. 65).   [2] Which is justifiable on other grounds.

admettre que la lumière a une vitesse constante, et en particulier que sa vitesse est la même dans toutes les directions. C'est là un postulat sans lequel aucune mesure de cette vitesse ne pourrait être tentée."[1] If we once allowed that *A*, who was in a very fast aeroplane, found the velocity of light less than it was for *B*, stationary on the earth, we should, apparently, simplify matters. But really we should be making them more complex, because we would have upset the accuracy of our standard to simplify a minor point, and when we came to discuss what we meant by saying *B* was "at rest", we should be left with a whole host of complications regarding the movement of the earth relatively to other planets, "through space", and so on. To do that would be penny wise and pound foolish. As Poincaré remarked, "La simultanéité de deux évènements, ou l'ordre de leur succession, l'égalité de deux durées, doivent être définies de telle sorte que l'énoncé des lois naturelles soit aussi simple que possible",[2] and this brings us to the fundamental point that, if we "choose the simplest", we have *some* choice in the matter. The measurement of time-intervals, as has already been insisted, is in some degree conventional. The relevance of this in the present connection is that we *need* not have chosen light as our standard, but that the choice was guided by practical considerations. (The very experiments which assigned to light a finite velocity greater than all other known velocities led to its choice as an "absolute standard"—and hence to its apparently contradictory properties.) If this point is forgotten it is apt to seem as if Einstein *equated* time with light-signals—an obviously questionable procedure, which Benedicks, for instance, criticized—but Einstein clearly realized and pointed out in his exposition in *The Meaning of Relativity* that light is only chosen as the basis of time-measurement because more is known about it than about anything else. Hence the retention of a finite figure for the velocity of light can be explained as leaving open the possibility that the notion of time is not wholly to be analysed in terms of light-signals, and that therefore it can be applied to the propagation of light itself.[3]

[1] *La Valeur de la Science*, p. 54. [2] Ibid., p. 57.
[3] Compare Bridgman, *The Logic of Modern Physics*, p. 70: "In order to ascribe any simple significance to postulates about the velocity of light, it would seem that we must have an instrument for measuring this velocity, and therefore for measuring time, which does not itself involve the properties of light."

On the other hand, the anomalies which lead us to call the velocity of light "critical" are a direct result of the second conception of time as measured, and measurable only, by light.

The Generalized Theory does not, as sometimes suggested, deny the postulates on which the Restricted Theory rests, but it is broader in its scope, and so it is able to include the two aspects of time which in the Restricted Theory appear, if not in opposition, at least in uneasy partnership. Perhaps that is why the theory of Relativity should appear to have more relevance to metaphysics than do most physical theories: though essentially physical (and to deny this would be to commit the kind of mistake which Bergson repeatedly criticized, the illegitimate identification of physics and metaphysics), it yet emphasizes, in its own way, the danger of confusing the two conceptions of time.

The second point in connection with the velocity of light is a causal one. We are accustomed by now to paradoxes of the time-traveller who, like Rip Van Winkle, found that two hundred years had elapsed in what he thought was two days, and of the Young Lady of Bright who—

> Eloped one day
> In a relative way
> And returned the previous night.

We are still more tired of mythical travellers who, whizzing away from the earth into space with a velocity greater than light, 'see' the events of their lives happening 'backwards, as in Nordmann's example of the reversed battle of the Marne, or the adventures of Flammarion's Lumen.[1] At first sight it would seem as if Relativity is encouraging these plagues. But when Einstein says, "*If* I travel faster than light, events will happen in reverse order for me", he is not suggesting that this is possible: on the contrary, the inference goes the other way. It is *because* events do not happen in reverse order that the velocity of light cannot be exceeded. It is not, as it might seem at first sight, merely a question of finding a velocity

[1] Compare also Fechner, *Vier Paradoxa*, which, like *Lumen*, was written before the Theory of Relativity. Meyerson, in his *Identity and Reality*, p. 217; Breton, in *Les Mondes* of 1875; and Nordmann himself, show a healthy scepticism. But K. Pearson ought to have known better than to talk about reversibility as he did in the passages quoted earlier.

slightly greater than that of light, though the persistence of our old habit of thinking of velocities as additive makes us think so. Eddington expresses the point very clearly: "The limit to the velocity of signals is our bulwark against that topsy-turvydom of past and future, of which Einstein's theory is sometimes wrongfully accused. Expressed in the conventional way this limitation of the speed of signalling to 299,796 kilometres a second seems a rather arbitrary decree of nature. We almost feel it a challenge to find something that goes faster. But if we state it in the absolute form that signalling is only possible along a track of temporal relation and not along a track of spatial relation, the restriction seems rational. To violate it we have not merely to find something which goes just one kilometre per second better, but something which overleaps that distinction of time and space—which, we are all convinced, ought to be maintained in any sensible theory."[1] Eddington's discussion was in terms of his conception of Space-Time as a double cone; and he rightly objected that the overleaping of the critical velocity would be to confuse space and time. Alternatively it can be regarded as a confusion, not of space and time, but of cause and effect. In so far, of course, as cause and effect are regarded as interchangeable (as they would be, ideally, in the deterministic systems of last century), this does not matter a great deal. But we do normally regard cause and effect as distinct, and hence the weird effect of the reversed battle of the Marne, and of Breton's and Flammarion's examples. The weirdness is increased by the confusion into which, for instance, Flammarion falls. He persists in judging a sequence of events which essentially means that our everyday standards of causality have lost their validity, by these very standards. In other words, we may if we please indulge in unverifiable and even nonsensical speculations, but we have no right to attempt to relate them to the everyday conceptions on whose denial they are based. Either cause and effect are or are not equivalent[2]: if they are, then the paradoxes disappear in any case, and there is no need to drag in velocities greater than that of light: if they are not, the paradoxes remain paradoxes only because we apply our present standards to them. This point will need to

[1] *Nature of the Physical World*, pp. 57–8.
[2] I am, of course, using the phrase in a very rough sense and without definition (as it is generally used).

be more fully discussed in connection with what is often called the "irreversibility" of time: here it may be simply stated that the objection to speeds greater than light is that it would blur the distinction between cause and effect, and the (perhaps the same, perhaps more fundamental) distinction between space and time.

In placing the velocity of light, which is not, apparently, as unimpeachable as the other two fundamental distinctions, on a level with them, Einstein is not detracting from their integrity. On the contrary, he is pointing out that the consequence of the trend in physics towards defining time-intervals (such as simultaneity) in terms of light-signals, is to endue the velocity of light with their importance. Hence the moral of the Young Lady of Bright, whose feat was an impossibility, is that so is such a speed, if it leads to such impossible consequences. The velocity of light is no ordinary velocity: it is, *by definition*, the bar between past and future (or, as they appear in physics, before and after), and such a bar must not lightly be disregarded.

The last important doctrine to be discussed as illustrating the contemporary trend of thought in physics is the doctrine, arising out of the Theory of Relativity, but usually associated with the work of Minkowski, of the hyphenating of space and time. In Minkowski's celebrated words: "From henceforth space by itself and time by itself are doomed to fade away into mere shadows, and only a kind of union of the two will preserve an independent reality."[1]

Now why should this discovery, of the essential connectedness of space and time, be hailed as such an important discovery, and why is it that physics has apparently only just realized[2] what has been for a considerable time sufficiently obvious to the plain man? The answer is not that the physicist is more stupid than the plain man: but that the distinction which we have been concerned to make is still applicable. The importance is not in the connection of "space" and "time": rather is it in the discovery (which is a new one, and not by any means self-evident, as what the plain

---

[1] *The Theory of Relativity* (volume of collected monographs), English translation, p. 75.

[2] "Modern science must be defined pre-eminently by its aspiration to take time as an independent variable" (Bergson, *Creative Evolution*, English translation, p. 355).

man thinks he means is) that no satisfactory description of the world in *physical* terms can be constructed which does not emphasize the need for time co-ordinates as well as space ones. The discovery is essentially a mathematical, not a metaphysical, one: shorn of their mathematical coverings, the interpretation of x, y, z, and t, as "space" and "time", and the assertion of an essential connection between them, is liable to fall flat, since even the plainest of plain men has always suspected that they were connected, in certain obvious ways. Minkowski's celebrated truism: "Nobody has ever noticed a place except at a time, or a time except at a place",[1] is so obviously trite, if interpreted literally, that that alone ought to lead us to suspect that what Minkowski *meant* was something that can only be misleadingly translated from its native mathematical symbols, into ordinary language. It is once again the difficulty which the physicist finds in *interpreting* his results.

Having said how misleading ordinary language may be, to continue is to court disaster. But it is necessary.

The word "dimension", as it is at present used, has undergone an extension from its original use (to denote the three empirical dimensions of space) while unfortunately retaining, in ordinary usage, its original meaning. Thus, for instance, when Rice says:[2] "Our arrangement of events in a time-order is a three-dimensional being's mode of dealing with a static arrangement in a *space of four dimensions*," he is not talking about the familiar space of everyday experience; and the second "dimensions" is used in a highly technical sense, which is properly non-spatial (though the earlier phrase, "Three dimensional being", may make us overlook this). Very roughly speaking, "dimension" is now used to indicate any way in which an object can be measured.

Suppose that I am measuring a rectangular sheet of paper, *ABCD*. Besides *AB* and *AD*, I may, if I please, take measurements also along *AC* and *BD*. In practice I do not, merely because I find it *sufficient* to know *AB* and *AD*, and it is more convenient than bothering also with *AC*. In this we regard our own convenience—it is important to notice that the dimensions we take are largely conventions, not cast-iron structures, like the divisions of an egg-box, running inexorably through the world. In an interesting passage, Silberstein says: "The number of dimensions is

[1] Op. cit., p. 76.   [2] *Relativity*, p. 108. The italics are mine.

not an inherent property of space or the world or any manifold whatever. To endow it with dimensionality some ordering principle or other must be impressed upon it."[1] Or, as Eddington expressed it: "It is the relation of order which is intrinsic in nature, and which is the same for both squares and diamonds: shape is put into it by an observer when he has chosen his partitions."[2] We choose these partitions, our axes, with regard to our own convenience. It is less trouble to take our measurements in certain ways, and so we use those ways. It is also less trouble to make as few measurements as possible: if we know AB and AD, we can find BD without needing to bother with AC as well. This has sometimes been misleadingly expressed by saying that we need two dimensions at right angles, in this way confusing the truth that we need two independent variables with the error that in order to obtain two such variables we need axes at right angles. So when we talk about dimensions at right angles to each other, what we mean is not that if we actually measured the angle between the two we should find it to be 90°, but that by using two axes at right angles we get two coefficients, neither of which can be dispensed with, and which are the simplest and most economical way in which we can describe objects within that two-dimensional manifold. This last clause is necessary as a safeguard. It is conceivable that we might, for convenience, make our measurements in three directions, though, theoretically, two would have sufficed. In such a case we should not talk of three *dimensions*, but of three *axes* in a two-dimensional space. Similarly, we may use "oblique *axes*", but it is silly to talk of oblique *dimensions*—just as silly as it is to interpret "dimensions at right angles to each other" spatially and literally. It is only too easy to confuse *axis* and *dimension*.

The plain man, not unnaturally, has great difficulty in seeing what can be meant by talk about "ten dimensions, all at right angles to each other". What it comes to, is that "at right angles" is a compendious way of saying, "Ten dimensions are needed for the

---

[1] *Theory of Relativity*, p. 316.
[2] *Space, Time, and Gravitation*, p. 54. Later in the same book Eddington remarked that it is theoretically possible (but too cumbersome in practice) to describe phenomena without reference to *any* mesh-system, by a catalogue of coincidences.

complete description of this object. I have so chosen them that, though I might conceivably have needed more than ten co-ordinates, if I had chosen differently, I could not possibly have done with less. Ten is the *minimum*."

So, in the new physics, when it is said that the dimensions of "space-time" are at right angles to each other, that does not mean, as the plain man might think (and as too many writers on physics seem to think), that time is somehow reduced to a dimension of space. It means precisely the contrary. When we want to graph a time-interval, we must show that it is quite different from space, and to do this we put it at right angles to space, *otherwise we would be considering it as resolvable in terms of space*. It would be a delusion to suppose that the "at right angles" is spatial: its meaning is much wider than that. (Of course, in the example just given, by the very nature of graphing we are giving a *spatial* interpretation: but we must not conclude that this is all that is meant.)

And here we come to the second extension of "dimension", which really follows on from the first. "Dimension" loses all specifically spatial connotations: and though "at right angles" persists to delude us, we have seen that this is not necessarily spatial. (Nor, for that matter, is "space", which is sometimes used in a general and non-spatial sense where "continuum" or "manifold" would have been better.) Finally, "dimension" comes to stand for the number of coefficients necessary for a full description, whether they are spatial or not. Thus, supposing I wish to consider an object with respect to a certain characteristic x: the result will be a certain function of x. Later I may discover that this characteristic depends on others: in place of one variable I have now several, and the comparatively simple $f(x)$ is replaced by $f_1(y)$, $f_2(z)$, and so on. If these all vary independently of each other, they can be legitimately regarded as each a "dimension", in the extended sense in which physics now uses this word.

This long exposition has been directed towards establishing three points. The first is, that the notion of dimension is essentially connected with that of measurement. Secondly, dimensions and axes must be distinguished. Lastly, and most important, neither "dimension" nor "at right angles" nor "space", as they are at present used in physics, must be interpreted exclusively spatially.

Mathematically, of course, there is no reason why we should

content ourselves with three dimensions—that is a purely spatial limitation. That what holds good for two or three dimensions can be extended, as far as mathematics is concerned, to n dimensions, is perfectly possible. But it is when we come to the *interpretation* of these dimensions that we are puzzled. We may juggle with our equations involving four dimensions, but we find it as impossible to *picture* such a four-dimensional world as the inhabitants of Flatland found it to picture a sphere. But that "dimension" had originally spatial connotations does not justify us in assuming that Minkowski's four-dimensional continuum is "spatial" (except in a highly specialized sense). It is not the case that the distinction between space and time has been broken down: as Cassirer puts it, the hyphenation of space and time does not involve that there is no difference in their fundamental character. In his book, *The Meaning of Relativity*[1], Einstein himself said: "The non-divisibility of the four-dimensional continuum of events does not at all, however, involve the equivalents of the space co-ordinates with the time co-ordinate. On the contrary, we must remember that the time co-ordinate is defined physically wholly differently from the space co-ordinates." Consequently the plain man will do well to distrust any pictures he may see, even in newspapers, of what "the fourth dimension" "looks like".

When Minkowski gave his celebrated Cologne address, what was novel in it was *not* that time and space are related in *experience*, but that to get a satisfactory definition of the universe in *physical* terms we must abandon the old, static world-at-an-instant conception in favour of a new one which no longer ignores the lapse of time.[2] Consequently, the physicists no longer say that the distance between two points is given by the equation—

$$s = \sqrt{(x - x_1)^2 + (y - y_1)^2 + (z - z_1)^2},$$

and then calculate what has happened to s during the time-interval $t - t_1$: instead the two processes become welded into one. It need hardly be said that s now is not a space-interval, but an interval in space-time, and it is this interval which is so important. "It is

[1] English translation, p. 34.
[2] But though it includes the *lapse* of time, it still ignores the *passing* of time. (Compare Bergson's remark (*Durée et Simultanéité*, p. 85): "You will never get the idea of temporal flux from Minkowski's schema.")

neither the point in space, nor the instant in time, at which something happens that has physical reality, but only the event itself."[1]

But the "space-time" of the physicist is a compendious way of saying that, for physics, it is useful to formulate its equations in terms of a co-ordinate which stands for time as well as in terms of the more usual space ones. But the "space" is the x-y-z of physics, and the "time" is the 't' of physics: how, then, it can be supposed that the mixture of the two should readily yield to an extra-physical and philosophical interpretation, is hard to understand.[2] The point has been well put by Schlick and Whitehead. "It would be wrong to associate any metaphysical speculations with the introduction of the four-dimensional point of view",[3] and "Time and space are among the fundamental physical facts yielded by our knowledge of the external world. We cannot rest content with any theory of them which simply takes mathematical equations involving four variables, which are interpreted as space and time co-ordinates."[4]

In the foregoing, I have tried to examine three of the major issues concerning time raised by the new conceptions in physics. That the final conclusion should endorse the earlier one, which was that it is a mistake to suppose that physical theories can ultimately solve the *metaphysical* problem of time, is not to pretend to put 'paid' to the claims of physics. To show that 't' is a specialized abstraction differing in important ways from "time" is not, as Bergson sometimes seemed to think, a valid ground of criticism against physical theories: what it *is* valid to criticize are the metaphysical conclusions drawn from such theories.

[1] *Meaning of Relativity*, p. 33. For a general statement of what Minkowski has done, see Eddington, *Space, Time, and Relativity*, pp. 55–6.
[2] Thus Alexander's "space-time", for instance, is quite distinct from that of physics.
[3] *Space and Time in Contemporary Physics*, p. 51.
[4] *Principles of Natural Knowledge*, p. 45. See also Bridgman, op. cit., p. 74, and Cunningham, op. cit., p. 213.

CHAPTER III

LOGIC

IT is sufficiently evident from the foregoing that questions involving the notion of time may be discussed from any one of several different aspects. Corresponding to these different aspects there is also a difference in the connotation of the most important concepts: for instance, a psychologist would say that two events, such as a report from a gun M and a flash from another N, were simultaneous if a subject S sensed them together, while a physicist would disagree. He would say that the two firings were not simultaneous if S was standing at equal distances from both guns. Light travels quicker than sound, and for the report from M to be sensed at the same time as the flash from N, M must have been fired first. Again, assuming that the lightning flash and the thunderclap come from the same source, we calculate how far away the storm is by the time-interval between them.

In his own field, the psychologist or the physicist is quite safe. As long as his use of a technical term remains constant,[1] and as long as (if departing from general usage) he makes perfectly clear the sense in which he *is* using it, the scientist is at perfect liberty to use words in whatever sense he likes. Peter Pan may, if he chooses, write a novel in which 'kiss' and 'thimble' exchange the meanings that they ordinarily have: and his readers, once they realize this, need not complain. But such a procedure is in the highest degree inconvenient: not to me *qua* reader of Peter's novel, but to me *qua* reader *also* of *The Mill on the Floss*, *Pride and Prejudice*, and so on. Of course, in the hypothetical case above, we are in no danger of permanently confusing 'kiss' with 'thimble' because they stand for two very distinct things. But if I so confused two terms that are often used in the same context—if, for instance,

[1] Or, where this is not possible, varies only between well-defined and explicitly stated limits.

I used the word 'dactyl' indifferently for a dactyl and a trochee —the denotation of 'dactyl' would be enlarged, but with the blurring of the former distinction, it would be correspondingly less precise.

In the same way the use in similar but distinct contexts of the same word is bound to lead to confusion. It is because we do not keep our physics and our psychology and our metaphysics in separate compartments that it is desirable to examine our terminology, and to see what terms are used to express more than one notion. Systematic ambiguity may not be harmful, but it is liable to lead to real ambiguity: and the use of ambiguous language is hardly likely to produce clear thought. Hence the need for a logical clarification of the concepts we use. This chapter may be dull: it will, nevertheless, be important.

At the outset a distinction (which will reappear in particular form in many of the later distinctions that are drawn) must be made between time as it is perceived and the *concept* of Time. I do not wish to give the impression here that there is only one concept of time. If there were one consistent and adequate concept the task of the system-builder would be much easier! As it is, the metaphysician grumbles that the physicist's concept takes account of one aspect only, and the physicist retorts that the *various* metaphysical concepts are all inconsistent. But that does not prevent there being a very important sense in which all conceptual 'times', different though they may be, can be grouped together, as against time as it is perceived. To use a familiar analogy, which must not, however, be pressed too far, concept and percept bear to each other something of the relation between finished product and raw material. This leads on to another point—that however valid and useful the distinction we make may be, and however helpful it is in avoiding harmful ambiguity, we can never make it absolute. Paper and wood-pulp differ in many ways: but we would be stupid if we denied that, when all is said and done, paper is 'made of' wood-pulp. As Kant expressed it, in a slightly different connection, "Thoughts without content are empty, intuitions without concepts are blind."[1]

Nevertheless, as long as we remember these reservations, the distinction between concept and percept is an extremely useful

[1] *Critique of Pure Reason* (translated Kemp Smith), B.75.

one, and Gunn was right repeatedly to emphasize it. As he puts it: "We *perceive* time: we are aware of certain amounts of duration and also, usually, of a succession of events. This knowledge is at the perceptual level of experience. Time is a percept. But as we increase and organize our knowledge, and bring to bear our powers of analysis, synthesis, and abstraction, we come to a concept of Time. Perceptual time and conceptual time are not quite alike in their characteristics, or more strictly we may say that time as perceived is not identical with Time as conceived. It is most important to recognize this distinction and to bear it in mind, for some things which are true of time as *conceived* are not true of it as *perceived*. For instance, time as perceived is always limited. We never perceive the whole of time. It is also perceived as sensibly continuous, as having a certain directional quality: it is transitive and related in its content to the subject at the moment of experience. Only if the wider, *implied* temporal perspective and the time-span immediately experienced be apprehended as passing into one another can Time be grasped, and in this way it is grasped as a continuum. Time as conceived is unlimited in character, is regarded as infinitely divisible and mathematically continuous like an infinite series. Further, it is looked on as involving an objective order of before-and-after, which is not to be equated with the past, present, and future of a subject. This has unfortunately led some idealist critics to claim that past, present, and future are merely subjective and illusory distinctions which show the inherent self-contradiction and unreality of Time. This, however, is due in part to carelessness in the construction of the concept and to a failure to refer to our actual temporal experience in perception. Conceptual time is also conceived to be a unity in spite of the difficulty of ascribing to it any principle of coherence. Perceptual time, however, is rooted in experience, and professions of unity are not made in regard to it. There may on this level be many unrelated times."[1]

To these can be added another difference. What we perceive is not so much 'time' as the passage of events. We never perceive 'time' by itself in abstraction from events: for perception, the fundamental thing is the happening of events. *But*, we find it useful for some purposes to emphasize the successiveness of the happening

[1] Gunn, *The Problem of Time*, pp. 373–4. See also, Taylor, *Elements of Metaphysics*, Book III, chapter iv.

of events:[1] hence we conceive of events as happening 'in' time, where time is regarded as a compendious way of dealing with events in their aspect of 'happenings'. Carried to an extreme, this may result in a conception of time (as for instance in Newton) as being independent of events. On the other hand, there is Whitehead, who insists that absolute time is a mere hypostatized figment, and that time is only the passage of Nature considered in its creative aspect.[2] The question of the relation between time and events is a difficult one, not to be gone into fully here. We need only invoke what was said above—that though the distinction between percept and concept has its uses, we should beware of making an absolute separation between them.

To avoid confusion between perceptual and conceptual time, unless the context makes it clear which is being discussed, time as perceived will be called 'the specious present' and the word 'time' will be reserved for conceptual time.

It is generally admitted that the notions of time and change are closely connected: we cannot write about time without finding that 'change' crops up repeatedly. As Broad showed in his excellent analysis in the second chapter of his *Scientific Thought*, the word 'change', as it is commonly used, covers two fundamentally distinct notions. The first is change in a thing with respect to its characteristics, as when a signal lamp changes from red to green: the second is the change of the temporal characteristics themselves, as when a future event, as we say, 'becomes present', and a present one recedes into the past. The first is a qualitative change; but 'past' and 'present' and 'future' can in no valid sense be called 'qualities' of an object. An event has not the quality first of 'presentness' and then of 'pastness', as a signal lamp has first the quality of 'redness' and then of 'greenness'. As Broad put it, "We cannot reduce changes of Time to changes in Time, since Time would then need another Time to change in, and so on to infinity."[3]

In what follows, qualitative change will always be referred to

[1] I would make the reminder here that we have direct perception in the specious present of bare successiveness, hence it is not circular to talk in this way about successiveness.
[2] *Concept of Nature*, p. 73, and *Principles of Natural Knowledge*, chapter v.
[3] Op. cit., p. 65. While agreeing with the conclusion that changes of Time are irreducible, I am not sure whether his reason is valid.

as 'alteration'. A special, and very important, case of alteration is the alteration of particles with respect to their spatial positions. This is known as movement, and it is tempting to suppose that all alterations can ultimately be resolved into movements. (The prevalence of such beliefs, from Democritus to modern atomic theories, shows their attractiveness to the scientist.)[1]

In this connection, it is interesting to note that Aristotle, who defined time in terms of motion, not only considered that all alterations were movements, but also identified 'changes of time' with 'changes in time' (alterations): hence we should expect to find that his view of time is stunted, in that he considered only half, and the less important half at that, of the problem.

With regard to changes *of* time, Broad makes a further distinction, in the light of his theory of the nonentity of the future, between the change from present to past, and the change by which the future becomes present. It is the latter which he considers fundamental, and to which the other types of change are ultimately reducible. There are many who would reject Broad's view of the future, and with it this second distinction: but until we have discussed the matter, we may at least make a verbal distinction, for even if it is finally decided that there is no real distinction, it can do no harm. The change from present to past and then to the more remote past will be called *recession*: the passage of the present into the future, following Broad, will be called *becoming*. *Passage* will be used generally to cover both recession and becoming; *change* will retain the wide use that it ordinarily has, including passage and alteration.

Next comes a group of distinctions that are related in that the same fundamental distinction runs through them all. This is the distinction between time conceived, as mathematics conceives it, as a continuous line, infinite in length and infinitely divisible, and time as it is lived, and as it appears to the subject. In these following distinctions, we have, of course, the old distinction between percept and concept reappearing, but they primarily emphasize a distinction between percept and a particular kind of concept, between 'private' and 'public' times. First, we must distinguish between the various senses of 'present'. As has already been said, the saddle-backed specious present of immediate experience is very

[1] Compare Meyerson, *Identity and Reality*, chapter vii.

different from the durationless mathematical point which represents the present 'instant'. Just as a line in geometry, though continuous, is conceived as made up of separate points at infinitesimal distances apart, so a point of time is conceived as composed of *instants*. The *present instant*, on the one hand, is to be distinguished from other instants: on the other hand, it is to be distinguished from the *now* of which we are immediately aware in the specious present. Within the specious present, a further distinction must be made. Unfortunately, as has already been said, 'present' is ambiguous: it may be used to denote presentness in the temporal sense—the now, or to denote that which is presented to us spatially—the given, the here. The latter use will be avoided as far as possible.

Secondly, the various uses of 'past' need elucidating. It should be realized that 'past' is not synonymous with 'my past':[1] hence the conception of 'the past' as the sum-total of all events that have ever happened is not to be identified with memory, neither my own memory, nor everybody's memories put together. As James points out, "Even though we *were* to conceive the outer successions as forces stamping their images on the brain, and the brain's successions as forming their image on the mind, still, between the mind's own changes being successive, and *knowing their own succession*, lies as broad a chasm as between the object and subject of any case of cognition in the world. A succession of feelings, in and of itself, is not a feeling of succession. And since, to our successive feelings, a feeling of their own succession is added, that must be treated as an additional fact requiring its own special elucidation, which this talk about outer relations stamping copies of themselves within, leaves all untouched."[2]

Also, memory of an event is to be distinguished from memory of receiving information about that event. Strictly, the child who is given a history test does not 'remember' when the Spanish Armada was: what he remembers is that *he* has read in his history-book, or has been told, that it took place in 1588. In other words,

[1] See Gunn, op. cit., p. 377, and footnote.
[2] Op. cit., p. 628. Compare also Collingwood (*Proceedings of the Aristotelian Society*, 1925–6), who distinguishes between "my present memory of a past event", and "the present effect of that past event on my organism" Similar remarks are made in *Essays in Critical Realism*.

the past event to which the memory refers did not occur in 1588, but a few days previous to the test.[1]

Whether a distinction between 'the future' and 'my future', similar to the one between 'the past' and 'memory', can be made, I do not know. (Gunn would seem to imply that it can, in his criticisms of the work of Dunne and Osty.[2])

That time has a certain extension is not a mere extrapolation of the scientist: we are immediately conscious of time as 'going on', and we can remember events which happened 'quite a long time ago'. But the extendedness of time as it is immediately experienced by the conscious subject, as Bergson was never tired of pointing out, is a very different matter from the pointer-readings and objective measurements of the scientist. It is undesirable that both should be called duration: following Bergson, let us keep 'durée' for lived time, and express objectively measured duration (the 't' of physics) by 'time-interval'.

Different meanings of 'simultaneity' have received a good airing in the last few years. First, there is the fundamental distinction between our judgments of simultaneity, and objective (as we may for the present conveniently and vaguely call it), simultaneity. Nobody doubts that such a distinction can be drawn: the scientist points out with unction that if two characteristically different stimuli are presented in very rapid succession, they are apprehended as simultaneous. But when it comes to defining 'objective simultaneity', it is less easy, and indeed, this is a favourite battleground at present, since the advent of Relativity. Briefly, the difficulties result from the conception of simultaneity as relative to the frame of reference: if two such frames are in motion relatively to each other, how are we to decide between them? On the other hand, how are we to measure velocities, unless we are already in possession of some notion of simultaneity? Gunn, in a note at the end of his *Problem of Time*,[3] distinguishes four senses of simultaneity. Beside the fundamental distinction between subjective and objective simultaneity, he distinguishes three kinds of the latter. (*a*) "Syntopic (recorded by camera with revolving film), (*b*) spaced simul-

---

[1] Compare James, op. cit., p. 629: "I have shown that what is past, to be known as past, must be known *with* what is present, and *during* the 'present' spot of time."

[2] Gunn, op. cit., pp. 404–8.   [3] Page 424.

taneity of two kinds—(i) where only observers *not* in relative motion would agree as to the simultaneity of two given events, (ii) where not only these, but also observers in relative uniform motion would agree (some call this public simultaneity) and this is the simultaneity which Einstein denies."

The theory of Relativity, and the doctrine that simultaneity is only relative, does not affect, of course, the certainty of the observer that two events, to him, took place at the same time:[1] hence the great importance of drawing a particular distinction between experienced simultaneity, and simultaneity in the sense or senses in which it is used in physics.

Lastly, in ordinary language 'Eternity' has been used to signify unending time, and timelessness, and the transcending of time in infinity. It will be better if the word is kept only for the last of these senses: as it was used, for instance, by Meister Eckhart in the Middle Ages and by Baron von Hügel in recent times; "In eternity is no before and after: the happenings of the past millennium, and the future one, and now, in eternity are all the same. God's doings of a thousand years ago and now and a thousand years to come are but one single act."[2] Or, as Von Hügel puts it,[3] Eternal life precludes not only spatialized clock time, but even duration. Time is not a barrier against Eternal Life, but the means by which we apprehend life.

As regards the first usage, as equivalent to 'unending time', it is better avoided, for time conceived as somehow going on and on without end is still time (that is, if it is anything at all but a figment). As Aquinas pointed out[4] in his criticism of Boethius' definition of eternity as the "simultaneously whole and perfect possession of interminable life", 'interminable' is a weak, imperfect, negative term by which to describe the fullness and the completeness that is eternity.

On the other hand, it is equally undesirable to use 'eternal' as a kind of reach-me-down opposite of 'temporal', to be used when-

[1] And the absoluteness of simultaneity, in that sense.
[2] Eckhart's *Works* (translated Evans), Vol. I, p. 150.
[3] *Eternal Life*, p. 383.
[4] Aquinas, *Works* (English Dominicans' Edition), Vol. I, p. 97. But Boethius himself distinguishes very clearly between being conducted through a life of an infinite duration, and comprehending the whole of this duration as present. Duration, even if infinite, is not eternal.

ever 'temporal' does not apply. If we mean that temporal notions do not apply, let us use *timeless*, or (better) *non-temporal* rather than 'eternal'. Thus mathematical truths, such as $2 + 2 = 4$, are not *eternal*, although they are not temporal: rather is it better to call them non-temporal, meaning by that that they are out of time altogether, and that temporal notions have no relevance at all to them.

Following on from this, we have to note the ambiguous use of words like 'always' and 'sometimes'; and must be careful to distinguish between expressions which appear to have, but do not really have, a temporal element, and expressions which genuinely contain temporal elements.

We say of a propositional function, such as "$\phi\chi \supset \psi\chi$", that it is always, sometimes, or never true. It is easy to see that in such expressions the words 'always', 'sometimes', and 'never' have not the same meaning as they have, for instance, in "I have never told a lie; but sometimes I have knowingly misled people by my silence". There is a difference between saying, "He sometimes eats fish on Fridays" and saying "At 1 p.m. on Friday, 23rd November, 1934 —that is, at *some* (particular) time—he ate fish".

When we say, "*If $A \supset B$, and $B \supset C$, then $A \supset C$ is always true*", we do *not* primarily mean to assert that at any particular time the implication holds, though in fact it does: what we are chiefly concerned with is the *implication*, which is essentially non-temporal, in the sense that it has no *special* connection with time. It is true, but irrelevant, that the implication cannot be found to hold good on particular occasions *except* at a time: but if it comes to that, on every such occasion, some *place* is concerned. We might just as well say, "*If $A \supset B$, & $B \supset C$, then $A \supset C$ is everywhere true*", except of course, that it is easier to imagine our mental operations (and our perception of implications) as having position in time rather than position in space. But the point is that if we said "*If $A \supset B$, & $B \supset C$, then $A \supset C$ is everywhere true*", we should really be asserting that to change position in space makes *no difference*[1] *at all* to the implication: that is, that spatial position is irrelevant. Similarly when we say "*If $A \supset B$, & $B \supset C$, then $A \supset C$, is always true*", what we mean is that mere difference in date does not affect the implication: hence

---

[1] This is the minimum position: many people would go further than this, and say that the whole notion is absurd.

the expression is in a fundamental sense non-temporal, and the use of temporal language, if pressed too far, is bound to be misleading. The point can be put in another way. The propositional function "*If A* r *B* & *B* r *C, then A* r *C*", is exemplified on the sad occasion when I discover that my length is greater than the length of the tape-measure, and that greater than the length of the new mackintosh I have bought, and hence conclude that I shall be considerably longer than the mackintosh. Now this is obviously an event in time —I might, for instance, record it in my diary as happening on a certain day—and equally obviously the general function is not an event in time. Hardly anyone would make the gross mistake of supposing it to be *an* event, but I think that many people tend to look upon a propositional function as a kind of class of events, formed by the summation of particular events which are instances of the function, and this seems to me quite wrong. The trouble is, that they would usually not hold this view explicitly, but by overuse of temporal expressions in propositional functions they implicitly slur over the distinction, between their use in such functions and in ordinary temporal expressions. Suppose I say, "When I am in London, I always stay with X." This evidently means that on every *actual* occasion that I am in London, I stay with X. The reference to time here is essential. On the other hand, if I attempted to make a similar analysis of "*If A* ⊃ *B*, & *B* ⊃ *C, then A* ⊃ *C is* always true", and to say that it *meant* that on every occasion on which trial has been made of it, *A* ⊃ *C* was found to hold good, my analysis would be insufficient. For we do not merely mean by this general implication that it does *as a matter of fact* hold good in whatever particular instance we like to take, but that it holds of necessity. Now time and temporal events cannot yield necessity, but only matters of fact,[1] so that if we are concerned with functions that claim necessity for their implications, a temporal analysis is insufficient. It is, of course, true that it does hold 'always', in the sense that we cannot find any particular occasion on which it does not hold: but we mean more than that by our assertion. But the best way of showing that the use of 'always' in propositional functions is essentially non-temporal, is to find an example where we should not use the word 'always' twice. Let us grant, for the sake of the illustration, that whenever a man takes a certain quantity

[1] This is an assertion which will need discussion later on.

of arsenic under certain conditions, his death necessarily follows. Then it would be permissible[1] to say "$(x), \phi x \supset \psi x$", or, "The function $a,b,c,d, \ldots \supset x$ is always true." But in the ordinary, temporal sense of 'always', we should not say that people are 'always swallowing arsenic', that is, it is not always true that $a,b,c,d, \ldots$ are happening. The difference is between asserting the implication, "*If A then* (always) *B*" and between asserting "*A* and *B*" (always). Hence in a *temporal* sense it is only *sometimes* true that $a,b,c, \ldots x$ occur: whereas it is universally the case that given $a,b,c, \ldots, x$ results. In other words, *sometimes* we have $a,b,c,$: *if* we have a,b,c, then we *always* have x. But this 'always' is not a temporal, but a universal 'always'. To imagine that it was a temporal 'always' would lead us into the absurdity of supposing that somebody was, at every instant, in process of swallowing arsenic: actually of course, whether the non-temporal 'always' holds good also temporally, depends upon the antecedent facts, *to which it is subordinate*, and these may only be a 'sometimes'. There seem to be four possibilities, given that *A* has the relation *r* to *C*.[2]

(1) *A* always happens (temporally) and *r* is a universal relation (non-temporal 'always'). Then we have 'always *C*' in a temporal sense as well. I doubt if any example of this could be given.

(2) *A* sometimes happens, and *r* is a universal relation. Then we have 'always *C*' *only* in a non-temporal sense. An example is "*A* logically entails *C*".

(3) *A* always happens, and *r* is a particular relation. 'Always *C*' in neither sense.

(4) *A* sometimes happens, and *r* is a particular relation—'Always *C*' in neither sense. An example of this would be, "*A* is often followed by *C*".

Now, of course, nobody does believe that somebody is, at every instant, swallowing arsenic, so we do interpret the 'always *C*' in a non-temporal sense: but in other examples, where the results are not so obviously absurd, it is easy to interpret the 'always C' in a temporal sense, and to base important metaphysical arguments on mistakes in logical analysis.[3] It is desirable to introduce separate terminology: so in what follows, the non-temporal "always" will

---

[1] Though not, as regards the second alternative, desirable.
[2] *r* need not necessarily be a relation of implication.
[3] This is a possible criticism of McTaggart. See Chapter VII.

be replaced by "*holds good in all cases*", or "*universally*": the non-temporal "never" by "*holds good in no cases*": and the non-temporal "whenever" by "if . . . then".

A related cause of stumbling is to be found in the verbal ambiguity that arises in languages that do not possess a tenseless mood, such as English. Ontological arguments are a permanent warning of the ease with which we can slide from tenseless statements to affirmations about present existence. As Laird put it: "It is simply false to maintain that any assertion of existence is confined to the present tense. One might wish that European languages, like some Oriental ones, had a tenseless mood, but even a European can see the point. It is true that the past does not exist now, just as it is true that the present did not exist formerly, but existence itself means the whole of existence, not merely present existence, and past events, like present ones, have their determinate place in the determinate series of existence."[1]

A favourite metaphysical magic carpet is the miraculously easy transition from "The past does not exist" (now) through "The past *is* not" to "The past is not real". (I should like to see an analysis on similar lines of "The past is past": I fancy that this obviously true, even if tautological, statement might present insuperable difficulties.) The lack of a tenseless mood means that the present tense (particularly in the verb 'to be') has to do duty for two quite distinct purposes, only one of which is temporal. If I say, "*X* is a universal truth", I do *not* mean merely, "*X* is now true"; I mean precisely the opposite, since my emphasis is on the truth and not on the particular time. Of course if *X* really is universally true (if any meaning can be attached to this), it does, in fact, hold good now, but this immediate, particular application is the last thing I wish to emphasize. (And here it should be pointed out that in the above so-called 'elucidation' of the distinction between tensed and tenseless statements, there occur examples of each.) Short of inventing a new mood for every verb in the language—a task which certainly cannot be attempted here—these ambiguities are unavoidable, and unfortunately their frequency increases (also unavoidably) as we pass from ordinary conversation to any kind of analytical statement. As an example of the difficulty of distinguishing between temporal and non-temporal language, there is an

[1] *A Study in Realism*, p. 50.

argument of Broad's which it is interesting to analyse. This is the important argument in *Scientific Thought*[1] where Broad, in analysing the three statements "It has rained", "It is raining", and "It will rain", seeks to show that though the first two can be translated by expressions which do not contain a reference to tense, the last cannot be so translated, and the reference to the future remains outstanding. His formulation of "It has rained" is "There is an event which is characterized by raininess, and the sum-total of existence when the judgment is made includes all and more than all which it includes when this event becomes." This is easily open to the objection that it should be 'included' instead of 'includes'. Let us try to get rid of the debatable phrase "*includes all and more than all which it includes when this event becomes.*" Translated, the proposition now becomes "There (is) an event which (is) characterized by raininess, and the sum-total of existence when the judgment (is) made (is) *greater than the sum-total of existence* when this event (becomes)."[2] Similarly, "It is raining", can be translated "There (is) an event which (is) characterized by raininess, and the sum-total of existence when the judgment is made (*is*) *equal to* the sum-total of existence when this event (becomes)." All the verbs in these translations are tenseless; though, apparently, they are in the present tense, actually they are timeless.

Can the judgment "It will rain" be similarly translated? Yes. It becomes, "There (is) an event which (is) characterized by raininess, and the sum-total of existence when the judgment is made (*is*) *less than* the sum-total of existence when this event (becomes)." The verbs here too are timeless. Now this Broad denies. It seems that his argument is based on a confusion, due to his translation of "It has rained" as ". . . *includes all and more than all which it includes* when this event becomes." Is the second "includes" intended to be in the present tense or timeless? If the former, then he is wrong, and it ought to be "*included*": if the latter, then by parity of reasoning, his translation of "It will rain" should be equally tenseless. Broad's whole point is that it is impossible to get rid of the future tense; but I think the translation suggested might do it. Again, when Broad begins his translations by "*There is an event* . . ." and goes on to hold that this cannot be so in the case of events that have not yet happened, "for the only events that there

[1] Op. cit., p. 76.   [2] All the verbs enclosed in brackets are timeless.

are are the events that have become up to the time when the assertion was made: the sum-total of existence does not contain future events", he is doing one of two things. Either the "*is*" in "There is an event" is timeless, in which case he is giving a wrong reason for his rejection of the future, or, if it is not, there is equally no way of analysing away 'has been' and 'is now' that does not lead to an infinite regress. I cannot think that Broad has proved his case,[1] but if such an exact thinker can be misled by verbal similarity, that shows the insidiousness of the confusion.

Wherever possible, when tenseless language is used after this in an argument, the ambiguous word in question, generally the verb, will be enclosed in brackets. (But in all probability the greater number will creep past unobserved.)

From what has been said above, the importance of a firm logical basis to any self-respecting metaphysic can hardly be over-estimated. I would suggest that we cannot hope to solve the metaphysical problems connected with time unless we have first not only made an analysis of the concepts which we propose to employ, but also, and no less important, brought out explicitly the ease with which we can slide into confusion, if we fail to realize the pressing necessity of distinguishing between language which is genuinely temporal and that which is, in a fundamental sense, non-temporal.

[1] It is interesting to speculate whether it is ever possible, by strict logical tenseless language, to prove a *metaphysical* theory regarding *temporal* concepts.

CHAPTER IV

METAPHYSICS—KANT

I

THE first section of this chapter will be taken up with showing the gradual development of Kant's views on time within the *Critique of Pure Reason* and the conflicting tendencies which they reveal. For no other philosopher is it as necessary as it is with Kant to trace the different views which he holds at different times, and to write sections on "The Aesthetic", "The Analytic", and so on. Only after this has been done can we go on to discuss in greater detail the more interesting of the problems which he raises.

In "The Aesthetic", Kant said that space and time were empirically real, but transcendentally ideal: by this he attempted to reconcile two apparently contradictory findings of our experience. On the one hand, no one would say that space and time are real, if at all, in the same way that material objects are real. On the other hand, our experiences do seem to be arranged in spatial order, and to be serial in time, so that we should be loath to believe in the possibility of experience that is not in time or space. Admittedly, these are two important points, and their attempted reconciliation cannot but be interesting. But what is meant by 'transcendental'? Does it just mean that the criteria which are emphasized are those of material objects?—for instance, that while time is 'real' in so far as it is experienced, it is 'ideal' in that it is obviously different from material objects, which are thus held to be the only things that are 'real' in the strictest sense. Such materialism would be a possible position; but it is not Kant's. It is, above all, important to see that he goes farther than this (it may be said, farther than he logically need have done, on the evidence of the Aesthetic). For not only did he hold that space and time were transcendentally ideal, but he also held that material objects, as they are apprehended by us, are ideal, and distinct from the things as they are in themselves. We are not, then, asked to contrast the transcendentally ideal space and time with 'real' material objects: on the contrary, the intuitions of our senses, along with the 'forms' that condition these intuitions, are contrasted with a 'real' world that is completely non-sensuous. If anything, space and time as the conditioning forms of representation[1] should be treated with greater respect by transcendental philosophers, than the mere conditioned intuitions. In this case, the support which common sense would at first give to the doctrine (since the plain man would probably allow a vague 'reality' to space and time) can no longer be given.

Secondly, Kant emphasizes the *a priori* character of space and time—indeed, they are what make *a priori* synthetic judgments possible. Though they are an essential part of all experience, they are not given to us through experience, but *a priori*. He bases his belief in their *a priority* on three grounds:[2] firstly, that "neither coexistence nor succession would ever come within our perception, if the representation of time were not presupposed as underlying them all *a priori*."[3] That is, Time is logically prior to times. This, however, is later contradicted when Kant says that "only through successive synthesis of part to part in its apprehension can the whole be known."[4] Which of the two represents his real position is difficult to decide. Secondly, "we cannot . . . remove time itself, though we can well think time as void of appearances.[5] But, as Kemp Smith pointed out, even if time is necessary to our apprehensions, that does not alone prove it to be *a priori*. Lastly, Kant contrasts concepts, which "contain only partial representations",[6] with intuitions, and says that the infinity of time, and the fact that the whole of Time precedes its parts, shows that it is an intuition. But later he changes his mind and treats Time as a concept.

Thus, in the Aesthetic, Kant makes a distinction between empirical and transcendental reality which he considers fundamental: he emphasizes the view of space and time as "forms" which condition our sensible apprehensions; and, on the whole, he treats space and time as of equal importance, though sometimes he is inclined to

[1] According to Fouillée, however, time is a form of appetition and not of representation (*Psychologie des Idées Forces*, II, p. 104).
[2] The over-emphasized parallelism, in his language, between space and time is here a defect, and should be discounted, in so far as the confusions and unfortunate language are not an essential result of Kant's position.
[3] B 46 (Kemp Smith's translation).
[4] B 204.   [5] B 46.   [6] B 48.

hold that time, not only may, but must, be represented by space. But time, in Kant's philosophy, does not occupy the very minor position in the transcendental scheme as it would seem from the Aesthetic, the place where he is avowedly dealing with time. As the Critique progresses, time occupies a more important place, until it is fundamental, while the importance attached to space proportionately declines. Thus the "Schematism of the pure concepts of the understanding" in the Categories proceeds only through the postulation of modes of time, though it is doubtful how far "modes" are consistent with the notion of time as a pure intuition, one and indivisible, which he emphasized in the Aesthetic. And, by the time that the Antinomies are reached, nothing less than an Idea of Reason is needed to disentangle the First Antinomy!

Yet it should not be thought that this is the only trend in the middle of the Critique. Side by side with these, and inconsistent with them, are passages where Kant seems to have a purely spatial conception of time, and to earn Bergson's criticism that he conceived of Time as a homogeneous medium—though he could never make up his mind whether representation in space is merely convenient, or necessary. "We are unable to perceive any determination in time save through change in outer relations":[1] "In order that we may make inner alterations thinkable, we must represent time figuratively as a line."[2] "We cannot obtain for ourselves a representation of time, which is not an object of outer intuition, except under the image of a line."[3] On the other hand: "The synthesis of the manifold parts of space is successive, taking place in time and containing a series."[4] It would appear that Kant never completely made up his mind on this point, yet it would surely be inconsistent with his main position to hold that spatial representation is necessary, whereas it is a tenable position which nobody is likely to dispute, to say that such representation is often convenient. On the whole, Kant's main trend is definitely towards emphasizing the importance of time and relegating space to the background, in contrast to the rather forced parallelism of the Aesthetic. The abandonment of such parallelism is all to the good, as far as time is concerned, since when there is distortion to fit an architectonic scheme, it is invariably time that suffers, rather than space, just *because* the characteristics which are not common to both are

[1] B 277.   [2] B 292.   [3] B 156.   [4] B 439.

specifically temporal rather than specifically spatial. So the very pre-eminence of time is likely to put it at a disadvantage.

As soon as Kant proceeds to formulate and deduce the categories, he discovers that the position he took up in the "Aesthetic" with regard to space and time was insufficient. Now he says, "Space and time are represented *a priori* not merely as forms of sensible intuition, but as themselves intuitions which contain a manifold."[1] And, "Space and time contain a manifold of pure *a priori* intuition, but at the same time are conditions of the receptivity of our mind—conditions under which alone it can receive representations of objects, and which therefore must also always affect the concept of these objects."[2] In a footnote, perhaps aware of the flat contradiction as it stands with the Aesthetic, he says, "In the Aesthetic, I have treated this unity (of space) as belonging merely to sensibility, *simply in order to emphasize* that it precedes any concept, though as a matter of fact, it presupposes a synthesis which does not belong to the senses but through which all concepts of space and time first become possible."[3] Kant's position in the Transcendental Deduction would seem to be that time is not purely a matter of sensibility, but depends also upon the understanding and its "original power of combining the manifold of intuition".[4] Inner sense alone contains only the mere form of intuition, but no *determinate* intuition, which is possible only "through the consciousness of the determination of the manifold by the transcendental act of imagination".[5] When I am given an appearance in time, I necessarily represent to myself synthetic unity of the manifold, because otherwise I could not intuit that time-relation as being *determined* in time-sequence. This synthetic unity, if I abstract from the form of inner determination, gives the category of cause. (It should be noticed that Kant's main concern here is not with time as such, but with causation as necessary in order to refute Hume—hence possibly some of his inconsistencies.) By a similar abstraction from space we get the category of quantity.

Yet in the Schematism he has gone considerably farther than this position. It is no longer merely, that time, like space, is dependent upon the understanding. On the contrary, the categories are valueless unless time is there to mediate the subsumption of appear-

[1] B 160. [2] B 102.
[3] B 160-1. Italics mine. [4] B 153. [5] B 154.

ances under them. Secondly, whereas before space, equally with time, was concerned with a special category, now time is emphasized and space ignored. Time is the "formal condition of the manifold of inner sense, and therefore of the connection of all representations",[1] and, "time is contained in every empirical representation of the manifold".[2] More than that, "the schema of each category contains and makes capable of representation only a determination of time".[3] Thus the schema of magnitude, not now spatial, is the "generation of time in the successive apprehension of an object",[4] and similarly with the other schemata which "are *nothing but a priori* determinations of time in accordance with rules".[5] The categories can only be applied to appearances through the transcendental determination of time. Yet time is transcendentally ideal, according to the Aesthetic! But Kant sees that, in realizing the categories, the schemata inevitably restrict them to conditions of sensibility. Obviously, if schematism essentially involves time, and temporal predicates are inapplicable to things in themselves, he must hold that "the categories in their pure significance, apart from all conditions of sensibility, ought to apply to things as they are, and not represent them only as they appear".[6] Nevertheless he admits that although there is a meaning in the pure concepts of understanding, it is a purely logical one, and "such a representation I can put to no use, for it tells me nothing as to the nature of that which is thus to be viewed as a primary subject".[7] I would suggest that if this is so he has hardly an adequate ground for his distinction between phenomena and noumena, and that to say that time is transcendentally ideal is to say very little.

The newer viewpoint is developed throughout the Analytic of Principles, and especially in the Analogies. The Kant of the Aesthetic could not have said: "Even space and time, however free their concepts are from anything empirical, and however certain it is that they are represented in the mind completely *a priori*, would yet be without objective validity, senseless and meaningless, if their necessary application to the objects of experience were not established."[8] Here space and time are considered as concepts, and to allow this a distinction between pure and empirical concepts is necessary. What Kant can mean by 'objective validity' is dubious:

[1] B 177.   [2] B 178.   [3] B 184.   [4] B 184.
[5] B 184. Italics mine.   [6] B 186.   [7] B 186–7.   [8] B 195.

certainly it cannot mean 'transcendental reality', since at the same time he asserts their necessary application to objects of experience. It would seem that of the two expressions, the former is the important one. We saw, in dealing with the Aesthetic, that time is indubitably 'real' for our experience: if it is also allowed to have objective validity, it would appear to matter very little whether or not it has 'transcendental' reality. I would suggest that most of what is valuable in Kant's treatment of time is independent of this question.

In the Analogies, the three rules of all relations of appearances in time are conceived as corresponding with the three modes of time—duration, succession, and coexistence. But though it is unfortunate that Kant implied that these three 'modes' can be separately apprehended[1] (and, indeed, was never clear whether there are three such modes or only two), the important point is that he saw the essential part played by time in our apprehensions, especially in connection with causality. It is often said that the Analogies are the most important part of the Critique, as showing the necessary connections that are involved in perception: and the prime place given to time in these Analogies (rules which are "prior to all experience and indeed make it possible",[2] and which determine the existence of every appearance in respect of the unity of all time) should show the importance of time in Kant's philosophy, in spite of his occasional spatial language. In the first Analogy, if anything, he overdoes the emphasis on time: since the conception of a permanent enduring through change is not itself temporal. A simpler alternative would have been to connect this enduring permanence with space, as a background before which changes (such as those with which the Second Analogy deals) take place. Endurance and duration are not identical: granted that an object which endures 'in time' has duration, yet what we primarily mean when we say that an object endures is that the lapse of time, which duration measures, has not affected it, and is therefore largely irrelevant. As Kemp Smith expressed it, "Kant here . . . unduly ignores space, limiting his analysis to inner sense. He defines the schema of substance as the permanence of the real in time, i.e. as the representation of the real which persists while all else changes. . . . Consciousness is only possible through the

[1] Compare Kemp Smith, *Commentary*, p. 356.   [2] B 219.

representation of objects in *space*. Only in outer sense is a permanent given in contrast to which change may be perceived. The proof ought therefore to have proceeded in the following manner. Time can be conceived only as motion, and motion is perceivable only against a permanent background in space. Consciousness of time therefore involves consciousness of a permanent in space."[1]

But Kant's most important pronouncements about time, and his real originality, are to be found in the Second Analogy. His originality lies in his having grasped and formulated, even if he did not succeed in explaining satisfactorily, questions which are fundamental not only to his particular metaphysic, but to any attempt seriously to grapple with time. These questions, which will be more fully discussed in the next section, are: What is the relation between simultaneity and succession? How is it that although our sensations are discreet and successive, we attribute continuity through time to the object which occasions them? Does that involve a distinction between subjective and objective succession? If so, what is the criterion by which we distinguish them? Is that criterion infallible, or only reasonably satisfactory—does it rest on logical grounds, or only on matters of fact? (If the latter, has he succeeded in answering Hume?)

We are not concerned at present with these questions—some of which Kant raised explicitly, and some of which were only implicit, to be raised by later commentators—here we have only to consider the relation of the Analogy to the rest of the Critique.

It is difficult to see how Kant, if time, as he says over and over again, is entirely subjective and a form of our apprehension, can consistently distinguish between subjective and objective succession. On his premises, what can 'objective succession' be? Yet he holds that there can only be consciousness of times conditioning one another in a single objective time. (That he does this is certain, for without it he would have left a very obvious loophole open to Hume.) "Absolute time is not an object of perception . . . on the contrary, the appearances must determine for one another their position in time, and make their time-order a necessary order."[2] Though time cannot itself be experienced, its essential characters must be represented through appearances—which sounds like an

[1] *Commentary*, p. 360.   [2] B 245.

implicit distinction between Reality and Appearance. If so, why should time itself be relegated to the world of Appearance? With respect to his frequent use of spatial language in the Critique, it is interesting to note that in the Analogies he fully recognizes the essential irreversibility of time, using it as a premise in his argument for causality. This should go far to clear him of the charge of holding at bottom an unduly spatial conception of time, in spite of many passages in which his language is spatial, some of them even in the Analogies themselves.

Moreover, in the Analogies Kant raises the important problem —very foreign to the doctrines of the Aesthetic!—of motion and change, and the relation of them to the permanent. He emphasizes the *necessity* that our experiences should be connected, and that the changes should be determined by a *necessary* law. The Analogies are rules which are "prior to all experience and even make it possible",[1] and time plays a very important part in the formulation of this essential doctrine in Kant's reply to Hume.

In the light of this, if time is given *a priori*, and prior to all experience—more than that, making experience possible—it is curious why time should be considered as having no validity apart from the conditions of possible experience: and the solution of the First Antinomy, which might have passed muster in the Aesthetic, is queer after the doctrines of the Analytic.[2] The Antinomy is concerned to point out the unthinkableness of both the alternatives that the world had or had not a beginning in time. Commentators have sufficiently exercised themselves in criticism and emendation: in particular, they have objected to the question-begging use of 'verfliessen', to Kant's wrong conceptions of the infinite, and to the undesirable dichotomy of 'the world' and 'time'. This last point links on to other places where Kant speaks as if time is something apart from events, and so it can be considered here. Bergson objected that Kant conceived time as a homogeneous medium. Whether or not that is entirely true, it is certainly the case that Kant's language in some places suggests this. We should expect to find it in the Aesthetic, where the whole treatment of time is

[1] B 219.
[2] See the short but clear article by Van Biéma in *Revue de Métaphysique et de Morale*, 1908.

defective through formality:[1] but when he says in the First Analogy, "Change does not affect time itself, but only appearances in time",[2] that is more serious. Nevertheless it is doubtful whether he did really intend to hypostatize time in this manner: in the Postulates of Empirical Thought he contradicts what he had said in the First Analogy: "Space alone is determined as permanent, while time and therefore everything that is in inner sense is in constant flux."[3] But though Kant can be criticized for inconsistency and unsatisfactoriness on particular points—his spatialization, his subjectivity, his illegitimate transition to physics in the First Analogy, his dubious assumption that time is only given to us through successive representations—the importance of his treatment of time remains. It is unfortunate that his most valuable remarks on time should come as it were incidentally and implicitly (for instance, in the Analogies, where he is primarily dealing with causality) rather than in the places where he is specifically dealing with time (the Aesthetic and the First Antinomy), more especially as the former develop into something quite different from, and in many ways conflicting with, the latter.

II

After this indispensable introduction, it is now possible to attempt to discuss in greater detail the more interesting questions which Kant raises, especially those in the Second Analogy.

Looking in a certain direction, I observe a brownish object, roughly elliptical in shape, surrounded by water. I move my head slightly and still see such an object, still surrounded by water. But there is a slight difference in that my field of vision formerly included some trees[4] directly behind the object, and now it does not.

On another occasion I am looking at a brick erection, in which are gaps at regularly spaced intervals. I move my head slightly, and still see such an object, in which there are still gaps. But I see slight changes in detail—the gaps are smaller, or differently coloured.

---

[1] As, for instance, in B 58: "Time itself does not change, but only something which is in time."
[2] B 226.   [3] B 291.
[4] How soon the attempt to describe sensa only and to exclude 'interpretation' fails!

On both occasions my perceptions are successive. There seems to be little to choose between them; yet I, with my admirable capacity for inference, say that in the first case I have 'seen' a boat moving downstream, in the second I have 'seen' first the lower storeys of a house and then the upper. A child would perform the same complicated inference also. On what grounds do we distinguish between the two and say (in Kantian language) that though our perceptions were in each case successive, the first genuinely is an example of successive appearances of the object in different places, while the second is not? This was Kant's problem—familiar enough to seem absurd to us, who make such discriminations every day without thinking: and yet for all that extremely difficult if not impossible to explain logically.[1]

On the two occasions, my perceptions before and after I turn my head resemble each other in a number of ways: but in other respects they are unlike. Why should my two judgments regarding what has 'really' happened differ so markedly?

It may be said that my judgment is based on some pattern of similarity and dissimilarity: in one case, the likenesses are grouped in a certain way, in the other, in another. Thus in the example of the boat the similarities concern the main feature—the brownish object—and the dissimilarities, comparatively unimportant, are in the background. So I say that what I have seen is the *same* object in different positions. In the second case, there is no one 'object' to which I can attribute self-identity: on the contrary, the dissimilarities are not *localized* as they were in the previous example, but scattered and blatantly obvious. (No door in the first floor; window-boxes on the second floor; dormer windows in the attics, and so on.) I fail in my search for a unity: consequently, I group the whole lot together and call it a 'thing', of which I have successively observed the parts.

With regard to this, three remarks may be made: (1) We do not, in attributing 'thinghood', follow the procedure indicated in the last sentence. Kant's example might have been of looking along a row of bungalows in a suburb. Unity is markedly absent: yet we do not say that we have been looking at the parts of one 'thing'.

[1] And Kant had to explain it logically if he was to answer Hume—it would have been useless to insist that we do *in fact* make such distinctions, since Hume would never have denied this.

In attributing thinghood, we follow our own convenience more than this allows. (2) It would follow, that there may be degrees in the certainty of our judgment. For instance, suppose that a moving object[1] presents a 'pattern' of likenesses and unlikenesses characteristic of our second case, should we not hesitate in our judgment, or even make a mistake? This whole suggestion rests upon a double conception of what is 'right' and what is 'mistaken'. A motorcycle, with a badly smoking exhaust, moves slowly along: I see first 'front of motor-cycle', then 'back of motor-cycle', then 'dense blue smoke', then 'rarer white smoke'. Ah! I say: all these perceptions exhibit characteristic differences—they then belong to one coexistent object. Should I not be wrong in this? Of course you would, says common sense. *But*, if our criterion is, as it is *ex hypothesi*, characteristic patterns, why are we dragging in common sense? The argument, which was meant to be a *reductio ad absurdum*, fails because the introduction of common sense is illegitimate. If our criterion really *were* the one suggested, it would be impossible to say that in a case like that of the motor-cycle we had 'made a mistake'. I suggest that though such a criterion may be possible it is not the one which we do in fact use. (3) Even if it were, it would not solve Kant's problem. It says, in effect, that the difference beetweeen the two cases is one of degree only, and is purely relative.

A second attempt at solution might be based on the modern doctrine of the specious present. My glances at the house and at the boat are not instantaneous, but occupy a finite, though small, time-interval. May the difference not be, essentially, that in the second case the time which elapses is sufficient for me *directly to sense* that the pattern set out before me in space changes very slightly —comparable to the blurring of a photograph by slight movement—while in the first case there is no such blurring? Psychologists repeatedly insist that we must distinguish between 'seeing that a change has occurred' and 'seeing a change', and declare that the latter as well as the former can be perceived—rightly, as each of us can test for himself. This solution would probably not be acceptable to Kant: but that might easily be overlooked. Unfortunately, however, I doubt whether it suits the question which

---

[1] Begging the question for a minute and assuming that we know what 'object' means.

Kant raised any better. It would, if allowed as valid, solve the particular example which Kant gives without any difficulty, but Kant could, with no more difficulty, frame another which the explanation could not meet.

A snail moves along the ground. He is a leisurely specimen, even of his kind, and my specious present, which may comprehend the movements of boats, is far too clumsy an instrument for the present task. Of course, I could keep my eye on him, and observe that, after a certain time-interval, he *has moved*. But that is an entirely different matter, as the psychologists assert, and in the present case it is begging the point at issue, which is how we are going to give logical *justification* for what we do in practice without a thought. It must again be insisted that it is useless to appeal to our conception, conveniently vague, of what constitutes thinghood, and to argue, "The snail is a thing. This thing is in a different spatial configuration from that which it was in a moment before. *Therefore*, this thing has moved"; because, in the first place, at most we can only assert relative movement, and, in the second place, our criterion of thinghood is itself in question, and must itself be justified before it can provide metaphysical alibis for its dependants. Secondly, it must be realized that it is not valid to condemn Kant for resorting to a highly abstruse argument to do what any child can do without any fuss. For his object is not *the distinguishing* between the two cases: it is the logical *justification* of our behaviour when we make that distinction.

Kant's problem still remains, then: What criterion have we by which we are *logically justified* in distinguishing, as we do unthinkingly, between subjective and objective succession? Short cuts having failed, what does Kant himself say, and how does he attempt to solve his problem?

In the first place, he starts from the belief that all sensations are successive. This in itself is very dubious: and it makes his task needlessly difficult, since it is hard to see how, given only successiveness, we ever managed to get hold of the concept of simultaneity, except by a very involved process. Yet he is far from denying that we have such a concept, though his treatment of simultaneity, as will later appear, is not satisfactory. Granted, then, his premises, in each case we have successive and characteristically different sensations, and we also have certain kinaesthetic sensations consequent on the movement of our head. Yet in the one case we attribute the differences *solely* to our movement, while in the other we say that the object itself has moved. But to state it thus, in a form which makes it a mere corollary of relative motion, is to miss the main part of Kant's problem. He is not concerned so much with the difficulty of distinguishing motion and rest as with the difficulty of distinguishing when our sensations are in every case successive, objective succession from succession that is merely subjective. The latter distinction conditions the former.

In the first place, what, to Kant, can 'objective' succession be held to mean? (Incidentally, that he admitted that there can be 'objective coexistence' makes it harder than ever to see why, in defiance of common sense, he thought fit to deny that our sensations may coexist.) We certainly do, in practice, distinguish between subjective and objective succession: but if Kant was doing more than paying lip-service to common language, if he really meant to insist that there *is* a genuine distinction—and probably he did— then the question arises how far that squares with his former insistence that time is essentially a way in which men regard things, and of no account outside the realms of possible experience. Time is here treated as being very much more than a mere form of intuition. Further, his solution depends upon the distinction. The only relevant difference between the two cases, says Kant, is that when I am looking at a house I can reverse the order of my perceptions at will: but I cannot do this in the case of the boat. Consequently, since in the second case whatever I do I cannot get my original sensation back, I conclude that this is an example of objective succession. I consider my various sensations as showing different positions of the same object at different times: and in the case of the house, as being successive glimpses of parts of a single whole[1] persisting in time. But what is this 'time' in which such an object is conceived to persist? Evidently not time, as imme-

[1] As was said above, it is missing the point to object that our successive glimpses may not be 'parts' of one 'whole', but of different 'objects'. Kant's argument does not depend on, though of course it is more easily exemplified by, the distinction between *an* object moving on the one hand, and *an* object persisting unchanged on the other. It is also a misapprehension to think that his problem is of distinguishing between *motion* and *rest*—it is more general than that, being the distinction between an object which is *changing in time*, and one which *persists unchanged through time*.

diately perceived. On the other hand, although an inference is necessary when we say that the successive appearances of the boat are objectively successive, while those of the house 'really' coexist though we see them (subjectively) in succession, it is an inference which we make immediately and without demur. Kant's point is that this inference is not made as a *mere matter of fact* (though conditioned by a factual criterion, whether or not what we do makes any difference), but that it is a *necessary* one. We necessarily make the inference to the time-order in which, objectively, events are arranged, *because* there can only be consciousness of times as conditioning one another in a single objective time. In other words, though to consciousness our subjective time-series (Bergson's durée) is prior, logically it is dependent upon the existence of an objective series, since without the latter there would be no consciousness of the former. Hence, time-order is determined, not merely casual, and from this follows Kant's attempt to rehabilitate causality.

First, the criterion which Kant offers needs examination. It is that, when whatever we do or do not do makes no difference, we attribute objectivity.

Case I.—I do not like a glaring advertisement on the wall of a tube station. I turn my head, and my former sensation is replaced by another. It would be gratuitous to assume that, as I turned my head (and that I *did* turn my head, kinaesthetic sensations assure me), one object vanished and another appeared, though that is the impression I get. I attribute the change entirely to the movement of my head; and this opinion is confirmed if, turning my head back again, the original sensation reappears. Consequently, on purely empirical grounds (since it is *possible* that my head-turnings coincided with the objective vanishing of one advertisement) I say that though, in my private time-order, the two sensations were successive, the objects which occasioned these sensations did not come into and go out of existence in a corresponding manner: on the contrary, they endured for a finite length of time.

Case II.—I am standing in a railway station. Near me is a tall thin man. My attention wanders and I glance away. In a second position I see the tall thin man. I look back again and see a short fat man with a suitcase. I look at the second place and see nobody. I look once more at the first place and see the two men talking to the guard of the train. In this experience there is a complexity not to be explained by the simplicity of my action—the mere turning of my head between two points. The vanishing and reappearance at another place of the tall man: the miraculous conjuring up of the guard: three men where only one man was before—all these are inexplicable as long as we confine ourselves to my actions. We have to introduce other sources of change: we say that the men moved, and that my successive sensations were occasioned by objectively successive events.

Case III.[1]—I keep my head still and stare at the advertisement. Nothing happens.

Case IV.—I keep my head still and observe comings and goings on the platform. I attribute these to the movements of others.

So far, the criterion would seem to justify its use. But, it may be said, it is possible with rolled advertisements that in the first case my turning of the head just *happened* to coincide every time with the appearance of "Yardley's Soap". I *might* have looked back in time to see "Ovaltine" or "Dubarry's Powder", or a formless blur as they coalesced. Of course, it is possible, but it is very unlikely, especially if I looked back at irregular intervals. Nevertheless, the attempt to avoid this objection plainly affirms that the criterion is purely empirical, and that there is no *logical* justification for our extrapolation, for however unlikely, the possibility of mistake still remains. The question is whether this empiricism tells against Kant's attempt to show the 'necessity' of the causal relation. But, important as this question is, it is better postponed.

A second objection is one formulated at length by Gunn. "Kant's criterion of objective sequence is inadequate. It needs to be checked by other considerations, for, if an observer stood near[2] a gun, then whatever he did the flash would invariably precede the roar, but if he acted on Kant's criterion he would assume that the flash objectively preceded the roar, and this would be incorrect. Again, if an observer were between two guns firing successive rounds together, and he stood in such a position that the sounds were simultaneous, then if he moved in one direction—say north—

---

[1] The last two cases were not considered by Kant, but they are added here for the sake of completeness. They present little difficulty, for if no change takes place in me, it must be attributed to outside events.

[2] Surely, "at some distance from"?

he would get a different sequence from that which he would get if he moved south. Such an observer, on Kant's criterion, would arrive at a judgment about simultaneities or coexistences which would be erroneous."[1] The first half of this is easily answered. A man at a distance from a gun may see the flash before he hears the report, but he has only to walk nearer and nearer the gun for the sound and the flash eventually to coincide. The second half, too, proves no more than the relevance of *position* in the determining of the objective sequence of sounds. Granted that a man south of the point midway between the two guns[2] would make a different judgment from a man north, if each made only one estimate, their judgments have no more grounds than mine would have if, because I saw a tall man at a certain point, I judged that he remained there for some time. But if the man south moves north, as Gunn says, "he would get a different sequence from that which he would get if he moved south". Surely that very fact, on Kant's criterion, would serve to make him suspicious about the objectivity of his judgments of succession and simultaneity?

The second part of Kant's argument which needs examination, is his use of a concept of 'objective time'. It has already been indicated that this is hard to square with some of his own principles: a more important topic, is, however, how far it is on any principles defensible. If it can be defended as leading to fruitful results, there are few who would criticize Kant harshly for inconsistency with the rather barren formalism of the Aesthetic.

Before he treats the separate analogies in detail, he gives a proof of the general principle of the analogies, which is that experience is possible only through the representation of a necessary connection of perceptions. In this proof he says: "Since time, however, cannot itself be perceived, the determination of the existence of objects in time can take place only through their relation in time in general, and therefore only through concepts that connect them *a priori*. Since these always carry necessity with them, it follows that experience is only possible through a representation of necessary connection of perceptions . . . The general principle of the three analogies rests on the necessary *unity* of apperception, in respect

[1] *Problem of Time*, p. 108. Cf. also article by Broad (from whom the criticism is taken) in *Aris. Soc. Proc.*, 1925–6, p. 200.
[2] Allow to each of them a characteristic sound, to assist identification.

of all possible empirical consciousness, that is, of all perception, at every instant of time. . . . This synthetic unity in the time-relations of all perceptions, as thus determined *a priori*, is the law that all empirical time-determinations must stand under rules of universal time-determination."[1]

In the deduction of the Categories, Kant laid great stress on the Transcendental Unity of Apperception. Synthesis, he said, is prior to analysis, and is logically presupposed by it. Here he is applying these findings to the problem how we from observation of particulars, as Hume would have put it, arrive at the belief that *some* of our perceptions are determined by others: and he again stresses the importance of unity. Just as previously he had said, "All the manifold, therefore, so far as it is given in one empirical intuition, is *determined* in respect of one of the logical functions of judgment, and is thereby brought into one consciousness. Now the categories are just these functions of judgment . . ."[2] so now he insists that we could not have consciousness of times unless there were first a single objective time in which events are determined in accordance with the principle of causation. *But* what is this objective time? It is open to the obvious objection that it is a return to the Newtonian absolute time, and is a mere hypostatized figment. Certain passages lend support to this: "Time cannot itself be perceived,"[3] and "Change does not affect time itself but only appearances in time."[4] Secondly, it is specially difficult to reconcile with Kant's own statements to the effect that time is not an ultimate constituent of reality. Lastly, how is this 'time' supposed to be related to space?

It is not to be supposed that these difficulties are slight ones: on the contrary, it is doubtful whether even his staunchest admirer could defend Kant completely on all these charges. Nevertheless, I am inclined to think that the very obviousness of some of these objections is likely to blind critics to the importance and the difficulty of what Kant was trying to formulate.

Let us grant his postulation of an objective time as a necessary unity, comparable in function to the Transcendental Unity of Apperception, and let us see what use he makes of it. Granted that we *necessarily* arrange events in a time order, how can that justify us in saying that "*A* causes *B*" is a relation such that if *A* occurs, *B* *must* (not merely 'does' as Hume said) follow? As Kant rightly

[1] B 219–20.   [2] B 143.   [3] B 219.   [4] B 226.

insisted, it cannot: but what it *can* do, is to provide "a rule according to which a unity of experience may arise from perception".[1] The whole paragraph[2] is of great importance as showing Kant's conception of the function of the three Analogies. "Since existence cannot be constructed, the principles can apply only to the relations of existence, and can yield only regulative principles. We cannot, therefore, expect either axioms or anticipations. If, however, a perception is given in a time-relation to some other perception, then even although this latter is indeterminate, and we consequently cannot decide *what* it is, or what its *magnitude* may be, we may none the less assert that in its existence it is necessarily connected with the former in this mode of time. In philosophy analogies signify something very different from what they represent in mathematics . . . in philosophy the analogy is not the equality of two *quantitative* but of two *qualitative* relations: and from three given members we can obtain *a priori* knowledge only of the relation to a fourth, not of the fourth member itself." The essential purport of this passage is the antithesis between constitutive and regulative: we cannot decide *what* the indeterminate second perception is, but we do know that it is *necessarily* connected with the former "in this mode of time" (in the case of causality, succession). We know the rule, but we do not know the particulars to which it applies. We have no constitutive principle that would enable us to say "M causes N" where M and N stand for particulars, but we can say that events are so related that the bond between them is a necessary one.

Expressed differently, it may be said—Kant looks upon the causal relation as a principle of the connectivity of events. It is concerned with the synthetic unity which conditions all apprehension of a manifold and, as such, it is necessary. He does not bother with particular exemplifications of the general causal principle, such as those which (as Hume pointed out) are discovered by empirical and inductive methods. On the contrary, he says that the general causal principle does not depend for its validity on particular causal "laws": rather do they derive from the unity of apperception without which experience itself would be impossible. Causation, then,

[1] See on this point Ewing, *Kant's Treatment of Causality*, p. 72 n., where he takes exception to Kant's use of the term 'analogy'. His remarks on that argument of Kant's in the Second Analogy which differs from all the rest are very sound (pp. 73–6). [2] B 222.

is necessary as being a principle of the connectivity of events: and the essential part played by time is, that it is in time that events are, and must be, regarded as being connected.

III

There are now two questions which must be answered: they are, Is this view of time a satisfactory one? and, Has Kant succeeded in proving the necessity of causation? These two questions are distinct: it is useless to criticize Kant (as Gunn is inclined to do[1]) on the first head because his proof of causation is not watertight. There are two stages in his proof of causation—first, that we are in possession of a criterion to enable us to arrange events as occurring in order of time: secondly, that given this time order, we necessarily believe that events are causally connected, though the process by which we discover particular causal connections is not itself a necessary one. Failure in the proof of causation is not necessarily to be laid to the account of the second stage, and my opinion is that the second stage, and the account of time which it contains, is both valid and valuable.

Returning to the earlier objections, in so far as Kant keeps to his main contentions (which is not always, and so he cannot be cleared entirely), it cannot be said that he uses his 'objective time' as a mere hypostatization like Newton's absolute time. On the contrary, there is the fundamental doctrine of time considered as a principle of the connectivity of events—it is objective in that it is a way in which we necessarily regard events as connected. (Space is another, and that answers the third objection.) But that is as far removed as possible from the undesirable assumption of time as being something apart from events and, indeed, there is much in common between Kant and Whitehead. Lastly, the second and least important objection—of inconsistency—could to a certain degree be met, since to say that we *must* regard events as being objectively determined in time, is not necessarily to say that apart from the conditions of our sensibility, time and causality are something in themselves.

But with the first stage of the proof of causation, and with its more particular treatment of time, a less satisfactory conclusion is

[1] As, for instance, op. cit., p. 109.

reached. The question was raised in the previous section, and there left unanswered, how far the *empirical* criterion according to which we arrange events in a time-order is a blemish that affects the whole argument. If (however unlikely it be) it is *possible* that I should make a mistake in my arrangement, does that vitiate the whole of the subsequent proceedings? It does, if my aim is to *prove* that Y necessarily follows on X, since my earlier mistake may have been to reverse the order of M and N, antecedents of X and Y. But it does not necessarily affect the general conclusion that events in time exhibit necessary connections. For Kant might reply that when we talk about "a mistake in my arrangement", that is itself postulating an order in which events are objectively arranged, and that that is all his argument requires.

Nevertheless, whether or no we decide that this criterion, and with it, Kant's proof of the necessity of regarding events as exhibiting causal determinations, is valid, the question remains of Kant's treatment of particular aspects of time (simultaneity, succession, etc.) in the first stage. It cannot be denied that this is not wholly successful. As Kemp Smith emphasized,[1] Kant's treatment of simultaneity, as elsewhere in the Critique, is unsatisfactory. Starting from the position that all our sensations are successive, the passage to objective simultaneity would be a difficult one—if it were fully explained: but it is glossed over with an ease that is almost miraculous, not to say suspicious. Then, too, Kant is never certain whether simultaneity is or is not a mode of time: and the argument of the second analogy, as of the other two analogies, is not helped, but rather hindered, by his tendency to assign to each, as a guardian angel, one of the so-called "modes of time". It is unsatisfactory to treat, as he does where he remembers the requirements of his architectonic scheme, 'duration' and 'succession' and 'simultaneity' as if they could be considered apart from each other.

A last important point arises which must be faced. In his treatment of succession in what we have called the 'first stage'—long before causation can rightly be invoked—is his procedure circular, due to the surreptitious introduction of causal notions? As Gunn puts it: "He is here on very dangerous ground, for it requires only a little reflection to see that, in general, we form our conception of causal connection because of the succession of events. How,

[1] *Commentary*, pp. 135-8 and 356-9.

then ... can we invoke the principle of causality in order to determine time-order when we really base our principle of causality on the sequence of events?"[1] Of course, it must be remembered that the connection between time and causality is admittedly a very close one, and that something akin to verbal tight-rope walking is needed to preserve a distinction. Kant did not shine at this—he could be condemned out of his own mouth for almost anything—and it is no wonder if he transgresses verbally. The question is whether there is more to it than that—whether his whole treatment is in essence a circular one, presupposing causality to prove objective time, and then using that to prove the necessity of causation. Sigwart said: "The use of these standards of time for the temporal determination of subjective events, and still more for the determination of the objective events of which they are perceptions, necessitates the determination of the relation between the time of the event and the time of the perception, and the reduction of the subjective series of perceptions to the objective series of changes in things. This reduction can *only be carried out by assuming causal laws*, in which the sensation is regarded as a temporally determined effect of objective change: but *to establish such laws is possible only again by assuming that* in the case of continuous events *the succession of sensations corresponds to the succession of the events*."[2] And—"Before we can establish a causal connection, a rule according to which B follows A, we must be able to affirm with objective validity that B has followed A: but before we can affirm this with objective validity we must have recognized a causal connection between A and B."[3] Sigwart's argument, essentially, is that in his attempt to distinguish between subjective and objective succession, Kant makes illegitimate use of the idea of causation. In the examples given earlier, my mere turning of my head is not thought to be sufficient to account for the complex differences which my successive perceptions on the railway station exhibit. I am forced to postulate other *causes* for these differences. But granted that there is some circularity, it is not necessarily a vicious circularity. It must be remembered that Kant is dealing with notions that are extremely abstract and general and fundamental: we have the greatest diffi-

---

[1] Op. cit., p. 106.   [2] Sigwart, *Logic*, p. 237. Italics mine.
[3] Ibid., p. 246. The whole of the section (pp. 236–52) is important in this connection.

culty in formulating a sentence without presupposing them and so committing verbal fallacies—but, Kant might reply, that is the very thing he is trying to urge, that we *must* regard events as causally connected. Let anyone try the experiment of formulating, as precisely as he can, the exact difference between a house persisting in time, the parts of which are successively apprehended, and the series of events which are the successive appearances at different places of a moving object, such as a boat, and it will be seen how difficult it is not to make use of the notion of cause. And then he may settle for himself whether the introduction of cause here is viciously circular, invalidating Kant's whole argument, or whether it does not itself show the necessity we are under of regarding events as subject to determinations of causality.

A somewhat different criticism, and one which can be summarily treated, is that which says that the use Kant makes of the notion of cause is ridiculous. The position of the boat earlier is not the cause of the later position of the boat. But Kant never said it was: all he said was that we are bound to postulate the existence of a causal chain linking together the two events. Schopenhauer's criticism[1] that on Kant's view the first event is regarded as the cause of the second (so that day would cause night, a man's walking under a roof cause a tile to drop on him, and the first notes of a melody cause the last notes), rests on a misunderstanding of Kant's position, for he was not concerned with particular applications, but with the principle of causality in general.

Kant's view of time is open to, and has received, many criticisms from very different quarters. It is loosely phrased, inconsistent, and obscure. As Kemp Smith said, Kant's view of time "is the most vulnerable tenet in his whole system."[2] On the one hand, Gunn grumbles at his subjectivism: on the other hand, there are passages where Kant is so 'objective' that he earns Bergson's criticism of conceiving an absolute time which, like Newton's, is a homogeneous and spatialized medium. Russell ridicules the view of the infinite on which the First Antinomy rests: on humbler ground, the

---

[1] *Fourfold Root of the Principle of Sufficient Reason*, section 23. For good discussions of the value of Schopenhauer's criticisms, see Gunn, op. cit., pp. 124–6; Ewing, op. cit., pp. 86–90; Kemp Smith, op. cit., pp. 365–6 377–9 (with references to other discussions), and 387–9.

[2] *Commentary*, p. 137.

psychologist cavils at the view that all sensations are subjective. The physicist finds Kant's criterion of objectivity unsatisfactory, and his treatment of simultaneity impracticable: and the commentator murmurs at his frequent contradictions. The logician scoffs at the architectonic formality of the Aesthetic: and the historian of philosophy decides that he has not succeeded in answering Hume.

Nevertheless, discounting all these, however justified, the value of Kant's treatment of time remains: in his formulation of, rather than his answer to, the difficult problems which he first opened up: in his insistence upon the importance of time in metaphysical speculation: and, more specifically, in his treatment of time as a principle by which events are given as connected in experience.

CHAPTER V

BERGSON

IT would be rash to assert that to any one man is chiefly due the important place which time and temporal notions occupy in present-day thought. Yet if that assertion were to be made, I think that it would be generally agreed that M. Bergson was that man. Nobody has done as much as he to insist on the importance of time, "La clef des plus gros problèmes philosophiques est là,"[1] and to ensure that we should, in Alexander's phrase, "take Time seriously".[2] He himself was the first, with the single exception of Kant, whose view of time he criticized, to do this.

And the importance of time and change in his metaphysic cannot be denied. One of his most prominent English adherents, Wildon Carr, entitled a book that he wrote on Bergson, *The Philosophy of Change*. Time is conceived by Bergson as 'durée', and this durée is not mere blank lastingness, enduring through a hypostatized, spatialized Time—it is a ceaseless, continuous flow, in which, as in Aristotle's God, all things live and move and have their being. Durée is not only real (as against those who would deny that time is real): it is itself Reality. Like Heraclitus, Bergson insists that the notion of process, of ceaseless change, is fundamental: unlike him, he does not proceed to stultify the notion by allowing cyclic repetition, but considers that durée evolves ever new and newer forms—that it is really, and not only figuratively, creative.

The influence of Bergson's notions has been widespread. Perhaps for that very reason the value of his work is liable to be wrongly estimated, in some ways, at the present day. Ideas which we take very much for granted are difficult to consider critically. That

[1] *Durée et Simultanéité*, Preface, p. viii.
[2] *Spinoza and Time*, p. 15. See also P. W. Lewis, *Time and Western Man*, who thinks that time is being taken *too* seriously, and who inveighs against time as much as Bergson against space.

may mean, on the one hand, an uncritical acceptance of Bergson. On the other hand, it makes it difficult for us to realize that such ideas—as, for instance, the need of taking Time seriously—have not always been as generally accepted as they are now. Hence we fail to appreciate the real originality of Bergson, and the importance of his protest against the spatialization of time, at the date at which he wrote. In what follows, we shall be concerned with the exposition and criticism in detail of Bergson's views, but it should be clearly realized at the outset that such detailed treatment is in a sense almost irrelevant to the main issue, since whatever the result reached by further inquiry, it will stand unaffected. The importance of Bergson can be summed up in a few words. It is that it was he who first saw and insisted on the importance of time, and that he was responsible for the awakening of modern philosophy from its dogmatic slumbers in this respect. His (if the comparison may be pardoned) is the function of Modestine's goad. Criticism, then, though by no means otiose on particular points, is unable to detract from his real achievement, which remains, whatever the conclusion reached. It is well that this should be emphasized to start with.

First of all, a note on terminology. Bergson sometimes uses 'time' in a narrow sense, as meaning spatialized or clock time, as opposed to real time, or durée. Granted that he had some excuse for the narrow usage, in that writers on 'time' invariably spatialized it, yet it will probably be found more convenient not to use the word 'time' unqualified, for spatialized time, as it is likely to lead to confusions—and Bergson himself was not always strict in his usage. 'Time', then (except of course in quotations), will continue to be used generally to cover both *spatialized time* and *durée*. Otherwise, there is no means of escaping verbal confusions if 'time' is finally rejected as not being 'really temporal'. This, of course, is not a serious criticism, in so far as Bergson, by verbal re-statements, could avoid it. And since he does, on occasion, point out that spatialized time is not time[1] at all, and that the only

---

[1] "When we make time a homogeneous medium in which conscious states unfold themselves, we take it to be given all at once, which amounts to saying that we abstract it from duration. This simple consideration ought to warn us that we are thus unwittingly falling back upon space and really giving up time" (*Time and Free Will*, p. 98). See also, ibid., p. 91.

real time is durée, I think that we may take it that this usage is correct, and throw over the unprofitable distinction between 'time' and 'durée'.

The first point, then, on which Bergson insists is that we must make a fundamental distinction between what he calls 'spatialized' time and real time, which he identifies with durée.[1] But, secondly, durée, even as it appears in his earlier books before he had erected it into a mystical absolute almost as hypostatized as the 'time' that he so often criticized, is not to be equated with mere duration, as we in England understand the word. Though, like it, it is subjective in the sense that it is closely bound up with the experience of the individual, in some respects it goes further than does 'duration'. We have *immediate* apprehension of durée in a way in which we do not have immediate apprehension of duration. It would not normally be held, as was pointed out in the chapter on Psychology, that we directly apprehend *intervals*, other than very short ones. Bergson on the other hand insists that durée is directly and intimately experienced as a ceaseless *flow*. The two words italicized in the last two sentences give the key to the difference —more often felt than expressed—between 'durée' as Bergson uses it and 'duration' as it is commonly understood in English. The difference is one of emphasis. When we talk of duration we think of something enduring through a period of time, of *lastingness*. This lastingness is the very antithesis of what Bergson wishes to express: his durée is not endurance, but *flow*.

Secondly, we often use the word 'duration' to stand also for 'objective' measurements abstracted from the direct judgments of individuals. This, of course, is the very conception of time against which Bergson is tilting, and it provides a further reason why we should be careful to avoid confusing durée with duration. Even the first sense of duration as subjective, though, is not what Bergson means, and he could easily criticize the 'lastingness' which is in most English readers' minds when they read the word 'duration', as being the overflow from the second, so-called 'objective' conception, and hence as being itself open to criticism.

It is, then, very important that we should not distinguish

[1] Compare also Oakeley, *History and the Self*, passim. On the unsoundness of drawing an analogy between space and time, see Broad's article on "Time" in the *Encyclopedia of Religion and Ethics*.

between *duration* (with all its, from Bergson's point of view, 'spatial' connections) and spatialized time, since in that case half the point of Bergson's distinction will have vanished: but between *durée* and spatialized time.

What, then, is this spatialized time about which so much has already been said? Bergson himself, very lucidly, supplies the answer.[1] "When we speak of time we generally think of a homogeneous medium in which our conscious states are ranged alongside one another as in space, so as to form a discrete multiplicity. Would not time, thus understood, be to the multiplicity of our psychic states what intensity is to certain of them—a sign, a symbol, absolutely distinct from true durée? . . . Does the multiplicity of our conscious states bear the slightest resemblance to the multiplicity of the units of a number? Has true durée anything to do with space? . . . For if time, as the reflective consciousness represents it, is a medium in which our conscious states form a discrete series so as to admit of being counted, and if on the other hand our conception of number ends in spreading out in space everything which can be directly counted, it is to be presumed that time, understood in the sense of a medium in which we make distinctions and count, is nothing but space. . . . It follows that pure durée must be something different."

So far, there can be little doubt that the distinction is not only justified but valuable.[2] But Bergson goes on to push the distinction into regions where it would not be generally admitted that it applied, and this is a source of possible criticism. Transitional between these is his doctrine of interpenetration. Durée is not merely a continuum (in mathematical language which Bergson would never have used)—it is characterized by the complete interpenetration of its parts. Nay more: 'parts' is a misnomer: it suggests that durée first has parts which are then mixed up and shuffled together, like the ingredients of a Christmas pudding, whereas on the contrary it is only *secondarily* that we even try to distinguish parts in what is, essentially, an integral unity. And just as interpenetration characterizes real time, so does discreteness

---

[1] *Time and Free Will*, p. 91. For reasons already stated, I have replaced, for the 'duration' of the translation, the original word 'durée'.

[2] See also *Durée et Simultanéité*. "The analogy between time and space is merely exterior and superficial" (Preface, p. vii).

characterize space. If we go on, then, with our attempt to partition time, we shall find that the reality, the durée, has eluded us, and that what we are partitioning is really space. Bergson takes some trouble to show that "if space is to be defined as the homogeneous, it seems that inversely every homogeneous and unbounded medium will be space",[1] and thereafter he assumes that all homogeneity is spatial. (In passing, it may be remarked that it is very doubtful whether he has proved this point. His view of space is exceedingly arbitrary, and he uses it, none too circumspectly, as a kind of reach-me-down contradictory of pure durée, and the consequent recipient of many uncomplimentary adjectives. His later excesses are in part to be attributed to his stunted view of space.[2] It must always be remembered that 'space' and 'spatial' in his usage have not the meaning they have in ordinary life, and finally become little more than convenient Aunt Sallies.)

The second step is to point out two different ways of regarding the self, and their analogy with space and time. In the first place, I may think of my memories, my perceptions, my tendencies—a motley crowd. Alternatively, I may realize their essential interconnection and unity in *me*. This latter is the fundamental view.

"All these clearly defined elements appear more distinct from me, the more distinct they are from each other.... But if I draw myself in from the periphery towards the centre, if I search in the depth of my being that which is most uniformly, most constantly and most enduringly myself, I find an altogether different thing. There is, beneath these sharply cut crystals and this frozen surface, a continuous flux which is not comparable to any flux I have ever seen. There is a succession of states, each of which announces that which follows and contains that which precedes it. They can, properly speaking, only be said to form multiple states when I have already passed them and turn back to observe their track. Whilst I was experiencing them they were so solidly organized, so profoundly animated with a common life, that I could not have said where any one of them finished or where another commenced. In

[1] *Time and Free Will*, p. 98.
[2] But Wildon Carr, in a sympathetic criticism, says that this is not so, and that Bergson only protests against *excessive* spatialization (British Academy, 1918: "Time and History in Contemporary Philosophy").

reality no one of them begins or ends, but all extend into each other."[1]

This passage has been quoted in full, as it is important in bringing together several strands of Bergson's thought.[2] Besides the opposition between time and space, between continuous flux and frozen surface, three other important points are made in this and the succeeding paragraph. The first is, that the opposition is conceived analogously to the opposition between two ways of regarding the self, of which one is much more fundamental than the other. This is the germ of the conception of time as analogous to mind, in contradistinction to the dead matter of space. (It is interesting to compare and contrast with this Alexander's view, that time is the mind of space.) Secondly, there is the important notion of time as creative, which was fully developed in "Creative Evolution". Thirdly, the notion of "turning back" to observe "multiple states" forms the basis of the celebrated distinction between time as passing and time as passed.

It should go without saying that Bergson does not regard these as separable and distinct notions. The most he could allow would be that we may sometimes find it convenient to regard things from one aspect, and sometimes from another. But always it is the same Reality, which is ceaseless flux. The critic may, however, argue: "You tell me that the motley crowd of sensations, memories, etc., are spatial and unessential, and that only the perception of the self as a unity is fundamental. Nevertheless, when you talk of heterogeneity and homogeneity, you make the latter correspond with space and the former with time. I really do not see *how* you know which corresponds to which in all these

---

[1] *Introduction to Metaphysics*, pp. 9–10. See also *Time and Free Will*, pp. 98–9, and *Creative Evolution*, p. 6.

[2] This phrase would be exceedingly unacceptable to Bergson, and with reason. For he repeatedly insists that such partial, fragmentary views are useless, and his whole point is that 'strands' cannot be distinguished. The disadvantage of such a method, too, must be obvious when compared with his brilliant and glowing passages. Yet I use the phrase deliberately. He may be right in holding that the method of analysis, which is intellectual, misses the heart of Reality, which is only accessible to intuition: nevertheless the aim here is much more humble. Whatever the limitations of analysis, it should at least be possible to hope that the results of intuition should not prove to be in *contradiction* with those of analysis!

distinctions." Bergson would probably regard this last as a silly question: but whether it is or is not, the apparent inconsistency with regard to homogeneity still remains. Most probably, however, it is not an important criticism, and could easily be avoided by a further distinction between real homogeneity, which is spatial, and the homogeneity which is not mere likeness, but unity and interpenetration: and between the fundamental heterogeneity of time, and the blank, irreducible diverseness which is spatial.[1] Whether such distinctions are desirable is another matter.

Justifiably or not, then, Bergson extended the original distinction between spatialized time and durée to include (what common sense would call) other distinctions, though he would never have admitted, in consequence of his doctrine of interpenetration, that there was any otherness about them. It seems at first sight that his conclusion does not follow from his premises: what his argument comes to, is that because time is a unity of interpenetration, and the self is also such a unity, *therefore* there is an intimate connection between the two unities, so that it is illegitimate to talk of "two unities" or "two strands of Bergson's thought", since they themselves interpenetrate, and can only be distinguished by a convenient, but ultimately unsound, intellectual process. Now all this is not to say that Bergson is wrong: he may quite well be right when he inveighs against artificial intellectual partitions, and insists that the perfect way of regarding the universe would be synthetic, rather than analytic. But it must be clearly seen, that if we start from durée, from pure memory, from mind, from life, however much we agree that each is a unity and cannot be divided into parts, it is a *further* step to say that all these together form a unity and that the division into aspects is secondary. A metaphysical intuition of interpenetration is implied from the start: it is impossible to divide his argument into stages, as has been attempted here. And this, of course, is what Bergson has insisted all along: consequently for him the method of metaphysics is intuitional rather than intellectual. "A true empiricism is that which proposes to get as near to the original itself as possible, to search deeply into its life, and so, by a kind of *intellectual auscultation*, to feel the throbbings of its soul: and this true empiricism is

[1] Compare his distinction between the two kinds of multiplicity (*Time and Free Will*, p. 85); but see also ibid., p. 98.

the true metaphysics. It is true that the task is an extremely difficult one, for none of the ready-made conceptions which thought employs in its daily operations can be of any use. . . . Philosophy thus defined does not consist in the choice of certain concepts, and in taking sides with a school, but in the search for a unique intuition from which we can descend with equal ease to different concepts, because we are placed above the divisions of the schools."[1] In contrast to this is the barrenness and artificiality of intellectual abstraction: "Instead of attaching ourselves to the inner becoming of things, we place ourselves outside them in order to recompose their becoming artificially. We take snapshots, as it were, of the passing reality."[2] It is not necessary here to go further into his championing of intuition, as long as it is realized that the distinction between intellect and intuition, like all the other distinctions, is in alignment with the first distinction between durée and spatialized time.

So far, it may be said, Bergson's view of time is not very startling. He began by drawing a distinction between real time, and space masquerading as time, but proceeded to carry it to such extremes in 'other' directions, that its effect was to blur its significance for *time*, and by its very wideness to become rather vague. But the importance of his view of time lies in his constant orientation towards those characteristics of time which are fundamentally temporal, and his rejection of those that are unessential. To this extent, therefore, the distinctions help him, but in his applications, he again takes them too far, and may be criticized. There are three applications which will be considered: his view of the past and memory; his insistence on creativeness; and, lastly, his remarks on reversibility and causality.

Bergson distinguishes very clearly between time in its passage and time as passed. The latter may be treated like space and divided: the former is a unity—"Nous divisons le déroulé, mais non pas le déroulement."[3] "Time is not a line on which we can pass again. Certainly, once it has elapsed, we are justified in picturing the successive moments as external to one another and in thus thinking of a line traversing space: but it must then be under-

---

[1] *Introduction to Metaphysics*, pp. 31 and 32.
[2] *Creative Evolution*, p. 322. See also p. 362.
[3] *Durée et Simultanéité*, p. 63.

stood that this line does not symbolize the time which is passing but the time which has passed."[1] It is a familiar fact, with which everyone would agree, that we can look back on events which have happened as if they were spread out in front of us all at once.[2] We may, and very often do, adopt the metaphor of looking back along a road that has been traversed: we regard the various happenings as points on the road: we talk of life as a "journey" from the cradle to the grave, and of certain events, such as leaving school, obtaining a post, and getting married, as "milestones" on that journey. From the notion of looking back on our past life as spread out, it is an easy transition to the notion of *time* as a "spreading out". But Bergson insists that this transition is fallacious, that time as passed is not time at all, but space, and that it is illegitimate to extend a metaphorical conception of events that have happened to their *happening*. And he reiterates that it is the last alone which is temporal.[3]

An illustration may make the point clear. Looking back, I see or seem to see, a connection between two events, M and N. There is a certain curious inevitability about them, just as if I looked back along a straight road and saw, first, the milestone, then Halfway House, and then World's End. But, when I was at World's End this morning, I knew that I would come to the Halfway House before the milestone—*it was all mapped out already, waiting for me to come and walk along it*. Now though, empirically, we have no such analogous knowledge at M of N and O, in our humbleness of heart we are ready to attribute it to our ignorance, and to hold that, objectively, it is all laid out. It is to this that Bergson objects. To say that it is all laid out, that "tout est donné", is an unwarrantable intrusion of spatial conceptions. Though we find it useful to schematize in space events after they have happened, we must not extend this schematism to events in their happening. "The duration *wherein we see ourselves acting*, and in which it is useful that we should see ourselves, is a duration whose elements are dissociated

---

[1] *Time and Free Will*, pp. 181-2.
[2] The spatial language of "in front of us" is noteworthy: so also is the *elimination* of time implicit in the phrase "all at once".
[3] "Can time be adequately represented by space? . . . Yes, if you are dealing with time flown. No, if you speak of time flowing" (*Time and Free Will*, p. 221).

and juxtaposed. The duration *wherein we act* is a duration wherein our states melt into each other."[1] Bergson rejects whole-heartedly the conception of time as a line, and of ourselves walking to meet future events that have "been there" all the time.

This distinction seems to me not only valid, but of the highest importance.

Secondly, the condemnation of the spatialized schema is fundamental for the view of freedom adopted in his first important book, *Time and Free Will*. We are not here concerned with this view in detail, and it will be sufficient to note that Bergson regards the usual alternatives—"I did X, but I could have done Y" and "I did X, and I couldn't have done Y"—as both open to the same criticism. This is that they rest on a wrong conception of X and

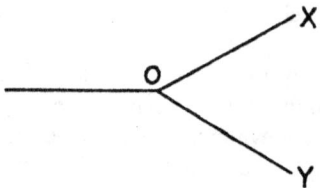

Y as mapped out in space, with a junction of roads at O, and it does not matter whether we hold that road Y was or was not open, for the criticism holds in either case. Bergson condemns the view of duration on which the conception is based, and urges that the problem is a pseudo one. It is because we look back and seem to see that if we had done something other than we did in fact do at O, we might by now be experiencing Y instead of X. "If only" is a familiar theme, from the child detected in mischief and punished, to *Othello* and *Far from the Madding Crowd*, and in retrospect it is valid. But, Bergson insists, at O we cannot talk about the alternatives X and Y in this glib way: what is valid enough for past time is not valid for time in its passing. And Bergson does not merely mean that at O we are ignorant of X and Y—which would involve

[1] *Matter and Memory*, p. 243. See also the discussion in *Time and Free Will*, chapter ii. He insisted that it is wrong to suppose "that the symbolical diagram which we draw in our own way for representing the action *when completed* has been drawn by the action itself *whilst progressing*, and drawn by it in an automatic manner" (*Time and Free Will*, p. 190).

that the distinction between past and future is an *epistemological* one only—he means that we *could* not know X and Y, for the distinction is an ontological one.[1] Any other view, he holds, depends on a fallacious and spatialized conception of duration.

Thirdly, he evolves a new theory of memory to fit in with his view of the past, and with his fundamental distinction between real and spatialized time. Corresponding to this is a distinction between habit-memory and true memory. Habit-memory is merely a crystallization of oft-repeated actions and movements, and is purely mechanical—it is only called "memory" by courtesy. On the other hand, true memory is unique and incapable of repetition, because it is intimately connected with durée. "The capital error of associationism is that it substitutes for this continuity of becoming, which is the living reality, a discontinuous multiplicity of elements, inert and juxtaposed."[2] In this connection his view of the relation between past and present is very interesting: the past is not a 'dead' past, but lives on into the present. As Bergson says, "The pure present is only the invisible progress of the present gnawing into the future."[3] It is doubtful here what is meant by "pure", and it is also doubtful how far the immediately preceding statement that we perceive only the past should be taken. As regards his general theory of memory, though it can be agreed that 'memory' and 'repetition' are not identical, yet when Bergson comes to a detailed working-out in terms of neurones, he is less convincing, and it may be the case that his distinction is not sufficient to bear the weight of the 'absolute' interpretation that he is trying to put upon it. It is, indeed, throughout a difficulty in dealing with Bergson to know just how far his metaphorical language is to be interpreted literally, and this is especially the case in connection with some of his remarks about the relation between the past and the present.

The second topic to be discussed is Bergson's conception of time as creative. The old idea, expressed in Ecclesiastes, that "there is nothing new under the sun", is vehemently opposed by Bergson. On the contrary, he urges, if we hold a right conception

---

[1] "Reality has appeared to us as a perpetual becoming. It makes itself or it unmakes itself, but it is never something made" (*Creative Evolution*, p. 287).
[2] *Matter and Memory*, p. 171.   [3] Ibid., p. 194.

of durée as a ceaseless flow, we are bound to hold some kind of evolutionary view in conjunction with it. Time is not a stable measure: it is a process, and a process which is continually working towards ever new forms, which it is impossible to predict. This point of view is developed at length, and with splendid imagery, in Bergson's most celebrated book *Creative Evolution.*—"The painter is before his canvas, the colours are on the palette: the model is sitting—all this we see, and also we know the painter's style: do we foresee what will appear on the canvas? We possess the elements of the problem: we know, in an abstract way, how it will be solved, for the portrait will surely resemble the model and will surely resemble also the artist: but the concrete solution brings with it that unforeseeable nothing which is everything in a work of art. And it is this nothing that takes time. Nought as matter, it creates itself as form. . . . Succession, or continuation of interpenetration in time (is) irreducible to a mere instantaneous juxtaposition in space. This is why the idea of reading in a present state of the material universe the future of living forms, and of unfolding now their history yet to come, involves a veritable absurdity. But this absurdity is difficult to bring out, because our memory is accustomed to place alongside of each other, in an ideal space, the terms it perceives in turn, because it always represents *past* succession in the form of juxtaposition. It is able to do so, indeed, just because the past belongs to that which is already invented, to the dead, and no longer to creation and life."[1] For the fundamental reality, according to Bergson, is not a static changeless Being, but a living and changing Becoming; and it is the great defect of Greek philosophy that it does not admit such a fundamental Becoming. "He who instals himself in becoming sees in duration the very life of things, the fundamental reality. The Forms, which the mind isolates and stores up in concepts, are then only snapshots of the changing reality. They are moments gathered along the course of time, and just because we have cut the thread that binds them to time, they no longer endure. . . . They enter into eternity, if you will: but what is eternal in them is just what is unreal."[2]

It should be clearly realized that Bergson is not taking the abstract view (which is often taken) of evolution as development

[1] *Creative Evolution*, p. 360.   [2] Ibid., pp. 334–5.

"through the ages"—"through" time in that vague sense only—he is insisting throughout that time itself plays an essential part in evolutionary process, and is itself creative.[1] Slightly differently expressed, time is not only the *medium* of evolution, but it is also its force.

It is possible to criticize this view—the splendour of which cannot be denied—as being based on a hypostatization of durée. Bergson had justifiably criticized,[2] in his earlier books, the 'receptacle' view of time as an illegitimate hypostatization, but he laid himself open to a similar criticism of durée. The precise connection between durée and the *élan vital* is (perhaps wisely) never made quite clear, but there are passages which read almost as if he was conceiving of the *élan vital* as a definite force, and others which read as if he was conceiving durée as the *élan vital*. But here again it is difficult to be sure how far to take what he says metaphorically.

If his remarks regarding the various courses open to the *élan vital*—the way of intellect, the way of intuition, and (in some books) the way of instinct—are taken literally, it would seem that he has laid himself open to the criticisms which he himself made in *Time and Free Will* against a wrong conception of the process of choice. He diagnosed this view of choice as being the result of holding a spatialized view of time, and this is rather significant if compared with his later remarks in *Creative Evolution*. Unless he is to be interpreted entirely metaphorically on these last two points, it certainly seems that he did press his conception of durée too far, and endued it with an almost mystical creative power.

Secondly, it may be objected that his whole view is incomprehensible and irrational. Objectors on this score point out the increasing vigour with which he distinguishes between intellect and intuition. The eulogies of intuition in the *Introduction to Metaphysics*[3] seem quite mild beside what he has to say in *Creative Evolution*. Finally, intellect is dismissed from philosophy with the assurance that its proper home is in the sciences. "Science can work

[1] But see Macmurray, who says that neither physical determinism nor evolution can give real change (Symposium on *Time and Change*, Aristotelian Supplement VIII, p. 149). Broad, however, later in the Symposium, criticizes Macmurray's view of change.

[2] See especially *Time and Free Will*, chapter ii and Conclusion. But he was probably wrong in dismissing Kant as he did.

[3] Op. cit., passim, but especially pp. 22–5.

only on what is supposed to repeat itself—that is to say, on what is withdrawn, by hypothesis, from the action of real time. Anything that is irreducible and irreversible in the successive movements of a history eludes science. To get a notion of this irreducibility and irreversibility, we must break with scientific habits which are adapted to the fundamental requirements of thought, we must do violence to the mind, go counter to the natural vent of the intellect. But that is just the function of philosophy."[1] And, a few pages farther on, he adds: "Time is here deprived of efficacy, and if it does nothing, it is nothing. Radical mechanism implies a metaphysics in which the totality of the real is postulated complete in eternity, and in which the apparent duration of things expresses merely the infirmity of a mind that cannot know everything at once. But duration is something very different from this for our consciousness, that is to say, for that which is most indisputable in our experience. We perceive duration as a stream against which we cannot go."[2] Again, Bergson repeatedly insists that the creative 'becoming' or process of Nature is of necessity irreducible to mathematical terms, and that it can never be explained by logic alone. *"Time is invention or it is nothing at all. But of time-invention physics can take no account, restricted as it is to the cinematographical method. It is limited to counting simultaneities between the events that make up this time and the positions of the mobile time on its trajectory. It detaches these events from the whole, which at every moment puts on a new form and which communicates to them something of its novelty. It considers them in the abstract, such as they would be outside of the living whole, that is to say, in a time unrolled in space. It retains only the events or systems of events that can be thus isolated without being made to undergo too profound a deformation, because only these lend themselves to the application of its method. Our physics dates from the day when it was known how to isolate such systems. To sum up—while modern physics is distinguished from ancient physics by the fact that it considers any moment of time whatever, it rests altogether on a substitution of time-length for time-invention."*[3] In all probability, Bergson was right about the irreducibility of time,

---

[1] *Creative Evolution*, p. 31. [2] Ibid., p. 41.
[3] Ibid., p. 361. Compare also p. 48: "Concentrated on that which repeats, solely preoccupied in welding the same to the same, intellect turns away from the vision of time."

but that is hardly likely to be a recommendation of his views in some quarters. It was, perhaps, unfortunate that Bergson should have taken such a very definite anti-intellectualist position, since it leaves him open to very obvious criticisms. And though, on his principles, he could not have been an extreme rationalist, he could yet, I think, consistently with them, have considerably modified the blast of his invective against intelligence. There must be many who would agree that synthesis is as important as analysis (for this is one way of expressing his distinction) and that on some occasions[1] we can get nearer to what is essential by intuition and sympathy (in the Bergsonian sense) than by abstract reasoning. And often we are certain of something without being able at all to give reasons for our certainty. But it is a different position, and one which does not follow logically from it, that *always* intuition can get nearer to what is fundamental, to the true Reality, than intellect, and that intellect is merely an intruder, seeking to divide what in truth is interconnected. In taking this second position, Bergson went too far. The logical conclusion of such a view, as his critics have not been slow to point out, would be chaos. Intuitions might not be successfully communicated, logical fallacies would be condoned as a mere breaking of the letter of the law, and there could be no philosophy. It has been partly my intention in treating of Bergson in an analytical way with "secondlys" and "thirdlys" and "fourthlys" (which certainly is to exhibit him in the worst possible light), to show that he has not taken advantage of leniency in the demands of logic. On the contrary, even from the logical point of view, there is little to cavil at—indeed, the extraordinary coherence and consistency of his ideas one with another (which he calls interpenetration) make it difficult to know in what order to deal with them. Consequently, M. Bergson's view of time is "irrational" only in the sense that it is irreducible to purely logical terms, not in the sense that it abounds in logical fallacies, and the extreme anti-intellectualist position, to which exception has been taken,[2] could be modified consistently with Bergson's main contentions.

[1] Bergson usually takes the example of a work of art. See also his book on *Laughter*, especially the last chapter.
[2] "The proof of the essential unintelligibility of a theory seems to me to establish a very strong presumption against its ontological value" (Cunningham, "Bergson's Conception of Duration", *Philosophical Review*, 1914, p. 530).

I have gone in some detail into the "anti-intellectualism" criticism of Bergson because I believe his view of time as a creative becoming, in spite of this and the hypostatization criticism, to be a valid and a fundamental one. It is necessary to get clear how far such a view of time as alogical and as creative *involves* anti-intellectualism, and how far that was a non-essential addition.

The third topic to be discussed is the 'irreversibility' of time, which follows from his other positions. If you hold that time passed and time passing are distinct, and that it is the latter which is fundamental, and also hold that time is, in some sense (however vaguely that 'is' may be interpreted) creative, you are forced to hold the 'irreversibility' of time. On his own principles, then, Bergson was quite right to reject the 't' of physics as having nothing to do with time. I do not propose to discuss *Durée et Simultanéité* in detail here: and still less the whole question of "physical time": it will be sufficient to say that Bergson is unquestionably right in his main thesis, and probably[1] right in insisting that 't' depends on durée which is prior to it.

Except for extreme physical fanatics, however, there are few who would deny, at first sight, the so-called 'irreversibility' of time. Bergson is on safe ground here. But it is possible to hold that time is "irreversible" in the vague sense that, empirically, it is "going one way", and also to hold some doctrine of recurrence in cycles. To a certain extent, we all hold that view, since we talk of "things happening several times", and even of "events recurring". But carried to an extreme, it is one which robs "change" and "irreversibility" of all real meaning, even though we continue to talk of irreversibility in the sense mentioned above. Bergson has a decided advantage over Heraclitean doctrines of universal flux in that he rejects the notion of recurrence.[2] The distinction which has here been made between "irreversibility" (at least, as it is commonly understood) and "non-recurrent" is one which Bergson does not, to my knowledge, make explicitly: but it needs to be

[1] I say "probably", not because I doubt it, but because it has been doubted.
[2] "Real duration is that duration which gnaws on things, and leaves on them the mark of its tooth. If everything is in time, everything changes inwardly, and the same concrete reality never recurs. Repetition is, therefore, possible only in the abstract" (*Creative Evolution*, p. 48).

made since it marks the point at which he diverges from these other views. This point will be returned to in a later chapter.

The separate treatment of aspects which Bergson regards as interconnected may have its advantages, but it certainly has also corresponding defects, the chief of which is its piecemeal and fragmentary character. Unity is strength: and Bergson might very well complain that single 'strands', when separated artificially from their neighbours and regarded from an alien angle, may appear more vulnerable than they in fact are. It will therefore be advisable to insist that single criticisms of isolated points have little weight against such a coherent system as Bergson's, and to make some general criticisms on the whole.

The first is directed against Bergson's anti-intellectualism. This point has already been discussed in detail, as arising from one particular aspect of his thought, but what was said there does, I think, hold good generally.

Secondly, a common criticism against durée is that it is essentially subjective: that the only criterion which Bergson admits is that of immediate apprehension. And this, of course, is true. Whether it is an important criticism is another matter. It seems to me that there are two ways in which the criticism of subjectivism can be levelled against Bergson: one is superficial, the other not. The superficial criticism is that which condemns as 'subjective' Bergson's reliance on immediate apprehension, without pausing to consider whether there is, in fact, any other criterion by which we correct our judgments of time. "Objective" methods (so-called) may, as has been said earlier, essentially depend on immediate apprehension. It is a mere begging of the question to call something "subjective" and then to condemn it out of hand: we must also know *why* we consider such subjectivity inadequate. The second criticism is much more important, if substantiated: it is also correspondingly more difficult to fix upon Bergson. It is this: Time, it may be asserted, is not merely my psychological apprehension of time, and yours, and his and hers, and . . . and still less is it any one of these. On the contrary, it is the essential going-on-ness of things, the happening of events, the growth of acorn into oak. Evidently this is very much what Bergson was all along emphasizing! But, it may be said, Bergson's real position was an insistence upon *our* awareness of process. In so far as this is so, then perhaps there is vicious subjectivity in Bergson's view. It is, however, extraordinarily difficult to decide how far it is reasonable to distinguish between "knower" and "known". Would there be time in a mindless universe? We shall never answer this question, and it may even, as framed by us, be nonsensical. Kant pointed out that apprehension involved a co-implication of object and subject: if we take this seriously, we cannot criticize Bergson for insisting on one aspect *to the exclusion of the other* since that would be impossible. Can we criticize him for inconsistency in his unheralded transition from "my apprehension of durée" to "a world of becoming"? To a certain extent, yes: beyond that, no. In so far as Kant is right, and they are ultimately co-implicant, it would be stupid to talk of inconsistency. Nevertheless, Bergson does leave us rather in the dark as to how exactly the transition (which, even if it be not ultimate, is certainly regarded as a transition in ordinary language) is mediated, and I think that probably he *was* inconsistent on this point, and that he would be hard put to it to explain the change of emphasis in *Time and Free Will* and in *Creative Evolution*. But the inconsistency was one which did not matter very much, and Bergson was wiser than he knew. Such is the power of intuition!

Thirdly, can be grouped together all those criticisms regarding illegitimate extensions of durée. Bergson conceived of durée so widely that it is often vague: he hypostatized it into Reality and Creativity and several other things beside: at the same time he left conveniently misty what he meant by "Real". It would, of course, be stupid to expect an analytic definition of "Reality": but it *is* insufficient to tell us that it is temporal, or worse still, that it is Time, and to let it go at that. And this Bergson was inclined to do, as, for example, when he says of Time—"It is the foundation of our being, and, as we feel, the very substance of the world in which we live."[1] *Creative Evolution*, though less open than *Time and Free Will* to criticism on the score of subjectivity, is more open to the objection that in it time becomes almost a mystical entity. This objection, of course, is only fundamental if the disadvantages of mysticism outweigh all other advantages of Bergson's conception of time. But that is not to say that his system would not have been better without it, in so far as it is separable from the main tenor of his work.

[1] *Creative Evolution*, p. 41.

METAPHYSICS—BERGSON

On the other hand, Bergson's great merit was to emphasize three points which are fundamental for a proper view of time. First, he saw that the analogy with space, though apparently plausible, was fallacious in that it overlooked characteristics which are fundamental to time. These characters are the irreversibility and the "becoming" of time, and his emphasis on these makes the second and third points. In consequence, he insisted on time as creative, as analogous to life, and as fundamentally irreducible to mathematical terms; and made a valuable distinction between time in its passage and time as passed.

All these are of great importance. It is Bergson's merit not only to have shown that "no question has been more neglected by philosophers than that of time, although all agree in declaring it to be vital",[1] and to have made us try to take Time more seriously: but also to have shown the essential characteristics which a truly temporal theory of time must not fail to take into account.

[1] *Durée et Simultanéité*, Preface, p. vii.

CHAPTER VI

ALEXANDER

IT would be impossible to omit from a discussion of modern theories of time the view of Alexander. And this not only because he insisted on the need to take Time seriously, and showed in an interesting exegesis how Spinoza's philosophy would have been improved had he paid more attention to time, but because the title of his great work, *Space, Time and Deity*, does not belie its contents, or ascribe to time an importance in his system which it does not really possess. There can be no two opinions about the substantial correctness of Alexander's criticisms of Spinoza as put forward in his lecture "Spinoza and Time": this chapter will therefore be concerned with the more debatable though brilliant speculations of *Space, Time and Deity*.

The close conjunction in one sentence of 'space' and 'time', and more particularly their hyphenation, are far from unfamiliar to us in this twentieth century. The work of Einstein and Minkowski has made 'space-time' at least verbally familiar to us all. Consequently, when Alexander, beginning with 'space' and 'time', shows that each involves the other, and thereafter speaks of 'space-time' as formed from their union, yet differing from both, we are apt to assume that we know at once what he means. But it cannot be too strongly emphasized that the 'space-time' of Alexander's conception is different from that of Minkowski's, as Alexander himself points out: " . . . this inquiry which, be it observed, is entirely non-mathematical . . . "[1] and "We have thus *by purely analytical or metaphysical and non-mathematical methods* applied to a subject-matter presented in experience, arrived at a notion of Space-Time which at least in spirit is not different from the notion of a world in Space and Time which was formulated *by mathe-*

[1] *Space, Time and Deity*, i, 57. Unless otherwise stated, all references in this chapter are to this work.

matical methods by the late H. Minkowski in 1908."[1] For the mathematician is concerned with space-time as *measurable*: Alexander's claim is the different one that not only psychologically and physically, but also *ontologically*, space and time are intimately connected. It would be a mistake to imagine that there is any special connection, other than that of verbal similarity, between Alexander's metaphysic and current physical theories. On the contrary, if one science more than another supplies the dominant ideas of *Space, Time and Deity*, that science is biology, with its doctrine of 'emergence', rather than physics. It would, therefore, be superficial to criticize Alexander on the ground that he imported into metaphysics notions whose proper home is physics. It should be clearly realized that Alexander was concerned throughout with metaphysics and not with physics.

A second preliminary remark can usefully be made before we go on to consider Alexander's views in detail. That is the obvious, if not always sufficiently heeded, one that it is a mistake to come to metaphysics with too rigid preconceptions of what the terms used should mean. It was wrong to equate Space-Time with the space-time of physics: it would be equally wrong to equate it with motion. That does not mean, of course, that the metaphysician is freed from the need of making clear how he is using his terms—if he departs from common usage the need is all the greater that he should make his own usage clear, and if this is not done, the obscurity of his conceptions is a major criticism against him. But criticisms based on misunderstanding are only too common, especially in the case of such a writer as Alexander.

It is almost an impertinence to attempt to expound what is already so lucidly expressed. Alexander's own introduction is the best. "Space and Time as presented in ordinary experience are what are commonly known as extension and duration, entities (let us say provisionally) or forms of existence, in which bodies occupy places, and events occur at times or moments, these events being either external or mental. We shall deal first with physical Space and Time, leaving mental occurrences to a later stage. Now

[1] i, 58. Italics mine. For a very clear statement of the relation of the Theory of Relativity to metaphysics, see also i, 87-92.

in order to examine empirically what Space and Time are, it is necessary to consider them by themselves, in abstraction from the bodies and events that occupy them, and this may seem to some illegitimate. The difficulty is partly derived from our practical habits, for we are not accustomed to think about Space and Time themselves, but about things contained in them. But it also has a theoretical basis. For we have not any sense-organ for Space or Time: we only apprehend them in and through our sensible apprehension of their filling: by what mode of our apprehension we shall inquire later. I shall call it intuition. It is only by analytic attention that we can think of them for themselves."[1] It will be seen that Alexander's starting-point is the space and the time of ordinary experience: he does not deny their reality. On the other hand, he does not rush to the other extreme which consists in forgetting that space and time are only abstractions from events, and in hypostatizing them. It may be that in the end we must decide that Alexander *did* hypostatize them, but it should not be overlooked that he showed himself aware of this danger, and rightly said that it must be risked. For, from an extreme point of view, even to talk of 'space' and 'time' is a hypostatization. Such a criticism we must all risk; and it is insufficient to point out that Alexander always used capital letters for 'space' and 'time', and, *a fortiori*, for 'space-time'. The attitude that he here takes up in regard to the relation between time and events seems to me entirely justified.

Secondly, as he points out, we can regard temporal phenomena as either external or mental—giving rise to the familiar dichotomy of 'physical' and 'psychological' time. In either case he is concerned to show that the same conclusions follow. His starting-point, then, is beyond reproach.

The whole of his subsequent procedure with regard to time can be summed up very shortly as follows. Time and space cannot exist apart: they involve and are interdependent upon each other. Their interdependence, which may be called for convenience space-time, is, however, not the mere sum of space and time, but is *more* than that: from their union something new has emerged. Now evidently these two stages might not be held together—at least, the first might be granted without the second, though the

[1] i, 37.

second could not be held[1] without the first. It will therefore be more convenient to discuss them separately.

Space and time, says Alexander, "are often thought to be independent and separate (whether treated as entities as here[2] or as systems of relations). But a little reflective consideration is sufficient to show that they are interdependent, so that there neither is Space without Time nor Time without Space: any more than life exists without a body or a body which can function as a living body exists without life: that Space is in its very nature temporal and Time spatial."[3]

A possible criticism (that though *we* never perceive one without the other, as in Minkowski's celebrated truism, that does not prove that *ontologically* they are connected) is quickly forestalled. Alexander is not concerned to elaborate the obvious: he is not merely talking about what we experience: he goes further, and tries to show that space and time are necessarily, and not merely factually connected, since one without the other would fall into contradictions. "The mere temporality of Time, its successiveness leaves no place for its continuity or togetherness and seems to be contradictory to its continuity. Yet the two are found together in Time as we experience it. If, therefore, the past instant is not to be lost as it otherwise would be, or rather since this is not the case in fact, there must needs be some continuum other than Time which can secure and sustain the togetherness of past and future. . . . This other form of being is Space: that is, Space supplies us with the second continuum needed in order to save Time from being a mere 'now'."[4] The realism of Alexander (in contrast, for instance, to Bradley or McTaggart) is well brought out by his search for a "second continuum" to save Time from contradiction. Whereas they are content to conclude that Time is unreal, he starts from the position that it is real as "an object given to us empiri-

[1] That is rather a sweeping statement. It would be possible for a man to hold that space and time were not necessarily interdependent, and yet to hold a doctrine of emergence in space-time. But its unlikelihood may allow the statement in the text to stand.

[2] The reference here is to his discussion, mentioned earlier, of the alternative conceptions of time as being apart from events, or of being only relations between events. See the criticism of what he believes to be a radical inconsistency in Alexander by Murphy (*Monist*, 1927 and 1928).

[3] i, 44.   [4] i, 46.

cally",[1] and hence has to find some means by which the apparent contradictions can be dissolved.

Similarly, space is only saved from blank negation by time—"Time is discovered to supply the element in Space without which Space would be a blank."[2] For different reasons, but fundamentally in each case for continuity, space and time involve each other. "Without Space there would be no connection in Time. Without Time there would be no points to connect."[3] Then comes the great jump, from Space and Time, involving each other, to Space-Time. "There are no such things as points or instants by themselves. There are only point-instants or *pure events*. In like manner there is no mere Space or mere Time, but only Space-Time or Time-Space. Space and Time by themselves are abstractions from Space-Time, and if they are taken to exist in their own right without the tacit assumption of the other they are illegitimate abstractions of the sort that Berkeley censured.[4] How they come to be distinguished apart from each other, and on what terms this is legitimate and useful will appear in due course. But at least they are not merely two concurrent though correlated continua. The real existence is Space-Time, the continuum of point instants or pure events."[5] This passage is of the last importance. Yet Alexander does not seek to consolidate his new position, as yet, but turns back and shows in more detail some of the ways in which space and time involve each other. First, he deals with the question of repetition in space and time, and shows that a one-one correspondence of points and instants would be insufficient to save space and time from the misfortunes threatened earlier, blankness and perishingness. But he adds[6] that he conceives of "this abstract or elementary relation" of Space and Time analogously to the familiar one of identity-in-difference, of a thing changing and yet remaining 'the same' thing. Nay more, he holds that it is this interdependence of space and time which is the explanation of how we can say that a thing changes and yet is the same. This passage is difficult and

[1] i, 46. In connection with the charge of hypostatization, it is interesting to note his language here. Time surely is *not* given to us empirically as an "object"?
[2] i, 47.   [3] i, 48.
[4] The former tentative criticism of hypostatization is thus ingeniously made to serve as an argument for Alexander's own view!
[5] i, 48.   [6] i, 50.

not to be taken in isolation: evidently it is very important, especially in connection with the topic, which is later raised, of emergence. For the logical question raised by all emergence theories is at root the familiar one of identity-in-difference. Here we can only note the rather abrupt transition from space and time to "our experience of empirical substances". He gives no grounds for his assertion of the fundamental relevance of space and time to the question of identity in substances, but whether this is a cogent criticism it is difficult to say: on the whole I think it is not, for such a fundamental position is more likely to be the basis of reasons than itself based upon reasons. That, of course, leaves it quite open for anybody to disagree with Alexander. Nevertheless, it is, at least at first sight—its detailed implications must be considered later, when there is more data at our disposal—an attractive idea that the 'differences' which we allow in 'a' thing[1] should be ultimately resolvable in terms of the relations of time and space. But the full discussion of this belongs properly to the second half of Alexander's position.

In a very interesting passage, Alexander seeks to show in detail how the various characters of time—its successiveness, irreversibility, and transitivity—are connected with those of space. He insists that an extra dimension of space is needed to account for—more, to admit of there being—each of these characteristics. But, as he points out, "This inquiry . . . contains no attempt at a construction of Space and Time, as if we were giving reasons for them and for their experienced features, and in a manner affecting to preside over their creation. Such an attempt would be as foolish as it is unscientific. I have merely attempted to show how the various features of the one depend for their character on those of the other. The reason why Space has three dimensions is that Time is successive, irreversible, and uniform in direction. . . . The word 'must' or 'needs' which I have occasionally used means no more than that we are forced to look for something, which we may or may not find."[2] Such a warning is very necessary:

[1] I do not here inquire what we mean by 'a' thing, but take the common usage for granted.
[2] i, 57. Murphy, in the first of the three articles already cited, criticized Alexander's attempts to relate the characteristics of time with the dimensions of space.

and it clears Alexander entirely from suspicion that such a laying down of laws was what he was trying to do. But, secondly, it may be objected that Alexander's conception of time here is too spatial. In so far as it is his avowed intention to correlate temporal and spatial characteristics, it is spatial: but this can hardly be made a ground of criticism, unless he carries it too far. A more important criticism, if substantiated, is that the whole attempt at correlation is based on a fundamental fallacy. Alexander wants to show that space and time are necessarily connected: what he actually shows is that they are, in fact, so connected in our experience that we cannot think of the one without reference to the other. He is not proving that irreversibility, for instance, involves a two-dimensional space, but only that we cannot schematize it without a two-dimensional space. It is doubtful whether even this much of the criticism can be granted; Alexander could make out a very good case for himself that his proof holds good ontologically as well as psychologically. But even if the criticism were granted so far, the distinction between things as they are and as they seem to us to be is one which takes us into very deep waters. Granted that things may not be what they seem, then in that case we can have no inkling what they are, if the reality is to be for ever hidden from our apprehension. The distinction between ontology and epistemology is a dangerous one, for it can so easily be turned against its makers: "If the reality is such that it cannot be known, how do you know this, and what grounds have you for your assertion?" It becomes merely a case of conflicting assertions, with the *onus probandi* on him who would deny an ontological value to epistemological statements. As Alexander tersely put it in a different context, "We cannot believe that though the senses may confuse our apprehension . . . they are there to pervert it."[1] The question, it will be seen, is not only of this single point, but concerns the whole realist position; and it seems to me that the criticism fails.

Having shown the interdependence of space and time, Alexander returns to their union in Space-Time, and sums up his position, thus: "The elements of the one reality which is Space-Time, and not either Space or Time alone, owe their distinctness in either kind to the complementary element."[2] This passage shows very

[1] i, 73. [2] i, 60.

clearly the essential point which he thereafter takes as proved, that space-time is the reality on which both space and time are dependent—in other words, that space-time is logically prior to space and time.

I have kept closely to Alexander's arguments so far, since their consideration is necessary before any criticism is possible. But now the important question arises as to the exact relations between space and time and space-time on his theory. Unfortunately, as well as being important, it is difficult to answer, and indeed it is one of the most telling criticisms against Alexander that he has left these essential relationships obscure.

First, he holds that space-time is the reality from which space and time are derived. But what *is* space-time? Obviously, we must not fall into the crude error of taking 'derived' in a temporal sense, and of saying in effect, "first there was space-time, and *then* there was space and time", which would involve a super-time in which all this happened, and hence contradiction. On the other hand, Alexander is not denying that, psychologically, we are more familiar with space and time than with space-time. Nor is he merely asserting the truism that we do, as a matter of fact, always perceive things as 'in' space and time—never in one or the other alone. Again, though he takes advantage of modern physical theories regarding the interdependence of space and time, his space-time is not the same as that of physics, as had already been said. Lastly, space-time is not motion, though it is the source of motion. But such information is merely negative, and the prior question, what space-time *is*, still remains unanswered. A general answer to this question can be given, but only a general one. It is easy enough to say glibly that space-time is the matrix of being, that it is the stuff of which the universe is made, but it is difficult to go into detail. Anybody can make such assertions: and anybody, too, can set up as a critic of them. And that, I think, is the danger—of too facile criticism of Alexander on the ground of obscurity. For though, in nine cases out of ten, it is legitimate to assume that a notion that can only be expressed in vague and general terms is of little value, in the tenth case its very importance might preclude a cut-and-dried statement. Alexander's position, it seems to me, is that space-time is so fundamental that little can be said of it, except by analogies and in language that is bound to be misleading.

Whether he is right in holding that it is fundamental is the main point at issue. If he is, then it would be ungracious to talk too much of obscurity: if he is not, his whole metaphysic collapses at once, and the matter of obscurity does not enter. Evidently, the verdict on the question is the verdict on his system, and it cannot be given now. We are bound to take 'space-time' for granted at present, and to see what use he makes of it, before deciding whether or not his claim that it is fundamental is justified.

Alexander is definite on the relationship between space-time and space and time: what difficulties there are can be attributed entirely, I think, to the difficulty we find in conceiving of his space-time. "There is no mere Space or mere Time but only Space-Time.... Space and Time by themselves are abstractions from Space-Time, and if they are taken to exist in their own right . . . they are illegitimate assumptions. . . . They are not merely two concurrent though correlated continua. The real existence is Space-Time, the continuum of point-instants or pure events."[1]

But there is another way in which we can think of Space-Time in relation to space and time, and this is a way in which it is perhaps easier for us to think, but, as Alexander must in consistency hold, it is less fundamental. This is to think of the whole of Space-Time as the total of all 'perspectives' in space and time. "A perspective from an instant gives us a picture of Space: a perspective from a point gives us a picture of Time. If we attempted to combine the two pictures, and to get a 'perspective' of Space-Time from the point of view both of the place and time of the point-instant oO, we should have, as a little consideration will show, not a perspective at all but the whole of Space-Time."[2] And again—"Total Space-Time is the synthesis of all partial space-times or perspectives of Space-Time."[3] Space-Time, of course, cannot, consistently with Alexander's main position, be conceived of merely as a synthesis, nor can its relation to space and time be analogous to the relation, for instance, between a heap of books and one of the books.[4] Alexander sees that clearly, and also that such a process is itself secondary, presupposing (not presupposed) by space-time. "From considering the true perspectives of Space-Time we can arrive at the notion of Space occurring at one time or Time occu-

[1] i, 48.   [2] i, 76.   [3] i, 76.
[4] Nor could it be so, even if space and time were not themselves infinite

pying one place. But from these sections we cannot arrive at the notion of true perspectives or at true Space-Time."[1] "These perspectives are *of themselves* connected with one another, so that the synthesis of them is not an operation which we, human subjects who think, perform upon them, but one which they, as it were, perform on themselves. For a perspective of Space-Time is merely the whole of Space-Time as it is related to a point-instant *by virtue of the lines of connection* between it and other point-instants."[2] It is evident that no criticism can be made against Alexander on the score of inconsistency here.

Thirdly, there is the problem of the relation between time and space. Here, up to a point, the remarks made earlier apply—that it would be a mistake to lay too much store on obscurity as a criticism. For whatever its shortcomings, there can be no doubt that Alexander's attempt to relate space and time is important. It is in ways like these that Alexander has the advantage over Bergson, whom in some ways he resembles. For Bergson, though he may have been the first philosopher to "take Time seriously",[3] certainly did not take Space seriously enough, and this is his great defect. Alexander put the point at issue between himself and Bergson concisely when he said: "The main result of our discussion has been to show that Time is really laid out in Space, and is intrinsically spatial. The representation of Time as spatial, Mr. Bergson regards as depriving Time of its real character. What he regards as a habit founded upon the weakness of our imagination has now been shown to be vital to the nature of Time."[4] We need not go as far as that to agree with him, as against Bergson. It is one of Alexander's most important achievements that he should have seen that a one-sided glorification of time is as undesirable as its depreciation, and that time is, at least empirically, connected with space, and that this connection needs explanation. For it is not sufficient to say: "The mutual relation of Time and Space is so close and ramified that they cannot be considered as separate entities but only as the same entity described in terms of its different elements."[5] Important though this interdependence is, involving Space-Time (and admittedly never completely demonstrable), this is one of the places where we *are* justified in asking for further

[1] i, 81. [2] i, 76–7. Italics mine.
[3] i, 44. [4] i, 143. See also pp. 148–50. [5] i, 58.

details. The mere mention of 'space-time' is not to be regarded as "Shut, Sesame!" to *all* questions, or it would be vicious. It is only by its success in co-ordinating and providing a possible explanation of various questions that Alexander's, and any other metaphysical theory, stands or falls. Only so can its major premise be justified. It is not, then, inconsistent to be indulgent with so-called 'obscurity' in the notion of space-time, and also to be rigorous in rejecting obscurity in anything else. Space-time we do not know, until Alexander introduces it to us, so we must not hastily criticize: but space we know, and time we know, and familiarity breeds, if not contempt, at least a desire to criticize. It is vital to Alexander that he should make clear how space and time are related on his theory, since only so can he justify the appearance of Space-Time. Obscurity here cannot but be fatal.

First, there is the connection between the dimensions of space and the characteristics of time, an interesting idea which Alexander worked out in detail. Secondly, he expressed the relation between time and space more generally as being in some sense comparable to the relation between identity and diversity. "Either of the two" (space and time) "we may regard as playing the part of identity to the other's part of diversity. It is worth while observing this, because previously Time was shown to apply discrimination in the otherwise blank Space. But Space may equally well be regarded as introducing diversity into Time. For without Space, Time would be a bare 'now' always repeated, and there would be no such thing as diversity." And he adds, significantly, "But the reality of Space and Time is in Platonic phrase the 'substance' which contains the identity and the diversity in one."[1]

But it is not until the Third Book—and this is perhaps significant—that Alexander really treats of the relations between time and space, in an oft-quoted statement. "Time as a whole and in its parts bears to Space as a whole and in its corresponding parts a relation analogous to the relation of mind to its equivalent bodily or nervous basis, or to put the matter shortly, that Time is the mind of Space, and Space the body of Time. . . . In any point-instant the instant is the mind or soul of its point: in a group of points there is a mind of those points, which upon the primary

[1] i, 60.

level of Space-Time itself is the corresponding time of that complex. Qualities will be seen to be the special form which on each successive level of existence the mind element assumes. In Space-Time as a whole the total Time is the mind of total Space."[1] On the face of it, this is not very satisfactory, for though we have some (sufficiently vague) notion of the relation between mind and body, it is not obvious that the relation between time and space is identical with, or analogous to, this. Secondly, and more important, Alexander himself admits that "the statement is better made in the reverse and truer form that we are examples of a pattern which is universal and is followed not only by things but by Space-Time itself".[2] In that case, the similar relationships between space and time, and between body and mind, are surely better expressed in terms of the former?—especially as Alexander takes space and time as primary data, rather than body or mind. But if expressed in the form, "Mind is the time of body, and body the space of mind", it is evident that the exact relationship between time and space is still to be sought. The celebrated 'formula' lends precisely nothing to an exact formulation. Alexander, of course, never meant it as such, and he would urge that the expressing of a more fundamental in terms of a less fundamental relationship was not intended as clarification in the logical sense, but simply as a metaphor to enable his position to be more easily understood. But nevertheless I think that the criticism stands, at least in a modified form. It was necessary for Alexander to show how time and space are related and he did not do so. It may be replied that their relation is unique and indefinable. Up to a point the plea (as, for instance, that the relationship can never be *completely* adumbrated) might be accepted. But the wholesale introduction of 'ultimates' is undesirable as leading to intellectual defeatism: and in such case the metaphysical utility of 'Space-Time' is bound to be questioned.

But the criticism, that Alexander has not made clear the relation of time and space, does not detract at all from the interest and importance of his comparison with the mind-body relation. As he points out, the relations are not identical, since the mind-body relation is more developed than the time-space one—"Space does not exist of its own right, and therefore Time is not a new quality

[1] ii, 38–9.   [2] ii, 39.

which emerges from Space. . . . The relation of Time to Space is therefore something closer than that of being merely analogous to the relation of mind and its neural basis, and something less than that of being identical with it."[1] And—"in the matrix of all existence, Space-Time, there is an element Time which performs the same function in respect of the other element Space as mind performs in respect of its bodily equivalent".[2] Finally Alexander makes his position quite clear, and shows that though he is open to the important negative criticism above, on the positive side his position is unassailable. "Our hypothesis is merely that alike in the matrix of finite things and in all finite things there is something of which, on the highest level we know of finite existents, mind is the counterpart or correspondent. So far as the philosopher is concerned with empirical facts, it is his business to indicate what this element is on each level. On the bare level of Space-Time, it is Time. Rather than hold that Time is a form of mind, we must say that mind is a form of Time."[3] To sum up, the view that time and mind are analogous is a brilliant speculation, coherent with the rest of Alexander's work, and suggestive to many whose views are very different from Alexander's: but it does not release Alexander from the charge of obscurity in the relationship of space and time, an obscurity which even brilliant analogies cannot dispel. Until it is cleared up, there is no reason (apart from the negative one of consistency) why we should accept "Space-Time". It may be a changeling.

Even, however, if the doctrines of space and time had been complete, we could not have hoped to learn everything about 'Space-Time'. For it was the second great point emphasized in *Space, Time, and Deity* that Space-Time is more than the mere sum of Space and Time. As a corollary to this is the general doctrine of 'emergence', of ever-new forms emerging from the common matrix, Space-Time. This doctrine is of special importance for time, since it is time which, following Bergson, Alexander considers to be the generator of change and novelty. "Time is the principle of motion and change. . . . Commonly it is personified in the figure of a scythe-man mowing down the old to make room for the young. This figure represents rather the transitoriness of things than the real nature of Time. . . . It forgets that the same Time

[1] ii, 40.   [2] ii, 44.   [3] ii, 44.

which mows down the grass produces the new crop. . . . Time is in truth the abiding principle of impermanence which is the real creator."[1] Nobody disputes the connection of time with change: it is the introduction of the notion of creating new forms, of novelty, that is especially interesting here. In a sense, of course, all change is novelty, and a verbal case could be made out for anyone who held that the rearrangement of a hand of cards was a novelty. But it is more convenient to keep the wide sense of 'change' as including mere shuffling, and to use 'novelty' in a narrower sense which excludes shuffling. Nobody doubts that there are changes. But scientists and philosophers have from the time of the Greeks been divided on the question whether all changes are ultimately reducible to shufflings, or whether an element of novelty sometimes[2] enters in. Atomism, for instance, admits that there are changes, but rejects novelty: while on the other hand theories of emergence insist that the attempt to treat the universe as a large sum in arithmetic to which the answer is always the same is a mistake. Ordinary language can give little help here. For our usage of "this is a new thing" and "this is an old thing in a different guise" depends upon practical considerations, and not upon logical ones. Even when everyone would admit on reflection that shuffling is all that has happened, the resulting mixture may possess practical utility, and so is given a name of its own. We talk of "mincemeat" rather than of "currants, raisins, suet, and the rest": we say of a distribution at bridge that A has a good hand, B and C moderate ones, and D a poor one. But the mincemeat is exactly the same as the mixture of its various ingredients: the new name does not mean a new thing, if by 'new thing' is meant, not the slipshod, common-sense usage, but something other than what has already been given. The atomist is quick to take advantage of this illogicality in ordinary usage, and he points out that mincemeat is 'nothing but' the mixture of its ingredients. In a similar way, he confidently asserts, every change is the result of shuffling. The Universe is a gigantic pack of cards and the changes that we talk

---

[1] ii, 48. See also ii, 337. Time "is creative: something comes into being which before was not".

[2] The extreme view that there is *always* novelty, even in successive rearrangements of three cards, is rarely held, and depends upon a hypostatized view of time as 'creative', even in a vacuum.

of in things are only different collocations.[1] It may be objected that such a view would not account for the orderliness and coherence of the world, and that the changes which occur are not the result of mere haphazard shuffling, but are connected with one another. Nevertheless, the atomist need not be, as this argument would appear to assume, a tychist. On the contrary, it is quite consistent to believe in atomism and determinism together. The use of the word 'shuffling' here is perhaps misleading: but all that it need involve is that the number of the 'cards' remains unchanged, without excluding the possibility that the so-called shuffling process is one in which certain changes determine others. Evidently, this tolerance of determinism makes atomism much more attractive to scientists than it would be if it postulated only chance concurrences. One argument, then, against atomism, that it is incompatible with causality, cannot stand.

But, it may be urged, whereas the plain man gives a separate name to any collection that has particular utility for him, even if it is granted that the so-called "new thing" is merely a regrouping of the old, the atomist rushes to the other extreme, and rather than be content with saying "This is something new", goes to endless trouble to exhibit it as a regrouping. And, on the face of it, the trouble seems ill-spent if, as usually happens, the atomist cannot *completely* resolve the given into known elements. To say "M is made of $ax + by + cz$" is all very well as long as we know what x, y, and z are: but if even one of these is unknown, the whole question of novelty crops up again with regard to z, the unknown. The sceptic can so easily retort: "You cannot tell me what z is, and I find no reason to believe in your hypothetical z: it seems to me that I might as well admit novelty, in M, first as last. I admit that I can never *disprove* what you say, for every time that you are attacked you shift your ground. If on one occasion the promised equivalence of M with its 'elements' does not materialize, you postulate another 'unknown', and approximate ever closer to the desired equivalence. But until you reach it—if you ever do—the

---

[1] Some such view is assumed in chemistry, and, indeed, the general atomic view is an extension from the "Water is hydrogen and oxygen" of chemistry. In what follows, I use "atomism" in a very general sense, and not in a specifically chemical one.

theoretical difficulty is as great for you as it is for me." The sceptic is right here, for the question at issue is not whether M is *partially* resolvable into known elements, and if even a small discrepancy remains, the logical consequences of the admission of novelty are as momentous as ever.

Meyerson deals[1] in great detail with the postulate of identity in science: and he shows, giving definite examples, how science seeks by successive approximations to reach the ideal of equality between left and right hand sides of a chemical 'equation'. "Beyond and beneath the produced phenomenon ... we believe that we see something else: we believe, we at least wish to believe, that the totality of the antecedents if we were able to embrace them at a glance and recognize their intimate nature, would be recognized as equal to the totality of the consequents and identical with it."[2] But, as he pointed out, principles of conservation are contradicted by the dissipation of heat. The heat, once dissipated, is lost: so that the last state is not, as what I have called 'atomism' assumes, quantitatively equal to the first. This is the first real check to atomism.

Secondly, and more positively from the point of view of the upholder of novelty, there is a certain class of objects for which analysis into 'elements' is curiously insufficient. The whole forms a unity which is integral, and which is more than the mere sum of its parts. Living matter forms the most familiar example of this. A living body is not merely head plus arms plus trunk plus legs: it is also—living. The anatomist who divides the body may make an exact inventory of the separate parts: but let him try to put them together again exactly as they were, and he will fail. "Life has gone out of the body", we say, our language vainly aping our atomistic prepossessions. But what and where is this 'life'? The anatomist made a list of the parts: 'life' was not on that list. The truth of the matter is that we cannot talk of 'life' as if it were a self-existent entity, a material element that goes, like carbon, to the making of John Smith. On the contrary, John Smith is more than the mere sum of his parts: he is alive, and he is an organic unity. Examples of integral wholes, though most familiar in, are not confined to, living organisms. Organic unities are well known

[1] In *Identity and Reality*, passim.
[2] Op. cit., p. 226.

in ethics; and in works of art their parts are fused into a single whole.[1]

> "Turn away no more
> Why wilt thou turn away?
> The starry floor
> The watery shore
> Is given thee till the break of day."

It would be madness to attempt to analyse this into 'parts'. Meaning (especially perhaps aesthetic meaning), no more than life, is to be interpreted in terms of an atomistic adding machine.

There are, then, two separate grounds for rejecting atomism: the first is, that it does not allow for irreparable loss; the second is, that it cannot measure incalculable gain. I have dealt with the first for completeness' sake, though Alexander is chiefly concerned with the latter, as it is a good opportunity to get clear on the general question of what is involved by novelty as against atomism, before considering Alexander's specific views.

It should be noticed that the two rejections of atomism are distinct, and that only the latter involves novelty. Consequently, it would be no argument against novelty as such, if a chemist were to discover that the energy 'lost' in cooling was really conserved, and that the process of the degradation of energy, leading ultimately to the 'heat death', need no longer be feared. But, on the other hand, as long as the Second Law of Thermodynamics is taken seriously—as long, that is, as the ideal of a frictionless machine of perfect efficiency is regarded as a mathematical fiction —indirect support is given to the upholders of novelty in making atomism less plausible. Its rationality is atomism's greatest advantage, and that explains the attraction it has had for scientists. But if science, as soon as it deals with the concrete, is forced to introduce makeweights and camouflaging factors such as 'friction', atomism immediately loses a great part of its advantage. The degradation of energy, then, can be used as an indirect argument for novelty; its denial can never be an argument against it.

Nevertheless, it cannot be denied that the difficulty, if not impossibility, of formulating any doctrine of novelty in a logical

---

[1] Compare the recent newspaper controversy on 'the inevitable' Bach! His decriers did not appear to realize the involuntary compliment.

form is at first sight a grave disadvantage. We have to be very sure of ourselves before we can afford to ignore the maxim "ex nihilo nihil fit", and to turn a deaf ear to the devastating question, "By what logical process do you arrive at the idea of novelty?" It simply cannot be answered: the notion of novelty is irreducible to the laws of logic. By hypothesis, no possible combination of known premises can yield the conclusion, for there is fundamental discontinuity between them. This certainly will not satisfy the logician, and he objects. (Sometimes with reason, when the evolutionist adopts startling methods to display his fundamentally alogical position as being logically demonstrable.[1]) But there is no reason why the evolutionist should thus deliver himself bound into the hands of the enemy: once he tries to fight the battle on logical grounds, he is done for. On the other hand, as against the disadvantage of irreducibility to logic, he has the very strong weapon of ability to point to examples of novelty in the world. By this I do not merely mean what common sense regards, for practical purposes, as a 'new thing'; far stronger examples can be taken of living organisms, of artistic creations (the term is significant), and of values. If these are not sufficient to give him confidence to ignore logic, and to assert boldly the counterclaim that the abstract rules of logic are insufficient to account for concrete reality, then all theories of emergence must break down.

All this may seem a far cry from *Space, Time and Deity*. I have, however, been trying to make clear the position of emergence with regard to logic, and to show that though a belief in novelty can never be logically justified, there are fairly strong empirical grounds for ignoring logic. The vital question, which each must solve for himself, is—Are these grounds sufficiently strong? If you answer, Yes, you must be resigned never to be able to refute your opponents, and never to be able to reach agreement with them. But once you have taken the vital step, your way is clear

[1] As when Leibniz hoped, by constructing an arithmetic with only the two numbers 0 and 1, to explain creation mathematically—evidently, the whole point is in the passage from 0 to 1, not in the subsequent procedure. Or, worse, when Burke claimed (in *The Mystery of Life*) that from unreality we can deduce reality, just as from i (an imaginary number) we can pass to -1 (a real number). Needless to say, the 'passage' is the other way round: i is only a mathematical device for dealing with a problem that was *already* there.

to using novelty in almost any way you like, for no further theoretical difficulty is involved. That is why it has seemed to me important to deal in detail with the presuppositions on which all theories of emergence are based, in order to avoid misconceptions and too-facile criticisms on the score of 'irrationality'. The rest can be more quickly dealt with, since in spite of the brilliance and originality of Alexander's speculations, no new considerations arise. The universe of Space-Time is creative, and is constantly evolving ever new forms, of which the next higher to the highest yet attained is Deity. But even Deity is capable of further evolution. "There is a nisus in Space-Time which, as it has borne its creatures forward through matter and life to mind, will bear them forward to some higher level of existence. There is nothing in mind which requires us to stop and say this is the highest empirical quality which Time can produce from now throughout the infinite Time to come. It is only the last empirical quality which we who are minds happen to know. Time itself compels us to think of a later birth of Time. . . . Deity is the next higher empirical quality to mind, which the universe is engaged in bringing to birth. That the universe is pregnant with such a quality we are speculatively assured. What that quality is we cannot know: still less can we contemplate it. Our human altars still are raised to the unknown God."[1] And, "In the hierarchy of qualities the next higher quality to the highest attained is deity. God is the whole universe engaged in process towards the emergence of this new quality, and religion is the sentiment in us that we are drawn towards him, and caught in the movement of the world to a higher level of existence."[2]

Finally, this nisus is conceived as bound up with the notion of time—"Time is the principle of growth."[3] Again, "the restless movement of Time . . . is not the mere turning of a squirrel in its cage, but the nisus towards a higher birth".[4] This view of time as essentially creative has much in common with that of Bergson, and it is an exceedingly attractive view. If we decide to flout logic and admit the reality of process and novelty, it is in keeping with economy to hold that these are connected—it gives us one sin of irreverence rather than two! In common with Bergson, too, Alexander stresses rather the creativity of time than its destructiveness. Certainly, as he says, the view of time as a destructive

[1] ii, 346–7.   [2] ii, 429.   [3] ii, 346.   [4] ii, 348.

force is rather too much emphasized, and both aspects should be borne in mind. But it might perhaps be held as a criticism against him that he went too far in the opposite direction: and that he might have strengthened his position against the atomists by considering the degradation that time brings. (It is no accident, it may be remarked in passing, that from the *scientist's* point of view, Eddington has connected the increase of entropy with the passing of time.) There is much to be said for the common-sense view that time both creates and destroys. This, however, is a criticism of slight account in comparison with the splendour of Alexander's conception of the universe of Space-Time evolving ever higher and higher forms. There can be no doubt that, even to those who do not accept the premises of Alexander's metaphysic, his work is of the highest importance.

CHAPTER VII

McTAGGART

THE denial of reality to time is by no means a startling result for anyone to achieve: it is almost a commonplace in philosophy. Parmenides and Plato among the Greeks: Spinoza and Leibniz and possibly Kant among the leaders of modern thought: Hegel and Bradley in still more recent times—all have denied, with more or less vehemence, the claims of Time to be reckoned among the attributes of Reality. McTaggart has been like most other idealists in this respect. But where he is in very striking contrast to the others is, that he is not content merely to deny the reality of Time—though his arguments in the important chapter in the second volume of the *Nature of Existence* are widely known and often quoted—but that he sees the need *also* of explaining how we have (as we unquestionably *do* have) the illusion that makes us attribute temporal characteristics to existents. It is in this that his great originality consists.

McTaggart's remarks on time therefore fall under two headings —first, his proof that time is unreal; and secondly, his explanation of the 'misperception' by which we attribute temporal characteristics to a series that is really non-temporal, and the consequences of that explanation. The second, constructive part is naturally in terms of his own system, and could not be accepted without modification, if at all, by those who rejected his principles (as, for instance, that of Determining Correspondence). The first, on the other hand, starts from common-sense views of time in an attempt to show that time is, in Bradley's phrase, "riddled with contradictions", and is independent of the main tenets of McTaggart's system, so that the cogency of its argument can be admitted even by those not in agreement with his views. But the greater vulnerability of the second part—since it may be false and the first true, but if the first is false the second must also be false—does not detract from its importance as an amazingly well thought out doctrine.

McTaggart's arguments in the chapter on Time[1] are directed to show that the notion of Time is full of contradictions, and that these contradictions are not resolvable, but essential and ultimate, as long as we continue to use the notion of time. He assumes that nothing which is self-contradictory and impossible to thought can exist, and hence he concludes that time does not exist.

We commonly distinguish positions in time as having places in the series generated by the relation 'earlier than' (or, conversely, 'later than'), or in the series past-present-future. The latter McTaggart calls the A series, the former the B series. Although the distinctions to which the B series gives rise are permanent,[2] and those of the A series are not so (since of two events, L and M, the former may be past and the latter present, yet at a later time, both are past), the A series is more fundamental to time than the B series. McTaggart goes on to prove that the A series is essential to time, and the B series only derivative, since, he asserts, change is essential to time, and the B series alone could never give change. This part of his argument may be granted,[3] and also his conclusion that the A series is essential to time. The second stage is to show that the A series is inherently contradictory, or alternatively, that to avoid the contradictions we must indulge in a vicious circle or a vicious infinite regress.

Past, present and future are not qualities of objects or events as *red* and *hard* are. This is undeniable. Therefore, says McTaggart, they are relations—the relations in which events stand to *something* outside the time series. This unknown term cannot be in time, yet it plays an essential part in the determining of temporal characteristics. McTaggart's first criticism is that this term should be discovered, and that if this proves impossible, as he suspects, it

[1] Reprinted with a few alterations from *Mind*, 1908.
[2] McTaggart's own language. He means by 'permanent' that "if an event is *ever* earlier than another event it is *always* earlier".—*Nature of Existence*, sec. 305 (my italics).
[3] There can be no change without time. It may be held that the converse does not also hold, since we can talk of things enduring unchanged through time. But, McTaggart asserts, there could be no time if *nothing* changed. This assertion, of course, cannot be either proved or refuted. But probably it is justified.

reflects upon the genuineness of the A series. Secondly, past, present and future are incompatible characteristics, yet every event has them all—an obvious contradiction. And, McTaggart continues, we cannot avoid this in a way analogous to that we should take in explaining the *prima facie* contradiction of "X is red" and "X is not red"—that the redness and the non-redness are *at different times*. Besides committing the fallacy of regarding past, present and future as if they were qualities, it is useless to bring in "at different times" because it begs the question at once. If it is regarded as *not* question-begging, we must further analyse what we mean by saying, "*M is present and L is past* is future to *M is future and L is present*", which starts us off on an infinite regress. Both the circle and the regress are vicious, and they cannot, therefore, be said to have exorcized the other alternative—that past, present and future are frankly contradictory. Hence the A series dissolves in contradictions, and so time is unreal.

The criticisms that I wish to make about this second and essential stage of the argument are threefold. They relate, firstly, to the unknown 'something', secondly, to the alleged regress, and lastly, to what seems to be a logical confusion between temporal and non-temporal uses of language.

McTaggart said that past, present and future are relations in which events stand to something outside the time-series. I think that this is questionable.[1] To postulate an entity entirely *outside* the time-series is tantamount to admitting that there can be reality without time, and this is suspiciously like begging the question. McTaggart says that the relation must be to something outside the series because it is not to something inside[2] the series. But why not? It *is* not, because it *cannot* be, since purely temporal relations cannot change. He says: "The relations of the A series are changing relations, and no relations which are exclusively between members of the time-series can ever change."[3] It seems to me that he is inconsistent here, for the second half of the sentence assumes what he had denied in the earlier part of his argument, that the "unchanging" B series is sufficient to constitute a time-series. Thus the

[1] Compare also the criticisms made by Gotshalk in a sound article in *Mind* (1930).
[2] I apologize for the language, and hope that the meaning is clear.
[3] Op. cit., sec. 327.

example which he takes[1] refers to the *B* series only, though the *A* series is ostensibly mentioned. If he meant what he said earlier, that the *A* series is essential, then he is wrong here, for a relation between the *A* series and an entity in time—say you or me—*is* capable of changing. In relation to my experience, this moment now is present: two years hence it will be past. This view accords with the common-sense notion that events are past, present, future, in relation to a given event, the now, whereas McTaggart's view is paradoxical to experience, and gets its recommendation from the fact that any other view is supposedly impossible. McTaggart, then, contradicts himself when he says that no relations which are exclusively between members of the time-series can ever change: and he is wrong in supposing that the other term in the time-relation must be something outside the time-series. The *A* series, therefore, is "riddled with contradictions" *if* it is taken as being a relation to an entity outside the time-series—but not otherwise.

But it would be silly to suppose that such a small change is sufficient to take the sting out of all McTaggart's arguments against the reality of time. On the contrary, only one of them is at all affected (even if the suggested substitution be valid). If we grant, for argument's sake, that the suggested procedure does do away with the *contradiction*, we are still left to deal with a regress. For, obviously, to say: "In relation to me, this moment now is present; two years hence it will be past," does not at all account for the main point at issue, which is the recession into the past of the 'now', any more than does the other formulation which McTaggart criticized.[2] Both are on a level as regards the primary miracle, and both leave it blandly unexplained. What 'is' 'now' for me, 'will' in a week be 'past'. There is no difficulty here only if the question is begged at the start—otherwise we have started again on the regress to which McTaggart objected.

Here is where the second criticism comes in. I know that it is generally taken for granted—not only by McTaggart—that a certain type of analysis of temporal characteristics leads to an infinite regress, and to all the consequences, welcome or unwelcome, which are supposed to follow from that regress. But I cannot help

[1] Sec. 327.
[2] See, too, the formulations suggested by Wisdom in his article on "Time, Fact and Substance" (*Aristotelian Society Proceedings*, 1928-29).

thinking that such an analysis misses the point somewhere, and that the regress is not the last word on the subject, but arises from a wrong conception of time. In the next chapter, this question will be more fully treated, but the main conclusions may be briefly summarized here.

An infinite regress is inevitable if we start from the idea of 'now' as moving, and as taking time over its movement: that is, if we consider the so-called movement of the 'now' as analogous to the movement of an *object* in *space*. I suggest that this idea is without foundation, and that it arises from an entirely wrong view of time. The fallacy is in regarding "E is occurring now" as analysable in a way similar to the analysis of "X is red": not only is 'now' regarded as a quality like 'red', but a confusion is made between E, an event, and X, a substance. This is, of course, speculative and open to criticism. But the thoroughgoing Realist, if he be daring enough, has one simple and effective means left of cutting the regressive knot. He may retort to McTaggart, "All that you have said only shows what I have all along insisted, that this passage of the present into the past, which for you is inexplicable, is fundamental and irreducible. The whole of the problem of time is there. You have tried to explain it in terms of something else and have failed, so you call it contradictory and regressive. I, on the other hand, postulate that this irreducibility is the fundamental fact from which we must start: hence there arises no regress for me." In other words, the criticism is that McTaggart (and other idealists) find contradictions because they are not taking time seriously enough, and that to take time seriously, we have to begin with, not explain away, this idea of 'passage'.

Now, evidently, this criticism cannot be regarded as final: because all that it does is to oppose to McTaggart's remarks about infinite regresses a contradictory *assertion* that no regress is required. I say 'assertion', because no proof can be given for it: any disagreements that remain are ultimate ones. And though, as an unsupported assertion it cannot be accepted outright, ultimately I think that only this type of argument can weigh against McTaggart's. The other remarks, summarized earlier, on infinite regresses, in the end depend upon the acceptance of some such view as this—that any conception of time which leads to a regress is partial and incomplete. To McTaggart his critic can only retort, when all is said and done—"Time is so fundamental that it must be assumed. This you call begging the question. I call it common sense." But this, unfortunately, is no refutation!

The third and last criticism has to do with McTaggart's occasionally misleading use of temporal and non-temporal language. This may seem a small matter after the last topic, and, as has already been said, an ultimate disagreement has been reached, so that his main position is secured from refutation: but all the same, secondary positions may be attacked and insidious confusions cleared up.[1]

Firstly, as regards McTaggart's use of the notion of 'change' in connection with the *B* series. The *B* series is temporal in the sense that the terms it relates are temporal: but the relation itself is not a temporal but a *logical* relation. It is strictly analogous to the "in front-behind" of space. The fundamental point about the *B* series is that it is an *order*, and it is itself no more temporal than is the order of the number-series. It is, in the strict sense, nonsense to say either that the order of positions in the *B* series changes or that it does not change: when McTaggart says that the distinctions of the *B* series are 'permanent', his language is unfortunate, because we get the notion of contrasting it with 'changing'— whereas the only sense in which it is 'permanent' is that the notion of *change* is inapplicable to it. What McTaggart meant by saying that it is unchanging, is that it is *fixed*, in the sense that it has nothing to do with time or place, but is defined by reference to logical relations. It is, of course, the case that the statement "The Battle of Hastings is earlier than the Battle of Agincourt" holds good in 1500, 1600, 1700, and on any occasion when we like to examine it: but although it is not a *falsehood* to say that Hastings is "always earlier" than Agincourt, since at any time we like to take the statement holds good, it is yet an unsatisfactory way of expressing it, and one which is perilously near nonsense. The point has been dealt with fully in an earlier chapter, and reference here is sufficient. But a second point may be briefly mentioned: If *all* we mean by "The Battle of Hastings is always earlier than the Battle of Agincourt" is, that at the time x (where x stands for *any* time) the statement

[1] I am indebted for the following points to Professor L. S. Stebbing, who kindly allowed me to see, in manuscript, an article on "Some Ambiguities in Recent Discussions on Time", published in a volume entitled *Philosophy and History*.

"the event H is earlier than the event A" is true: then by parity of reasoning all that we mean by "The event H is always past to the event A" would be "at the time x (where x stands for *any* time) the statement *the event H is past to the event A* is true". Now there is obviously something badly wrong with this: there are two interpretations, and both are undesirable. On the first, it would commonly be said that the reference to the time x is unnecessary: on the second, that the statement is *false* for some values of x.

There is, therefore, an essential difference in the types of analysis of which the A and the B series are susceptible. McTaggart saw this, but he expressed it in misleading language. The point is *not*, that the distinctions of the terms of the B series are 'permanent', while those of the A series are 'changing': but that the sense in which the former are 'permanent' is not one which can be properly opposed to 'change'. 'Permanent' is ambiguous: standing both for "continuing unchanged" (in time), and for "fixed with regard to . . . " The distinctions of the B series are of this latter type: it is only the temporal reference in the terms of the B series that makes the other view, and the consequent confusion, as plausible as it is.

Secondly, it may be held—perhaps unjustly—that McTaggart in his discussion of the "changing distinctions of the A series" is confusing the two radically different types of change, passage and alteration. Several passages can be adduced in support of this view. "Can we say that, in a time which formed a B series but not an A series, the change consisted in the fact that the event ceased to be an event, while another event began to be an event?"[1] "Change, then, cannot arise from an event ceasing to be an event, nor from one event changing into another. In what other way can it arise? If the characteristics of an event change, then there is certainly change. But what characteristics of an event can change? It seems to me that there is only one class of such characteristics. And that class consists of the determinations of the event in question by the terms of the A series."[2] Nevertheless, it could plausibly be held that verbal alterations would suffice to clear McTaggart of this charge. Similarly, the criticism of his view of change that, loosely expressed, "everything affects everything else", or that all relations are internal

---

[1] *Nature of Existence*, Sec. 310.

[2] Ibid., Sec. 311. See also Gotshalk's remarks (loc. cit.) on McTaggart's view of change.

in the sense that Moore defined and criticized,[1] though justified, is not very pertinent. A more important criticism, in this connection, of his view of 'change', is the obverse to the criticisms already discussed of his view of the nature of the B series.

Lastly, there is the logical aspect of his analysis of the A series which led him to his infinite regress. His method of analysis of, for instance, "The Battle of Waterloo is present" consists essentially in regarding the "Battle of Waterloo" as a fixed and determinate object, and the "now" as a curious protean mystery that moors itself on to different and ever different of these conveniently solid events. But there is another point of view, no less legitimate, which holds that "the battle of Waterloo" is essentially indeterminate, a descriptive phrase whose proper analysis demands a propositional function, and that the now-reference is the only determinate part of it. There are, of course, two separate parts to this criticism, and one might be urged independently of the other. The first part is the objection that events are not such fixed and static things, and that to conceive them as such is half way to the old idea of events standing in definite relations to each other and to the 'time' 'in' which they occur, and to the consequent hypostatization of time. The second one says simply that it is a mistake to regard 'now' as needing further analysis along the lines of "the now is what is now *now*", which will never yield classification, but that the reference to the 'now' is fundamental and sufficient. This view, of course, is similar to the earlier one which would make short work of all regresses, and like it, its premises are essentially metaphysical (though couched in logical terms). We have to choose between this view and McTaggart's: for their divergence is irreconcilable.

The conclusion reached, then, about McTaggart's arguments to prove the unreality of time, cannot be a decisive one. It is suggested that he is definitely wrong on one point, that the A series is contradictory, and that on several others some of his statements can be questioned. But the denial of the need to search for a hypothetical

[1] See his conclusive paper on "External and Internal Relations" in *Philosophical Studies*. McTaggart's remark, which is open to this criticism, was: "If anything changes, then all other things change with it. For its change must change some of their relations to it, and so its relational qualities. The fall of a sand castle on the English coast changes the nature of the Great Pyramid" (ibid., Sec. 309).

"timeless entity" does not leave us any better off with regard to the alternatives of begging the question and starting on a vicious infinite regress, and to that fundamental question, no definite answer can be given. To some it will seem that McTaggart was evidently right on this point: to others it will be just as evident that he was wrong. And that is as far as we can go.

The second part of McTaggart's remarks on time is on an entirely different footing. McTaggart, unlike most idealist philosophers, saw clearly that it is not sufficient to dismiss time contemptuously from Reality as being (in Bradley's phrase) "riddled with contradictions"—an explanation is needed to show how it is that we come, as we *do* come, to perceive things *as if* happening in time. McTaggart's brilliantly speculative attempt to provide this explanation is one of the most important achievements of modern thought.

At the outset, it will be well if one or two necessary warnings are made clear. The first is, that we cannot take the line of criticism which against every other philosopher is so easy and effective. We cannot say to McTaggart that he is presupposing the notion of time all along the line: for it is an essential part of his claim that he can do this with impunity. Against Russell, for example, it can be pertinently objected that he is all the time presupposing something more fundamental than the cognitive relations which he gives us. A better example is that of Aristotle, who defined time as the number of motion, without apparently realizing that motion essentially depends on the notion of time. But such a line of criticism is not open against McTaggart, since he was neither denying time completely, nor seeking to define it. He freely admits that what we call time is really an appearance, though he asserts that our perception of things as in time is a *mis*perception of a Reality that is fundamentally non-temporal. It may very well be the case that temporal language and temporal analogies, though insufficient to express the full nature and glory of Reality, are best suited to finite intellects, and so, in spite of their imperfections, there is a definite advantage in using them. It would be stupid to criticize McTaggart for using occasional temporal analogies. Consequently, within limits, we must allow McTaggart more latitude than we would allow anyone else.

Within limits. For there comes a point when this tolerance must be withdrawn, and this is not a contradiction. All the foregoing is *not* to be interpreted as asserting freedom from criticism on these grounds, but only that we must be more circumspect than usual before objecting. But it is perfectly logical to hold that McTaggart may use temporal language to make his meaning more easily apprehensible, and *also* to hold that he can be criticized like any other idealist if his meaning is *only* to be apprehended with a temporal interpretation. Thus, for instance, as will appear later, though we cannot rush madly in to criticize when he talks about 'eternity' as being in 'the future'[1]—as long as there is a reasonable doubt he must be given the benefit of it—if his conceptions are *fundamentally* temporal he can and must be criticized. But *where* the line is to be drawn I do not know: probably no two people would agree on this.

Lastly, it should be remembered that this portion of McTaggart's work, more than his arguments against the reality of time, is definitely linked up with his general metaphysical position, and depends on the adoption of certain postulates that are by no means universally accepted. Consequently it is probable that many people will soon find themselves in a position of ultimate disagreement. Hence their only chance of coming to a definite conclusion would be, in spite of its difficulty, by the way mentioned earlier, of seeing whether or not his ideas essentially presuppose temporal notions.

After this preliminary, a summary of McTaggart's views on time as contained in Book VI of *The Nature of Existence* can now be given.

"If we are to find a single cause for error, we must find it in close connection with the appearance of time, and with the reality on which that series is based."[2] This brief sentence is the key to McTaggart's treatment of time, since it brings out three important points. The first is that time, though not itself real, is really an appearance: and the second is that things appear to us as in time as the result of misperception. Lastly, temporal appearance is of very great importance (as witness the length with which McTaggart deals with it), since all error is closely connected with the primary illusion that we have that events are 'in' time. But to say that misperception is at the root of our experience of time is not sufficient, as McTaggart clearly saw: in order that misperception should

[1] See his article in *Mind*, 1909, which was later incorporated in *The Nature of Existence*, chapter lxi.   [2] Op. cit., sec. 521.

produce an A series, it must be a misperception of something that is a series already, though not a time series. This real, non-temporal series McTaggart calls the C series. Of course, the misperception must be attributed to the percipient and not to the thing perceived: thus the C series which is misperceived by G as a time-series in H is in H, but the fact of the misperception can only be accounted for by the C series in G. It follows from this view of time as an error in perception that there are as many time-series as there are selves who perceive things in time, since each apparent time-series is really the series of misperceptions in the percipient. (But, in fact, they are closely enough correlated to enable different people to talk as if there were one series, common to all.)

The next question is, what this C series can be. It is of little use to postulate such a series, and leave it at that: the rejoinder could too easily be made that we have no reason to believe in such a hypothetical series, and that we have, empirically, reason to believe in the time-series. The presumption must be against such a vague 'explanation', until more precise information about the C series is given. MacTaggart lays down, altogether, twelve conditions[1] which must be satisfied before any theory can stand. These are: (1) The terms must be parts of a spiritual substance, divided into infinite parts by determining correspondence. (2) The theory must allow both for correct and for erroneous cognitions. (3) The different kinds of error must be accounted for. (4) The series must be one-dimensional, transitive, and asymmetrical. (5) It must have at least as many terms as the B series. (6) The theory must explain how it is that we do not *perceive* things as being infinitely divided. (7) It must allow for the recurrence of certain contents of present experience. (8) It must allow for the apparent oscillations in the extent of our experience, (9) in clearness of perception, (10) and in accuracy of knowledge. (11) It must explain the relation of the C series to the apparent time-series. (12) Lastly, no two terms of the series can be in the same set of its parts, for though the terms of the C series are all parts of the self in which they fall, they do not form a set of parts of that self.

The conditions having been stated, McTaggart goes on to discuss the nature of the terms and the nature of relations in the C series. At first sight, it would seem plausible that the terms in

[1] *The Nature of Existence*, chapters xlvi and xlviii.

the C series should be those of the Determining Correspondence series, but this McTaggart rejects. For the C series is one-dimensional, the determining correspondence series two-dimensional: in the latter the terms have no definite *place*, as they have in the ordered C series: and, most important, only one part within any primary part of the determining-correspondence series can have the same direct determinant. Hence, if the C series is distinct from the determining-correspondence series, its terms must be simple and indivisible, because infinite divisibility is only possible if the parts are determined by determining correspondence. "My view is, then, that whenever a self (or a part of a self determined by determining correspondence) appears as being in time, it is divided in another dimension besides those of its determining correspondence parts, and that the terms in this fresh dimension form the C series."[1]

The relations of the C series are transitive, asymmetrical, one-dimensional, and one is the converse of the other (as, for instance, "earlier" in the B series is the converse of "later"). McTaggart rejects the relations of "more accurate" and "less accurate", "more extensive" and "less extensive", and "more clear" and "less clear", in favour of *"included in"* and *"inclusive of"*. Although the terms of the C series have intensive magnitude only, the existence of another series—the D series—whose terms have *ex*tensive magnitudes, is involved by it. The nature of the increments in not an increase or decrease in the extent, clearness, or accuracy of perceptions—but an "additional perception of the perceptum" (in a specialized sense which he explains).[2]

Granted that his treatment so far is correct, McTaggart's next task is to discuss the relations between the C series and the two misperception series.[3] Important as this chapter is, no new points are raised in it, and its contents can be briefly summarized by two quotations. "When any self, G, at any point in his own misperception-series observes H as in time—that is, as a B series—then it will be the case that some terms, at least, of the inclusion series of H form a C series for G—that is, are the basis of G's erroneous perceptions of a B series."[4] "We know of no other sort of relation, except time, as which it would be possible that the relation of inclusion should be misperceived."[5] Though it is not impossible, it is

[1] Op. cit., sec. 541.   [2] Op. cit., sec. 572.
[3] Op. cit., chapter xlix.   [4] Op. cit., sec. 581.   [5] Op. cit., sec. 588.

very improbable, that a self should misperceive the inclusion series of another self, or its own, otherwise than as in time. "The theory of error . . . is very closely connected with the illusion of time."[1]

The rest of the exposition can be briefly dealt with, in spite of its importance. McTaggart goes on to show that the inclusion series fulfils all the conditions laid down earlier for the C series: the presumption then is that their identification is correct. He next deals with four points that have proved stumbling-blocks to many theories of time, and in an extraordinarily fascinating chapter shows how they can be interpreted on his theory. First, he reverts to the question raised earlier, how, if time-perception is a subjective error and the number of time-series is very great, we can have any kind of a common time-series. The answer is, that though time is only an appearance, it is none the less a real appearance—if the apparent contradiction can be forgiven. In Leibniz's phrase, time is a "phenomenon *bene fundatum*." Again, the distinction we commonly make between 'real' and 'apparent' duration can be maintained. Though both are 'appearances', in a second sense of 'appears' we can rightly say that one is more fundamental than the other, since it is a "phenomenon *bene fundatum*", and the other is not. As regards the difficult question of the infinity of time, McTaggart replies that every inclusion series is bounded in both directions, and so, "While the series of such stretches appears as a series of periods in time, time will appear as being finite in each direction."[2] Lastly, the question whether time is or is not infinitely divisible McTaggart leaves open: for, as he points out, the fact that time has simple parts—which is all he is concerned to maintain—is consistent with any hypothesis about divisibility.

The whole position that he takes up in Book VI is summed up at the end when he says: "This explanation of the possibility of erroneous perception depends, indeed, as has just been said, on the unreality of time. But the assertion of the unreality of time can scarcely be said to be so improbable as to throw doubt on any theory which includes it, especially when we consider how many philosophers, from Descartes to the present day, have agreed,

[1] Sec. 610.
[2] Sec. 620. The 'stretches' referred to are stretches of the inclusion series.

while differing on so many other points, to deny the reality of time."[1]

Before going on to discuss the "Practical Consequences" in Book VII, it will be as well to halt and examine how far McTaggart is open to criticism on the counts mentioned earlier. I do not think that McTaggart has ever laid himself open to the criticism that his presuppositions are essentially temporal, though it is to be expected that this criticism would be more likely to enter in connection with Practical Consequences. Nevertheless, a slight suspicion remains that though he has not *presupposed* time, he has not succeeded in *eliminating* it. It would seem, at first sight, possible to say "But is the 'most inclusive' term earlier or later than the 'least inclusive' term?" He himself, does, as it happens, raise this question. We shall have to scrutinize with particular care his formulation of, and his answer to, this question, for it is very important. He would say that in answering this question he is only saying which relation in the *C* series corresponds to which relation in the *B* series: on the other hand, it might be possible to maintain that the question is important as *bringing in extraneous notions between which all thought of 'correspondence' is insufficient to explain their juxtaposition.*

There is little that can be said about these opposing views. It is evident that the metaphysical postulates on which McTaggart's arguments depend are not such as to be immediately acceptable to all. Although he does not, for instance, assert a specific connection between the hypothetical *C* series and the determining correspondence series, yet his view of the *C* series is dependent upon the latter, in the sense that if there were no determining correspondence series, the *C* series would have to be modified, since in his system everything is bound up with everything else. Now there are many who would assert that McTaggart's view of determining correspondence is logically unsound, and who would therefore look on his view of time with a sceptical eye. Others, confirmed realists, deny the *a priori* probability of a view which starts by asserting the unreality of time. Yet again others, who have no particular prejudice either for or against time, point out the lack of economy involved in postulating a *C* and a *D* series as well as apparent *A* and *B* series, instead of the plain man's *A* and *B* series. But these are metaphysical objections, and cannot be *logically* conclusive, since

[1] Sec. 692.

they consist in denying premises. But the prior question still remains, whether the premises of McTaggart or of his critic are the better ones, and here, as may be expected, an ultimate disagreement is reached, beyond which further progress is impossible.

In Book VII, McTaggart goes on to deduce two consequences of his theory of the C series that are important for his view of time. The first concerns the answer to the question "Which relation of the B series corresponds to which relation of the C series" and the second deals with the important but obscure doctrine of the "Futurity of the Whole".[1] He points out that the direction from earlier to later in the B series is more important than the direction from later to earlier: and also that the passage from less inclusive to more inclusive in the C series is more important than its converse. Hence, he argues, it is plausible to suppose that the more important sense in each case corresponds to the other. We may say, though not with certainty, with great probability, that it is the relation "inclusive of" which appears as "later than". From this follows directly the conception of a final state in which everything is included, and in which, unlike the earlier terms, which are unstable in the direction of the final term, there is perfect stability. This is the true eternity. McTaggart remarks: "The perception of the whole from its own standpoint is never a perception of it as present, yet it is a perception which has an important similarity with the perception of anything as present."[2] This similarity is, that the perception is correct and free from error. But apart from this rather metaphorical sense in which McTaggart agrees that eternity may be spoken of as *present*, he insists that it is a mistake to conceive of it under the temporal analogy of present. "The view which connects the eternal as such, or the universe as a whole, with presentness rather than with pastness or futurity is wrong."[3] If a temporal analogy is to be used, it is more correct to say that eternity is in the future than that it is in the present: since the last term in the C series, which is completely inclusive, is what would be called, in the language of the B series, the 'latest event'.

An obvious criticism to this, that McTaggart denies time and

---

[1] I do not propose to deal with the other consequences, such as immortality or pre-existence, though these bear on the subject of time. But they depend, in very great part, upon the conclusions reached on the other two topics. [2] Sec. 728. [3] Sec. 377.

yet talks of eternity as 'future', is forestalled by McTaggart himself. "Of course, if heaven is timeless it cannot be really future. But, as we have seen, it may, if certain conditions are fulfilled, be as much future, and as little past and present, as breakfast tomorrow is. . . . The conditions in question were that nothing should be really in time, that whatever appeared to be later than another thing should really have to it a certain non-temporal relation, and that this relation should hold between the events of to-day and heaven, as it holds between the events of to-day and to-morrow's breakfast."[1] This answer is satisfactory: but nevertheless I do not feel that the last word has been said upon the subject. Expressed slightly differently, the criticism would be that the conception only gains *meaning* because we know what 'future' is, and that the appearance of the word 'future' is not a mere incidence to be explained away by our psychological predilection to perceive things 'as if' in time. The same criticism applies more strongly to the talk of a 'final stage' and of a 'last term': I would suggest that these both presuppose the notion of time. If they do, then the presupposition is vicious, because they occur in fundamental places in the argument where their occurrence could not be excused as due to an attempt to make the argument more easily comprehensible. On the contrary, the words 'last' and 'final' are used to apply to the terms of the *C* series *as well as* to those of the *B* series. If this is so, then temporal notions are, *ipso facto*, assumed to be more fundamental than, or, at the very least, different from, the *C* series. It is one thing to say: "Temporal language is metaphorical and misleading, but if you must use it, then it is less wrong to say that eternity is future than that it is present or past": it is quite another to use as presuppositions of the whole argument the temporal notions that are later denied—and it is this last which is here criticized.

Secondly, as suggested earlier, it may be objected that McTaggart's correlation of 'earlier' with 'less inclusive' and of 'later' with 'more inclusive' is a *discovery*: that is, it is by no means an analytical, but a synthetic statement. In one sense, the criticism falls to the ground at once. For McTaggart never meant to say that the statement "Earlier corresponds to less inclusive" is a tautology, otherwise he would still be saddled with the temporal characteristics

[1] Sec. 739.

that he was trying to eradicate. But even allowing for a difference of emphasis, which he could safely admit, I think that the discrepancy between the two notions is more than he could allow. In other words, it is by no means tautologous to ask the question, "Is a more inclusive term earlier or later than a less inclusive one?" and McTaggart does in fact ask that very question. It would, however, be unfair to condemn him for *asking* the question, since the same objection could be twisted round to apply to *all* speculative philosophy. But if it be decided that his question was not merely rhetorical, that he might (though he did not)[1] have given the opposite answer to the question, we must, I think, grant that he was giving us new information when he said that "inclusive of" corresponds to 'later'. In that case, time and temporal notions are still being covertly regarded as extraneous and irreducible—not because they mean nothing, but because they mean too much. The criticism is an extraordinarily difficult one, because it is so easy to state it in a manner unfair to McTaggart: and when it has been discounted several times we are rather apt to rush to the opposite extreme and declare that there is nothing in it. Nevertheless, when all due allowances have been made, I think that the residue is justified, and that McTaggart does lay himself open to this criticism.

Thirdly, it is perhaps suspicious that, whereas in the chapter denying the reality of time, it is repeatedly insisted that the A series is essential to time, yet in the later parts the B series does duty almost exclusively for time, and the A series is hardly mentioned. By itself, this could hardly be called a criticism, but taken in connection with other dubieties, it has considerable weight. It is difficult to see, for instance, how the correspondence between the A series and the C series could be worked out. A possible criticism is, that the choice of the B series to mediate the transformation of temporal unreality into inoffensive C and D series is significant—is in fact almost an admission that all is not quite what it appears to be. For the B series is not a temporal *series*, though the *terms* which it relates are events. I would suggest that the passage from the B to the C series is successful in so far as the B series is *not* temporal: and that the difficulties mentioned above are due to the occasional

[1] McTaggart could retort that there is no question of 'might' since he did not. But this extreme view is not often held, and it is justifiable, indeed necessary, to depart from it to criticize him.

appearances of the skeleton in the cupboard! As long as the *B* series is taken as a series, all is well: but as soon as reference is made to the specifically *temporal* connotation of the series, trouble begins. The ghost of time cannot be permanently laid.

It will be seen that these criticisms, however they trick themselves out in logical garb, depend ultimately on a metaphysical postulate, which is nothing more impressive than a mere incredulity, a disinclination to believe that a complete elimination of time is possible. If it were not for that accompanying belief, the critic would find no cogency in the objections against McTaggart on that score: on the contrary, he would willingly accept McTaggart's brilliant arguments, and see no need to question them. No one, however, whether sympathetic or questioning, can fail to admire the splendidly courageous and original attempt to do what idealists, in general, have so signally failed to do—to build up a coherent and satisfying explanation of temporal appearances, on the foundation of a metaphysic which denies the reality of Time.

CHAPTER VIII

DUNNE

A SIGN of the growing importance of time in modern thought is the interest aroused by the publication of Mr. J. W. Dunne's two books, *An Experiment with Time* and *The Serial Universe*. The first is divided into two halves, one of which is a detailed and interesting account of some remarkable dreams, which led Mr. Dunne to formulate a theory of the future. Having gone so far, he decided to see whether it linked up in any way with accepted facts of everyday life, and whether it could be deduced from these facts. He came to the conclusion that it could, and the second portion of the book is an attempt logically to deduce from agreed first principles a *metaphysical* theory of time. This theory is in agreement with the results of his former empirical and psychological investigation, but, as Dunne himself points out, it is logically independent of them. Thus it is useless to criticize his metaphysical theory merely by saying that the dream-results are not scientific: equally we cannot discredit the dream-results by showing a neat array of fallacies on which the metaphysical theory is alleged to be based. If the dream-results can be substantiated—and Dunne's results are sufficiently interesting to stimulate investigation—it will mean that all future metaphysical theories about time must find room for revolutionary conceptions.[1] Theories (such as Broad's, for example) which hold that the future is nothing at all, will be ruled out: but that does not mean that Dunne's own theory is established.

Dunne's second book, *The Serial Universe*, repeats in an alternative form the arguments on which the theory of Serialism rests, and then applies the findings of Serialism to modern science. It is claimed that the Quantum Theory, for instance, can be exhibited as a consequence of Serialism. About this technical part, little will be said, firstly, because I am not qualified to deal with it, and

---

[1] Dunne is obviously right when, in his "Replies to Critics," he scoffs at those who, while accepting dream precognition, yet retain the old 'orthodox' view of time.

secondly, because it stands or falls with the theory of time. This chapter, then, will be mainly concerned with the theory of serial times as it is developed in these two books.

The notion of a regress as contained in time may be introduced by two quotations from Broad[1]: "We are naturally tempted to regard the history of the world as existing eternally in a certain order of events. Along this, and in a fixed direction, we imagine the characteristic of presentness as moving. . . . It is *present* at B when it is *past* at A. Thus all the problems which this analogy was invented to solve are simply taken out of other events to be heaped on that particular series of events which is the movement." And "We can hardly expect to reduce changes of time to changes in time, since time would then need another Time to change in, and so on to infinity."

The idea, then, that a certain method of analysing temporal predicates leads to an infinite regress is not peculiar to Dunne. But Dunne differs from Broad and McTaggart in his attitude to the regress. McTaggart regards it as a strong argument against the reality of time. Broad, though he does not go as far as McTaggart, considers a regress undesirable *per se*, and suggests that this type of analysis is fruitless *because* it leads to a regress. But Dunne not only considers a regress not undesirable: he sees in it the very nature of time itself, and the key to certain ultimate questions of psychology, and physics, and the philosophy of religion.[2] He reaches the infinite regress from an analysis of what we mean by 'now'. Obviously it is a relative term, belonging by divine right to no event, and constantly changing: what *was* present, *is* no longer present, and what *is* present, will not always be so. The tense reference remains: we must go a stage further back in our effort to find a unique reference for the 'now'. And so on *ad infinitum*—there (is) no such unique reference. Dunne makes this clearer by taking the example of three events, L, M and N, of which the first is past, the second happening now, the third in the future. Then I may write them $L(M)N$ with a mark round the present event M to show that it, and not one of the others, is now happening. Yesterday I should have written $(L)MN$, and tomorrow, perhaps, I shall write $LM(N)$. But *now* I am writing

[1] *Scientific Thought*, pp. 59–60 and 65.
[2] See *Serial Universe*, pp. 34–6, for a clear statement of his views on the utility of regresses.

$L(M)N$. It is obvious from this that the reference to tense is still not eliminated: faced by the alternatives $(L)MN$, $L(M)N$ and $LM(N)$, we have no valid reason for discriminating between them on that evidence alone. To show that the second of them is the correct one, we have to add another distinguishing mark—say by enclosing $L(M)N$ in an oblong. But, similarly, at a past date $(L)MN$ would be enclosed ... and so on. The infinite regress is fully launched.

```
3.      L        M       (N)
    ┌─────────────────────────┐
2.  │   L       (M)       N   │
    └─────────────────────────┘
2.          (L)      M       N
```

The preceding account is taken from *The Serial Universe*.[1] In the *Experiment with Time*, the same result is reached, but the language used often leaves Dunne open to the charge that he held an undesirably spatial view of time. As he expresses it in the *Experiment with Time*,[2] "We have seen that if time passes or grows or accumulates or expends itself or does anything whatsoever except stand rigid and changeless before a Time-fixed observer, there must be another Time which times the activity of, or along, the first Time, and another Time which times that second Time, and so on in an apparent series to infinity." The essential idea in *An Experiment with Time* is a development of the view of C. H. Hinton, as expressed in his book, *What is the Fourth Dimension?* Dunne summarized it very clearly as follows: "If AB were to travel thus" (in the direction indicated by the arrow), "the little bits of the full lines where these are intersected at C, D, E, F, G and H, would appear as moving either towards A or towards B —as moving, that is to say, in Space. ... A creature whose field of observation was thus limited to AB would be aware, therefore, of a little world of moving particles. But you and I, whose field of observation covers the whole diagram, perceive that the *actual bits* of the full lines intersected do not really move about on the page: what happens is merely that the sectional *views* of the lines move as our eyes follow the movement of AB. And the only thing which seems to us really to move over the page is the line AB. So, according to Hinton's theory, a being who could see

[1] Chapters vii and viii.   [2] P. 158. (References are to the Fourth Edition.)

Time's extension[1] as well as that of Space would regard the particles of our three-dimensional world as merely sectional views of fixed material threads extending in a fourth dimension, and would consider that the only thing in the entire Cosmos that really moved was that three-dimensional field of observation which we call 'the present moment'. Hinton assumes thus that the past and the future 'co-exist', and that our experience of change is due to a relative motion between this time extension and that 'narrow space and single moment' which is the present. But he refrained from noting that such relative motion must *take Time*."[2]

The essential point is the simplification such a generalization of

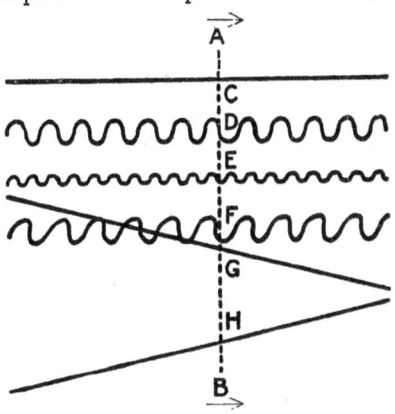

movement produces. Instead of numerous atoms 'moving in' space, we have objects *persisting:* all their apparent movements being replaced by the single movement of the present (that is, of time 1 in time 2). It does not, of course, get rid of *all* movement, and it is that fact that leads on to an infinite regress. At each stage in the regress the preceding time-dimension will be found to have 'turned into space'—but the reigning time-dimension itself 'takes time' over its movement, and is consequently superseded. As regards the 'turning into space', the conception may be illustrated by the familiar representation of time as a journey. The movement of

[1] This phrase seems suspiciously near to begging the question.
[2] *Experiment with Time*, pp. 139–40. A similar idea is expressed (in a much more readable form than in Hinton) in Abbott's *Flatland*, where the Flatlanders' mysterious circle, increasing and decreasing in size, is 'really' a sphere passing slowly through their plane. The extension of the idea to many dimensions is particularly noteworthy.

time is like a man walking along a road: every minute he has gone a bit farther than the preceding minute. Finally, he looks back and regards the *distance* he has traversed as a whole, artificially divided by him into what has been traversed (past) and what is still to be traversed (future). It is an essential point in Dunne's theory that the distinction between past and future is entirely subjective and epistemological, and that both have the same ontological status. But the originality and the fascination of Dunne's theory lies in his attempt to reconcile prediction with interference to falsify that prediction.[1] It is evident that if in a dream I saw myself in a motor accident, I should keep away from motors for a considerable time! Yet the prediction might none the less have been genuine, Dunne insists, as showing what *would* have happened *if* I had not interfered. Although the future is as objective as the past, I can interfere *now* in such a way as to modify the subsequent[2] course of the substratum.

Corresponding to the regress of times, there is a similar regress in the self-conscious observer. I am not only conscious, but conscious that I am conscious, and conscious that I am conscious that I am conscious . . . and so on endlessly, as Dunne shows in his example of the artist at the beginning of *The Serial Universe*. But, he points out, the first term of a series differs from all succeeding terms in the important respect of its lopsidedness. "In the *first* term of a series, the relation which links the terms is absent on one side: and this lopsidedness may have a very practical significance. Thus the first swing of a pendulum has no previous swing to determine it: it must be started by an external agency. The first furrow in a ploughed stretch differs in section from all the others. And the forces acting on the end members of our cantilever girder are balanced at the outer ends, not by pushes and pulls in similar members, as elsewhere in the series, but by the externally applied end-load."[3] From this he deduces the unendingness of both observer and time-series in all times except time 1—and this is, he claims, "the first scientific argument for human immortality".[4]

---

[1] *Experiment with Time*, p. 126 and pp. 219 ff.

[2] It seems to me that the word 'subsequent' here begs the question, and is a return to the common-sense view of the future. This point will be returned to later.

[3] *Experiment with Time*, p. 158.   [4] Ibid., p. 5. See also p. 197.

Added to which, in the *Serial Universe*, he relates his theory to modern scientific doctrines such as relativity, the quantum theory, Heisenberg's Principle of Indeterminacy: so that its importance, if it be substantiated, cannot be doubted. And even as far as time alone is concerned, when it is remembered that it treats of problems that are central to any metaphysical theory of time (such as the *A* series, the inexplicable 'movement' of the 'now', the irreversibility of time, the status of the future), its importance is in no danger of being under-estimated. The preponderance of destructive criticism in what follows is not to be interpreted as a lack of admiration for a very interesting synthesis.

The first criticism that can be brought against Dunne is that his conception of time is too spatial. As far as the *Serial Universe* (which is, in this respect, the better book) is concerned, this criticism is far from justified at first sight, and Dunne repeatedly warns his readers, that though he uses spatial illustrations, they must not be interpreted too literally. "We have nowhere used space order to represent time order. It is true that the counters in our bags[1] are spatially separated, but their space orders in the bags may be changed. . . . Next, we were particularly careful not to say that the now-marks *moved* from one state to another: for to do this would have been to declare that the states were being *presumed* to be spatially separated. We said, instead, that the marks 'changed from association with' the next in whatever series we had been hoping, previously, to regard as real time-order. The change, again, was not presupposed; it was discovered to be an empirical fact that our chance of interfering with any particular 'state' of the object system would vanish, and would be replaced by a chance of interfering with the 'state' which came next in what we were trying to regard as time-order."[2]

It must be remembered, too, that Dunne emphasizes the fundamental importance of the *A* series, and begins his analysis from it, and so we can assume that he did not start from a wholly spatial conception. It may be objected that his view eliminates time, since, at each stage, the preceding time-dimension turns into space, and if we stop the regress at any one point, we get an absolute and eternal 'now.' *But*, the fact of the regress remains unexplained and

[1] An example which he had taken as an illustration.
[2] *Serial Universe*, p. 81.

essentially temporal: after all, what is meant by 'preceding time-dimension'? The various dimensions are obviously irreversible.

The earlier book gives much more cause for the accusation. The quotation of passages said to exemplify spatialization, besides being irritating, is rather futile, since isolated passages may be made to prove anything: nevertheless dubious remarks are frequent.[1] A more important question to ask is whether Dunne's whole conception is spatial in its essence. The use of spatial diagrams in itself proves nothing: neither does the use of spatial language; but these, taken together with the 'turning' of time into space, the movement of the 'now' (seeming to posit a homogeneous medium through which the 'now' travels), and the citation of the *physical* scheme of Hinton, are more than suspicious.

The turning of time into space seems to me the crucial point, as it reappears, in a less blatant form, in the *Serial Universe*. We may take it for granted that it is an essential point in Dunne's theory, and see whether it can be shaken. At first sight, the criticism I wish to make appears merely a verbal one. If it is not, it goes to the whole basis of his theory.

When Dunne shows the regress involved in the analysis of the 'now', he rightly says that you cannot distinguish between the past state $(L)MN$, the present state $L(M)N$, and the future state $LM(N)$, by the first-term now-mark alone: to show that the state $L(M)N$ is the present one you need a second distinguishing mark. But he goes on to say that just as M is present, in first-term time, so "in the more comprehensive system known to us", LMN is present.[2] As it stands, this is going too far. It is not L, M and N that are present, but $L(M)N$ [as opposed to $(L)MN$ and $LM(N)$]—and the distinction between M, and L and N still remains. He might mean by the phrase, "present in the more comprehensive system known to us", that from the aspect of second-term time, we can see that there (is) no inherent difference between L, M and N, and that each (have) equal claims to be regarded as present. Thus, though there is (actually) a difference, and though M alone is present, it is contingent and might be otherwise—indeed, at another time it will be otherwise. If so, though it is a dubious use of 'present', it is valid enough. But

[1] For example, pp. 131, 148, 158, 165.
[2] See *Serial Universe*, pp. 77 and 90.

unfortunately it forms a convenient stepping-stone to the *different* view that, for second term time, there is *actually* no difference between L, M and N—and this step Dunne immediately takes by asserting that all three are "equally present". The question is, Is this view valid? If it is, his theory follows, in the spatialization of first-term time for second-term time. If not, it breaks down.

The phrase, "There is a difference between L and M", is ambiguous. (1) L and M may be of different stuff, for example, chalk and cheese. This has got nothing at all to do with time. When we are dealing with L, M and N as events, we are neither concerned to assert nor to deny that there may be differences between them in this sense. (2) There is a first-term temporal difference between L and M. M is different from L, because it *is* present and L *is* past. (3) The difference between L and M runs right through the temporal regress, apart from first-term time.

Nobody is likely to deny (2). The controversial one is (3), and Dunne would deny this. The point at issue, then, is not whether there is to ordinary experience a difference between M and L and N. Quite obviously, there is. But Dunne would say that this difference is *wholly* explicable in terms of first-term time, and that otherwise there is no difference: and in support of his view he adduces, what is hardly likely to be denied, that M's attribute of presentness is a contingent one, and that for second-term time, the first-term 'now' does not belong either to L or M or N. The question is whether his conclusion follows from this. After all, it may be said, the difference does run through the regress, in that we can never get rid of the 'now'. Then the 'present' for second-term time is not LMN, but $L(M)N$. To this Dunne might reply that it is only so because the second-term observer is using the first-term observer as his instrument, and so there is an essential reference to the first-term 'now', and a difference between M and L and N that is only then introduced. Here we reach two contrary assertions: that the difference does run through the regress and that it does not. I do not think that Dunne anywhere proves that it does not (it may even be inconsistent with his main position), and his conclusion does not follow logically. But that does not mean that the contrary assertion is justified, and Dunne may very well be right nevertheless. The point I wish to make is, that the omission of the first-term now-mark is not necessarily the obvious fallacy that it certainly seems at first, but opens up a very deep and perplexing problem. (Whether the problem *is* a problem on any other premises than Dunne's, is another matter.)

A second criticism, related to that of undue spatialization, is concerned with Dunne's use of the idea of movement 'in' time. Suppose that a man looks back over a number of past events. There is an evident and an unexceptionable analogy between this procedure, and looking back over a road traversed. We may, after Hinton's "narrow moving slit", which represents our present, has passed on, look back on past events and see them, as it were, all spread out together at once: But does it follow from that that we so conceive them *as they are happening?* Dunne seems to think it does: he tacitly assumes (what Bergson denied) that what is true of time passed may also be true of time passing. By this he may be begging the question: the essence of time, to put it very crudely, is in the happening of events rather than in their having happened.

Further, the notion of a 'thing moving in time' is one that demands further analysis. Dunne says that anything which moves in time must take time for its movement.[1] "We have seen that if Time passes or grows or accumulates or expends itself or does anything whatsoever except stand rigid and changeless before a Time-fixed observer, there must be another Time which times that activity of, or along, the first Time, and another Time which times that second Time, and so on in an apparent series to infinity."[2] From this comes the notion of the second-term time that is 'taken' by the movement of the first-term 'present'.

There seems to be a possible ambiguity in the phrase, "a thing moves in time". If only it were possible to find and formulate a non-spatial interpretation of 'moving in time', half the difficulties and the fallacies would be at once removed, I think.[3]

When a material object moves, it moves in space and its movement takes time. But to extend the anology and to say that the present 'moves' in space and that this movement can itself be timed,

---

[1] *Experiment with Time*, p. 144. See also pp. 172–3.   [2] Ibid., p. 158.
[3] His best statement is to be found ibid., p. 190 n. "Note the distinction drawn here between events in a system observed and observational events. The entire 'regress' of Time depends upon the fact that these two classes of events cannot be allotted positions in a single dimension."

is a very doubtful conception, and Dunne himself seems to recognize this, and attempts to avoid it. "It may be urged that the admission of this behaviour of the 'now-mark' is an admission that the states are separated in the same way that points in space are separated. Quite so. But this new view of the relationship between the states is a *development* of our original less explicit view—a development forced upon us by the logical development of the regress. The new view is one which we have endeavoured to avoid, and had successfully avoided up till that moment. It is a consequence of the regress, not a primary supposition causing the regress."[1] Nevertheless, he is not wholly successful in avoiding the criticism. He says, "The employment of references to a sort of Time behind Time is the legitimate consequence of having started with the hypothesis of a *movement* through Time's length."[2] That may be so, but the crucial question is whether this hypothesis is legitimate or not. The 'movement' of the 'now' has nothing in common with the movement of objects in space except the name: and it would be highly desirable to remove this verbal ambiguity. To say that the present moves is a bad statement which, if taken seriously, as Dunne takes it, is bound to lead to an infinite regress. Broad points out that if we think of the 'now' as a moving circle of light cast successively on different houses in the street by a policeman's lantern,[3] we can rightly say, "It illuminates No. 30 before No. 32 . . . " and that leads to an infinite regress. Certainly the movement of a lantern can be regarded as 'taking time': the question is whether the now (is) really analogous to the movement of a policeman's lantern. If it is, the rest follows: but it seems to be an undue hypostatization of time. I agree with Broad[4] that if we take the first step upon the regress, there is no halt short of infinity, but that there is no necessity at all to take that step. Put shortly, time is nothing apart from the happening of events (probably Dunne would agree to this[5]): are we justified in considering *that events happen* is itself an event? If so, then this new

[1] *Serial Universe*, pp. 81–2.   [2] *Experiment with Time*, p. 131.
[3] Broad, *Scientific Thought*, p. 59. I hope that in substituting Broad's example for Dunne's, where the fallacy is intentionally clearer, I have not misrepresented Dunne. See also Bradley, *Logic*, p. 54 (Second Edition).
[4] In his article on Dunne (*Philosophy*), 1935.
[5] See *Experiment with Time*, pp. 140–1.

event has temporal relations, but on a different level from the others ... and so on to infinity. If not, the phrase "the velocity of the *now*" is nonsense, and question-begging nonsense at that.

Or, to put the point in still another way, Dunne is regarding 'now' as an adjective or property like red or green. If we had to render consistent the two statements "*X* is red" and "*X* is not red", we should, as Broad showed,[1] say that they were not contradictory because they were true *at different times*. Dunne is inclined to analyse '*E* is *now*' and '*E* is not *now*' in a similar manner, saying that they are true *at different times*. But, although ordinary language might appear to support this, it is only because of an analogy with '*X* is red'—an analogy which is bound to be misleading because in the first case '*X*' stands for a *substance*, while '*E*' is an *event*, and because 'now' is *not* an adjective like red, but is an elliptical statement for "*occurring now*".

Thirdly, even assuming that the regress be valid, Dunne is never very explicit as to *how* exactly it is supposed to be explanatory of time, and he leaves essential parts very vague. In some places he seems to hold that time is the last term of the regress, that all the others are masquerading as time, but that each, from the point of view of the next higher dimension, turns out 'really' to be spatial; and in other places he seems to hold that the regress itself is time. This uncertainty is shown very clearly in his conception of the serial observer, which, like the time-series, is regressive. Usually he holds that the observer is 'the same' to infinity, but there does not seem to be much room left anywhere for other observers. Although Dunne says: " 'Observer at infinity' does not mean an observer infinitely *remote* in either Time or Space. 'Infinity' here refers merely to the number of terms in the series. The observer in question is merely your ordinary everyday self, 'here' and 'now' "[2]—he does not always stick to it. And the distinction between the 'observer at infinity' and the 'superlative general observer' who appears at the end of the "Experiment" is rather difficult to follow. But, however sceptical we may be of the possibility of working it out in detail, this conception of a regressive self-conscious observer is a very interesting one. In

---

[1] *Scientific Thought*, p. 62.

[2] *Experiment with Time*, p. 188. See also pp. 190 and 200, and *Serial Universe*, chapter lv.

many ways it is comparable to that of Leibniz' monads—in both there are degrees of 'clear perception', the continuity from the lowest to the highest is unbroken, and an endless relativity is involved. As in Leibniz, it is not clear whether God is the highest monad or outside the series of monads, so in Dunne, we are never sure whether the observer is the last term in the regress, or the whole sum of terms. Then, too, there is the same difficulty about interaction among the monads or observers. It would be very interesting if the likenesses and differences between the two were fully worked out.

To return from the digression—Dunne's conception of the observer is very unsatisfactory, and particularly in that *each* observer is implied to have his *own* regress of times, differing very slightly from those of other observers, it is true, but still differing. The whole network Dunne describes[1] seems to be a hypostatization of relativity doctrines, with the difference that each and all is supposed to have some kind of objective existence. This last sentence is vague, but that cannot be helped.

But more important for our immediate purpose than the unclearness of Dunne's views of an 'observer' is the corresponding uncertainty of his meaning in the time-regress itself. On the one hand, there is time as continually 'turning into space'—"Are we to try to imagine the more comprehensive system as embracing two kinds of time? Certainly not: the more comprehensive system possesses only one time order. . . . It contains, also, all present, the items of the time-order indicated by L, M and N: but that order is not time-order—in the more comprehensive system of affairs."[2] On the other hand, there is time as the regress. "In that way only—by the employment of this flagrantly regressive method of description—have we been able to convert our otherwise irrational knowledge into a systematic and serviceable scheme."[3] Again, this uncertainty as to his real meaning is reflected in the thoroughly dubious use of "absolute Time" and "absolute motion" in the earlier book. He says, for instance,[4] "The analysis will

[1] *Experiment with Time*, pp. 228 ff.
[2] *Serial Universe*, p. 77.
[3] Ibid., p. 35. See also *Experiment with Time*, p. 159, and *Serial Universe*, p. 91.
[4] pp. 186–7. Italics mine. See also ibid., pp. 204 and 290.

continue in the same fashion *to infinity*. There we shall have a single multi-dimensional field of presentation *in absolute motion*, travelling over a fixed substratum of objective elements extended in all the dimensions of Time.... At infinity, again, we shall have a Time which serves to time all movements of or in the various fields of presentation. This Time will be '*Absolute Time*', with an *absolute past, present and future*. The present moment of this absolute Time must *contain* all the moments 'past', 'present' and 'future', of all the subordinate dimensions of Time." This is really a very queer statement, and is the abandonment of what Dunne was chiefly concerned to emphasize—the subjectivity of past and future, and the unendingness of the regress. As Broad remarked,[1] it is a contradiction to talk of 'absolute Time' at the end of the regress, since the regress, by hypothesis, has no end. We shall be concerned later with his doubtful view of the future, and it is sufficient to remark here that the amazing persistence of past and future even in the absolute—amazing because of his reiterated assertion of their relativity—is due to an attempt to hedge, and to smuggle the common-sense notions in at the back door.

But even if Dunne had made up his mind between the two possible views of time as regressive, and had avoided a dubious absolute, a further criticism remains. It may be true, as Dunne insists—though reasons were given earlier for doubting it—that time *involves* a regress, but it does not thereby follow that the regress can *explain* time. And in fact Dunne has never properly worked out how a regress is supposed to give an explanation. He and Hinton may be right in asserting that all apparent movements of particles may be explained by one generalized movement in a higher dimension, but though, to a scientist, the possibility of reducing all movements to one generalized movement is attractive by reason of its greater simplicity—and it is evidently a much simpler conception—yet that does not help the metaphysician, because he is still confronted with *a* movement, and the need of finding an explanation for it. In other words, granted movement as a physical fact, it may be possible to get a simpler *physical* explanation in terms of Hinton's extra dimension. But this cannot be held to explain the *possibility of movement* itself, since *one* movement has always to be postulated. And with movement

[1] In the article referred to.

outstanding and unexplained, we have not eliminated time.[1] We cannot explain 'time' by the escapades of derivative 'times' that are really space; for at each stage of the regression 'time' itself eludes us. Dunne admits and emphasizes this, but the true conclusion to draw from it is neither that time 'is' the regress, nor that it is the last term in the regress (between which conclusions he wavers), but that the one thing which we do *not* get by the regress is time, which eludes us at every step. The regress, then, is not in any way *explanatory* of time: for the essential point which embarking on an infinite regress teaches us is, that at whatever term we stop, we are still confronted with time, in its pristine, unexplained splendour. For to say that a certain method of analysis of temporal facts (a vicious one, in my opinion) leads to an infinite regress does not mean that time *is* that regress. Dunne never saw this.

The last part of this chapter will be taken up with some remarks on prediction and the status of the future—both very important questions. For it stands to reason that if genuine prediction occurs, we should have to moderate the full blast of any Bergsonian argument against the spatializing of time, through conceiving of the future in a way analogous to the past. But that would not affect the other criticisms that have been made. *If* there is prediction, that disposes of Broad, but it does not necessarily justify Dunne, for as he himself rightly points out,[2] his *metaphysical* theory and his dream-evidence are logically independent of each other, though his position is, naturally, strengthened by having two separate lines of argument to go upon. It will be convenient to follow Dunne's practice, and treat of the two topics separately, but before doing this, it is advisable to make one point clear. That is, that in so far as Dunne means by 'prediction' a more or less probable forecast, he escapes the chief criticisms that can be directed against the notion of prediction, since nobody would doubt that we can make more or less probable statements about the future. On the other hand, if this is all that he means, his work loses in importance, and there is no need to construct a metaphysical theory postulating the equal status of past and future to

---

[1] Reasons were given above for rejecting this conception of movement and time. But, on Dunne's own principles, it follows that, to put it crudely, though all movements except one are eliminated, this one remains unexplained and inexplicable. [2] *Experiment with Time*, p. 198.

explain statements that are merely probable. It seems that here again Dunne hedges between two views: the one, postulating *certain* predictions, of the highest interest and importance if it can be substantiated: the other, more trivial, but also less paradoxical to hold. In what follows, I shall treat only of the first view, as long as it be remembered that there are passages[1] supporting the second.

Firstly, with regard to the dream results given in *An Experiment with Time*, they form a remarkable collection not lightly to be set aside. Granted that it is not scientific evidence, it is not easy to see how such could be collected on this point. And Dunne nowhere can be accused of stretching a point in his own favour: if anything, he under-estimates his cases for precognition. That is, on his own principles, if precognition is regarded as *equally* possible with retrospection. But that is just what seems to me questionable. I must admit to a prejudice against precognition, and to a wish to attribute a dream-event to anything *but* precognition. I hope that this is not a pigheadedness which flies in the face of *facts*. I prefer to think that the facts can be interpreted differently according to whether we start in favour of, or against, the *possibility* of prediction. This implies a metaphysical position, which will be defended in another chapter: assuming for the present that it is defensible, the pleasant conjurer's task of explaining Dunne away will occupy the next few pages.

In what follows, I shall not attempt to dispute the evidence that Dunne adduces, but to see whether 'precognitive' dreams cannot bear any other interpretation.

In the first place, there is the possibility of mistakes. Besides the obvious mistakes of identifying a merely general dream with a particular event, and of attributing a dream of a past event to a future event—mistakes which only insistence upon corroborative detail can avert—there are others, more difficult to pin down and therefore more insidious. We all have a strange feeling at times as if we had remembered something, or had seen it before. Dunne suggests that our vague stirrings of memory and our feelings of '*déjà vu*' are to be attributed to precognition. Nevertheless, alternative explanations can be given. The similarity, which gives us the feeling of familiarity, may be in the thought content (or general context) of the two occasions, not in any special 'belonging

[1] Op. cit., pp. 219, 223, 224, 227.

togetherness' of them. Lloyd Morgan gives an excellent example of this:[1] the two occasions are readily seen to be similar and could easily be classified together as "two occasions when I was walking with X", "two occasions when I talked about Y", "two occasions when I was in the neighbourhood of Z", etc. It is no wonder that one should revive the other: but that is very different from saying *either* that the latter is only a memory of the former *or* that the former is a precognition of the latter. To rush headlong into either of these two statements is in effect to deny that experiences can be roughly classified under groups. Again, it is common knowledge that while some of our associations are fairly easy to trace, others are peculiar to ourselves, and give a bias to our thoughts which it is difficult to explain on 'rational' grounds. Recently, I was trying to remember the phrasing of Wordsworth's ode:

"Though nothing can bring back the hour
Of splendour in the grass. . . ."

At that point the word "insufferable" flashed into my mind, and refused to depart. It linked itself insistently with "splendour"—a queer conjunction, certainly, and one that had nothing to do with Wordsworth. I remembered in the end De Quincey's phrase in the *Opium Eater*—"fretted with insufferable splendour", and was satisfied.[2] This example is intended to show the tangential behaviour of our thoughts, and that associations can remind on grounds which are, objectively, insufficient. The very irrationality of some of these darts of thought makes us feel that there is a missing connection somewhere, and we are tempted to overdo it by harking back to the *whole* previous incident, instead of to the one aspect of it which is relevant.

Secondly, there is always a preponderance of the past in a mixture of familiar things, though we are liable to overlook their familiarity, and attend to their new grouping. Most people have an idea what a place—Oxford, for instance—'looks like'—a generic image of colleges and lawns and churches. We have all seen churches and lawns, and photographs of well-known 'views' of Cambridge, and perhaps have read *The Scholar Gypsy*. It is

[1] *Emergent Evolution*, p. 125.
[2] An interesting point is that that is *not* De Quincey's phrase, which is ". . . into insufferable splendour that fretted my heart".

only the grouping which is unknown, but we are liable to forget how much was already familiar, if our generic image should be anything like the real thing. Or again, blending may result in a whole which answers fairly well to an altered object: thus a man may leave his birthplace at the age of seven, and never return to it until he is sixty. In the interval his memories become increasingly vague: he attributes to it a hideous red brick market-hall (that he has seen elsewhere) instead of the old one, and wider roads, large shops, 'super' cinemas, a new bank in the centre of the town, and ugly suburbs. As much the same thing is happening everywhere, he may very well be right in his so-called 'memories', and, coming back, may 'recognize' the bank and market-hall that had only been built five years, and later, when he learns this, attribute his 'knowledge' to prediction or second sight.

But prediction is not mere 'seeing A, and A comes true'. Though where we are to draw the line in all these examples between a more-or-less right general agreement, which is otherwise explainable, and the particular grasp of detail which predictions claim, is difficult to say. The distinction is a matter of plausibility, and cannot be made absolute. If A is sufficiently unlike anything we might reasonably expect, if it cannot be traced to anything else, if the number of alternatives of equal antecedent probability to A is great, the prediction is admitted, but as this is a pragmatic, not a logical test, it is always open for an opponent to hold that the 'prediction' was not genuine. For, lastly, it is very difficult to evaluate the probability of a dream, and proportionately easy to mistake coincidence or general correspondence for a particular prediction. Thus a man may dream that he is in a railway carriage with a number of market-people. He may rarely travel by rail, and he dislikes crowds: consequently this is a rare event. But the number of alternative modes of travel is after all limited: if his car breaks down—and this may just as well happen on market day as on any other day—and he is too old to cycle, and too lazy to walk, and his business is essential, the train is the only alternative. We are apt to assess probabilities inaccurately.

The unconscious is very much to the fore nowadays, and granted the basic principles of modern doctrines of the unconscious, some 'predictions' can be explained away. We may be unconsciously influenced to choose our subsequent actions in accordance with a dream. I dream that I am at X where I very rarely go, and only remember this dream when, a day or so later, I am at X. The memory has been latent, and has influenced my choice of an expedition. In such cases, are we to say that the action was because of the dream or vice versa? Again, there are accredited cases of unconscious perception. I see S, and 'forget' that I have seen it. A child who once saw Oxford when he was very young, may have a vivid and detailed dream of one street a night or two before he is going to Oxford, as he thinks, for the first time. Or S may be such as to make T probable—and I, unconsciously perceiving S and inferring from it to T, may dream that T happens, and be genuinely unable to realize *why* I dreamt of T. In cases of sudden illness, A, apparently in the best of health, may dream beforehand that he is seriously ill. It is not far-fetched to say that such cases may be due to unconscious knowledge all the time that he is not as well as he seems, and not to prediction. Finally, the distinction between the apparent and latent content of dreams makes it very difficult to say offhand to what the dream 'refers'.

Thirdly, whenever we think, plan or remember, it may be said loosely that our minds wander through time in an analogous fashion: planning in particular is important in connection with prediction. We do not, rightly, find any particular mystery in the fulfilment of our plans, and many dreams are of the planning type. Wish-fulfilments and fantasies are at least potential plans. Again, the persistence of an idea as well as its objective probability counts in evaluating the worth of a 'prediction'. It is not probable that a long-lost uncle will bequeath to me a million pounds: but if that chimerical fantasy were often in my mind, it would not be very strange if I dreamt of it shortly before the unexpected happened. We must, then, interpret 'unexpectedness' in two senses before we assess the probability of occurrences, and as well as the objective probability, we must remember the subjective attitude of mind. This second factor is often forgotten.

Fourthly, the foresight may be purely intellectual, as in the case of general prophecies. Economic crises follow wars: a cycle of good harvests cannot last for ever, and seven lean kine follow the fat ones: given the nature of Napoleon's activities in Europe, it was not difficult to foresee that his rule would not be a stable one: a railway time-table forecasts with fair accuracy the movements of trains: by induction from past low-pressure systems a fall in the barometer is believed to herald bad weather. But such intellectual foresights must be clearly distinguished from predictions proper. Swift has provided us[1] with a neat little distinction between the 'cause' of a man's death and the 'predicter' of it. How far would Isaac Bickerstaff have been regarded as hastening the end of Mr. Partridge, if, after the prediction that Mr. Partridge would die on a certain day, Mr. Partridge had taken the hint?

Explaining away one unknown faculty in terms of another unknown faculty is a highly undesirable procedure. Still, if, as seems probable, we have finally to admit the existence of what we now call 'supernormal faculties', it may be advisable to remember that some of the phenomena of telepathy and psychic research could account for some puzzling examples of 'precognition', without the need of postulating precognition as well. A man dreams of an event which actually happened some time before his dream, but which he is positive he did not know about. Shortly after he dreams it, he hears of it, as he avers, for the first time. In such cases, the fact that the event had happened *before* the dream makes unnecessary the postulation of precognition if telepathy is admitted. And, of the two, the latter seems to me much the less incredible.

Lastly, if all other explanations fail, there is always coincidence.

It is inevitable that these diverse explanations should ill bear comparison with Mr. Dunne's single explanation, and his discreet and scrupulous method of using it. Granted an equal antecedent probability, there can be no doubt which explanations should be accepted. But it seems to me that the notion of prediction raises so many difficulties that it is not worth having, and that in the long run the more cumbrous explanations above will prove simpler. These difficulties can only be stated here: they seem to me to be final. First, of course, there is the difficulty of interference, as Dunne recognizes. A prediction predicts what will happen; if then it does not happen, how can the prediction be a genuine one? But besides this evident difficulty, there are two others, less easy to see, but, I think, no less fundamental. What *exactly* do we mean when we say that we dream *of* a future event? What is the relation between dream and event such that the word 'of' can rightly be used? Thirdly, a stricter notion of cause is required: and my fundamental objection to prediction is not that some predictions do not come true, but that prediction is essentially incompatible with causality.

[1] *Bickerstaff Papers.*

METAPHYSICS—DUNNE

The rest of this chapter will be concerned with Dunne's metaphysical basis for his belief in precognition, and with his view of the general status of the future. The first difficulty mentioned above, that of intervention to alter, can best be dealt with in this connection: the other two must be postponed to another chapter, since Dunne never attempts to deal with them.

The distinction between past and future is one which exists only for time 1: for time 2, all events are equally 'present'. "Every Time-travelling field of presentation is contained within a field one dimension larger, travelling in another dimension of time, the larger field covering events which are 'past' and 'future', as well as 'present', to the smaller field."[1] The sole distinction between past and future, then, is the empirical one that observer 1, as a matter of fact, confines his attention to a single point in time 1, and travels slowly up it. Dunne must, of course, on these principles reject Bergson's view of a fundamental 'becoming'. He says, "In unnecessary addition, we have it that these extended objects must be conceived as being perpetually added to by a process of *creation*. This is a very strange proposition, and one for which we have no evidence whatsoever."[2] But I doubt whether it *is* possible to get rid of becoming: it is inescapable, and Dunne himself has to admit that AB 'moves along' in time 1. It seems to me more unnecessary than Bergson's view to assume: (1) At the moment Y, the whole contents of X-Z are objectively 'there'; (2) the movement of AB,

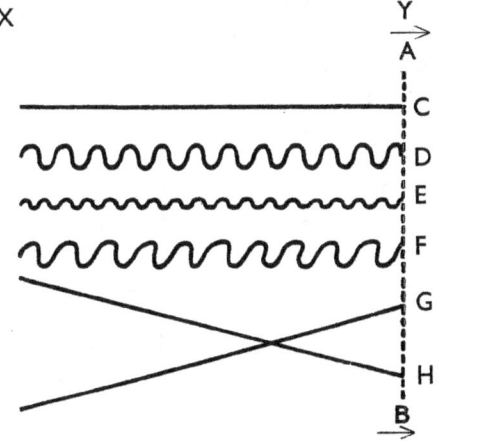

[1] *Experiment with Time*, p. 187. See also the corresponding passages in *Serial Universe*, already referred to.   [2] Ibid., p. 152. See also pp. 153–6.

which involves the 'becoming' to which Dunne objects, and also an extra dimension. Dunne cannot criticize Bergson on the score of economy: and to say that AB 'moves along' 'in' 'time 1'—which has already been criticized—is certainly no less dubious than is the notion of 'becoming'. To say that there is not a particle of evidence for 'becoming' is tantamount to saying that there is not a particle of evidence for the movement of AB in time 1. But probably what Dunne meant is that there is no evidence for 'becoming' as ultimate and irreducible, in which he may be right—though it is doubtful whether his own regressive system ever succeeds in eliminating or explaining becoming.

But the main criticism I wish to make is not against his rejection of 'becoming': it is that Dunne is running with the hare and hunting with the hounds in his view of the future. He asserts a view that is far removed from, and incompatible with, the common-sense one, yet he reverts to this on occasions. He is trying to have it both ways: in a very real sense—not merely a 'first-term time' sense, due to our limitations—A must happen *before B*, or else at A we could never modify the course of events, so that the predicted B does not occur. I suggest that the temporal language Dunne uses in this connection is significant: "He may never encounter the cerebral event . . . perceived in the dream—and may, instead . . . encounter a totally different event."[1] How is this to be interpreted? Also: "It is to be noticed that these breaks in the verticals are to be regarded, not as fixed substratum features which exist before (in absolute Time) observer 1 reaches O, but as *changes* in that substratum which occur at the instant when (in absolute Time) this observer reaches that point."[2] What is "absolute Time" but a confession that some events must occur before others, in a sense that is not merely due to our limitations?

It may be said that Dunne never denied the before-and-after relation—all he denied was the objectivity of past, present and future. But, in the first place, the former gains its essential meaning from the latter: and in the second place, if all events, as Dunne insists, are equally 'present',[3] it is difficult to see why the before-after relation should go from A-B, rather than from B-A. On Dunne's principles it would seem to be indifferent which we choose.

[1] *Experiment with Time*, p. 219. [2] *Ibid.*, p. 221. See also p. 226.
[3] *Serial Universe*, p. 82.

But though denying that 'events' are really in the future, he reverts to the more usual belief whenever it is convenient. An example will make my criticism clearer. In chess, I may plan an attack. Half-way through, at M, I realize that if I continue as I had intended, I shall inevitably be mated at N. But if I change to defence,

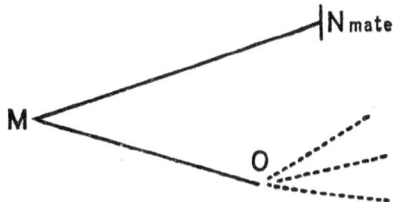

there is a chance that at O I may escape, and this in fact happens. But that I can modify my proposed plans, and reach O instead of N, does *not* mean that both cannot be 'really' future to me at M —on the contrary, the whole point of the situation is that M *does* occur before either N or O—otherwise there would be no object in my interfering at M.

I suggest that on the one hand, Dunne conceives of past, present and future spread out, and all equally accessible: and that on the other he reverts to the common conception of M being before N. In other words, 'first-term time' persists throughout. This, it will be remembered, was a point left undecided in an earlier criticism: that it should *not* do so was then his only loophole against a charge of fallacious reasoning. It is with regard to the future that the worst consequences of a too spatialized conception of time are revealed. Dunne's view of the future as being both 'there' and 'alterable' (which is a tacit admission that it is 'later than' what we do in the present) is, to put it bluntly, far too good to be true.

To sum up, the main defects of Dunne's theory of time are those resulting from spatialization and a too ready identification of time in its passage with time as passed. This leads to the fallacious view of time being taken by the 'movement' of time, and the idea that the 'now' has a velocity. It also results in the unsatisfactoriness of a regress which explains nothing, and in the thoroughly undesirable conception of the future. Lesser criticisms, such as that of failure to work out in detail the notion of an observer, only emphasize the fundamental defect.

But, at the end of a chapter given chiefly to destructive criticism, it must be emphasized that this is so because, among the very many advantages and obvious importance of Mr. Dunne's work, defects which are less striking but, I think, none the less radical, are apt to be overlooked.

NOTE

Mr. J. W. Dunne has kindly supplied the following statement:—

What is declared on page 90 of *The Serial Universe* to be 'present in the more comprehensive system known to us' is L M N *plus* ( ), the latter 'now-mark' being observer 1. L M N, regarded alone, represents a series of events in an objective world which the describer regards as existing independently of observer 1. This series is granted only those characteristics which are strictly necessary to a physicist's temporal sequence; that is to say, it exhibits an irreversible causal relation of earlier and later which I, following Eddington, style 'entropy order', but its describer attributes to it no *inherent* first-term 'now'. The physics of cause and effect recognizes no reality distinction between L, M and N.

The foregoing is the view of observer 2, who has been compelled to bring observer 1 into the picture. The latter individual, unaware of the part he plays in the matter, would describe the series of objective events as L (M) N, the 'now-mark' being inherent in the series so that (M) alone is real. Consequently, he does not spatialize time and is a pure Bergsonian. But (M), which he labels real, becomes M labelled unreal; so there is still a passage of the series of objective events (rendered possible by the fact that these are objective), and a regress, not the consequence of a spatialization of time, is fairly launched. But the second-term 'now' attributes equal second-term reality to four items: L, M, N and the present state of ( ), or observer 1. L, M and N become apparent then as point-events in a relativistic space-time continuum over which motion is possible. And the mysterious first-term 'now' turns out to be the first-term 'self.'

Observer 2 is a Bergsonian. Time, to him, is a fifth dimension and non-spatial, while he regards the past states of observer 1 as unreal. Observer 3 reinterprets that view after he has brought observer 2 into the picture . . . and so on.

The theory professes to show that the attempt of any observer to propound a metaphysics based upon observation must follow the lines of an infinite regress, and it claims that this regress, amounting to a perfectly logical account of how any possible external world would be bound to affect its observer, should be valid in experience if such external world exists. The physical tests of this claim (in *The Serial Universe*) and the psychological tests (in *An Experiment with Time*) provide, thus, the proofs of the existence of an external world and, so, a refutation of solipsism.

Needless to say, such a theory is not necessarily concerned with 'explaining' or 'getting rid of' time. Its value is that it provides new information, and it is this which distinguishes a valid regress from a 'vicious' circle.

J. W. DUNNE

PART II

CHAPTER IX

PREDICTION

I

THE power to predict future events has been claimed by many, by prophet and charlatan, by mystic and hysteric, from Joseph to the present day. Yet it is not a universal faculty, and those who lack it (or, *pace* Mr. Dunne, have never noticed it) are apt to be incredulous when confronted with alleged instances of precognition. Perhaps it is this lack of agreement about the possibility of precognition as well as the general interest it arouses —for who is there who has never wished to know, before deciding on a course of action, what the outcome of it will be?—which accounts for the avoidance of it by philosophers. What everyone dabbles in, is not likely to be the subject of a scholarly monograph. Yet it is an important topic, and one which it is necessary to get clear about before a satisfactory view of time can be reached. To Mr. Dunne is due the credit for the general, if belated, recognition of this.

If I say that a dream or a prophetic vision or a sudden foreboding was a genuine example of precognition, what do I mean by this? In the first place, I do not merely mean that I 'see' E, and that at a later date E 'happens'. At present, I have a grotesque mental image of A (a Londoner) sitting blissfully in the 'chair' on Cader Berwyn in his full City regalia. It is possible, though unlikely, that this will happen: but I have no intense, inner certainty that it will. On the contrary, the more I think of it, the more chimerical this pleasing sight seems. But genuine precognition is, as it were, anchored: it does not float through the mind as a pleasant or terrifying fantasy, but is insistent that it is to be related to actuality. If precognition is not distinguished from the mere thinking of something which comes true, every idle surmise will be dignified with the name of precognition, and the whole thing will be no more than a guessing game. Expressed differently, precognition is not vague dreaming, but is literally, precognition: that is, there is a certainty about it, *and* the precognition precedes the event which is precognized. It would seem from this latter statement that the precognition must be something other than the event precognized. In that case, what is meant by saying that on January 1st I dreamt *of* a future event? What is the relationship between the prediction and the event which justifies me in saying that the prediction is a prediction 'of' the event? How is this 'of' to be analysed? The quickest way would be to say that the event which is foretold in the prediction is the *same* event which 'happens'. But in that case, how are we to explain away the time-lapse? My dream that I am reading *Pickwick* is itself an event (E_1): and by hypothesis it has a place in the time-series different from my actual reading of the book (E_2). In the analogous case of memory, however, nobody argues from E_2 (the actual reading) and E_3 (the memory)'s being different events to the impossibility of memory. While it is granted that the analysis of 'of' in the phrase, "the memory of E_2", is more difficult than the plain man might suppose, it does not constitute a difficulty like the analysis of 'of' in the phrase, "the prediction of E_2". In other words, it is not the *difference* of the two events E_1 and E_2 that constitutes the especial difficulty, since this does not arise in connection with the different events E_2 and E_3: it is their *order*. The crucial question at the basis of prediction is: Can I have precognition of something unless that 'something' is already, *in some sense*, given? If the answer to this question is "No", the alleged precognition is no precognition, but perception, *unless* a meaning can be attached to the *"in some sense* already given" so that the prima facie contradiction is removed. If the answer to the question is "Yes", the supporters of precognition have to explain what other relationship between the precognition and what is precognized is possible. The *onus probandi* is on them, and in the absence of such proof sceptics are at liberty to hold that they are not dealing with genuine precognitions, but with mere "seeing *E*, and *E* comes true".

But before the question can be properly asked, it will be advisable to get clearer what is meant and what is not meant by prediction. A fertile source of confusion, already mentioned, must first be removed, by distinguishing between events and the contents of events. This does not imply that such a distinction can be made absolute, for that would be a great error. By the "content of an event" I mean, for instance, my reading of a book. But my reading of a book is always *datable*: it happens at a certain time, and however many times it happens,[1] it is a different *event* each time. Briefly, the content of an event is *what* happens: the event itself is *what* happens *when* it happens. There is an essential reference in the notion of an event both to content and to date: and the event, more fundamental than either, mediates between undated content and empty time. The danger of abstracting time from events is well known: the opposite danger of abstracting content from events is less realized, but may be no less serious.[2] Unless we are to allow strange amorphous "Universes of Discourse" wherein undated contents float, we must recognize that there cannot be a 'what happens' without a when at which it happens. The temporal reference in the verb 'to happen' is essential. However, as long as it be remembered that content cannot ultimately be abstracted from events, the distinction between them is a useful one, and makes it easier to avoid superficial arguments both for and against precognition.

My having of a precognitive dream of X going to China is itself an event, E_1. But what I precognize is not *the event* E_2 which later happens when X does go to China, but the *content* of that event, X's going to China, which I will call C for short. Thus what I precognize is not E_2, but C. In other words, the content of E_1 and E_2 is to a certain extent identical. This may seem a contradiction in terms, for either two things are identical or they are not. It remains to be seen whether this contradiction is a real one—for myself, I doubt whether precognition can be disposed of so easily. The supporter of precognition is bound to hold that there is more than a mere general similarity between the content of the dream and the content of the 'real' event, for the dream, he says (in the still unanalysed phrase), is a dream 'of' the event. On the other hand, there is a difference, and the difference

[1] I am taking 'happening' as ultimate and indefinable.
[2] Science proceeds by abstracting from particulars of time (and place) and by ignoring datable characters. This alone is not vicious, as long as it is not thought that this abstraction is anything more than a methodological device. When this further step is taken, trouble begins. Some of the perplexities and contradictions that beset modern scientists may be due to this error.

is just that vague, elusive, but nevertheless important one between dreams and 'real life'. Evidently, however, the difference that is alleged to contradict the identity of the two contents is not in the contents at all. Whether C happens in a dream or in reality does not alter C. The 'contradiction' is based upon an elementary misunderstanding.

The problem of precognition, however, as we have seen in the case of memory, is not how two events can have the same content; and it is not so much even how the content can be seen, thought of, or dreamt before it actually happens. For if that were so every idle remark, every chance fancy which 'came true' would be in the same case. Nobody finds any special difficulty in a man's saying, "When X comes over next time I want him to see the garden", and nobody feels the need of explaining how he came to say it before X's visit, when in due course X *did* see the garden. The point is not merely that he is a purposive agent and can plan what he and X shall do—it would be useless to explain away all reference to the future in terms of will, free or otherwise—the essence of the example is in the "*when X comes*", if X in fact does come. Arguments against precognition, then, which confine themselves to denying the *possibility* of C's being thought of, or dreamt of, before it actually happens prove too much, for they can apply equally to quite harmless anticipations and plannings. I am not suggesting that we know all that it means when we make plans involving the future, but I do suggest that, whatever the difficulties involved even in planning, additional and graver difficulties are involved in prediction. In other words, the earlier statement that the problem of precognition was not in the *difference* of the events E_1 and E_2, but in their *order*, needs modification. Not *only* in their order but in that extra corroboration and certainty that binds E_1 and E_2 together is the essence of the problem of prediction to be found. This last statement is vague. If I wished to uphold precognition, I should have to amplify it: as it is, the legacy is an interesting one.

It may be objected that the problem is an unreal one, and that there is no such extra corroboration and certainty in predictions as against mere thinking-that-comes-true. Mr. Dunne seems to hold that, since precognition is a normal faculty, we cannot tell, from the mere thinking over our dreams at breakfast, which of them will be verified and which will not.[1] He takes, as a sufficient criterion of prediction, the mere verification at a later date, and distinguishes prediction from coincidence only by the improbability of the occurrence. It may be granted that the comfortable use of the word 'coincidence' is often a shelter for ignorance, when a little trouble would have discovered a causal connection, and also that we do, in fact, give more credence to alleged verified predictions in proportion to their *a priori* improbability, and correctness in details. Nevertheless, the fallacy of "post hoc ergo propter hoc" lurks to trap the unwary. We are all, below a more or less superficial covering of reason, superstitious. We believe that our luck is out or in—"There is a tide in the affairs of men"—and that what is badly begun will end badly. We hate to hear others prophesy evil, even in jest, and if anything should happen, we blame them for it. Of course, this procedure is only half-conscious, and if our 'rational' selves heard of it, they would soon squash it as nonsense. But it is this unconscious proneness to irrational belief that makes it so dangerous. I chose, as a pleasing figment of the imagination, the spectacle of A sitting on the top of Cader Berwyn, and when I chose it, I said that even if it ever came true, it would not be a prediction on my part. Supposing, however, the improbable happened: would I not be inclined to look back on my chance fancy with uneasiness, and wonder whether, after all, some dim 'premonition' had not guided my thoughts to take that particular course? I might just as well, I might say, have thought of B instead of A, and of Cader Bronwen's bogs instead of the crag perched high over the lake: the way is easy to wondering *why* I should have thought as I did. An irrational feeling, perhaps: but it cannot be denied that we have a tendency, looking back, to see more than coincidence. It is one thing to say, if C did not happen, that would not make of my fancy a precognition: it is quite another to say, C has happened, but my previous picture of it was not a precognition. But it is 'another', not for any logical reason, but because of our psychological predilections. Yet we do not even carry our illogicality to its logical conclusions, and in the case of the fulfilment of a remark like "I hope we have carrots for dinner", we

[1] From my own experience, I have felt no more conviction at the time about dreams which were later verified than about those which were not. That seems to me to point to coincidence rather than to precognition.

have sufficient sense to see nothing mysterious. All this is very obvious: but the point that I am trying to make is that there is no *logical* difference between the 'carrot-fulfilment' and the 'crag-fulfilment', but only a difference of probability. Hence, if precognition is not to be on the same (logical) level as guesswork and idle fancy, it must be certain.

Now where is this certainty to come in? Emphatically, not *after* the event only: for we have seen how suggestible we are in finding causal connections after the fulfilment of a 'prediction'. Yet it would seem harsh to limit certainty to certainty before the fulfilment: some of Mr. Dunne's best examples, for instance, do not seem to have been attended with certainty that they would be fulfilled. It would be a mistake to weight the scales against prediction to start with: but we must protect ourselves against post-fulfilment suggestion. Even so, premonitions, however certain, are not always fulfilled.[1] We do not hear of the proportion of unfulfilled to fulfilled predictions: I suspect that it is large. Subjective certainty, then, is not a good enough criterion of precognition. We are thus forced back to the starting-point, short cuts having failed: the only criterion of genuine precognitions is in a peculiar relationship between the precognition and the event 'of' which it is a precognition. Failing the discovery and the analysis of this, we have no reason to believe that predictions, as distinct from guesswork, occur.

It might seem at first sight plausible that the relationship is a causal one. The coming event "casts its shadow before" (in the phrase which is so familiar that we never stop to examine if the analogy is a good one), and causes me to have an intimation of it, similar in kind to that particular type of intimation (of a *past* event) which I call memory. In terms of the analogy, in memory I look at a shadow, and know what the object[2] was that cast it— whether it was a tree, or a house, or a man. This is not at all a bad analogy for memory (as long as it is not pressed too far). But when applied to precognition it is self-contradictory. For the tree is

[1] Once, before a journey, I 'felt' that something would happen to the train. I had never had the feeling before or since, and the absence of any proper reason, if anything, increased the suggestion. I had sufficient sense not to postpone the journey, and nothing happened. The 'premonition', though strong, was (perhaps conveniently) vague—for if there had been a mishap, however slight, I fear that I would have been credulous.

[2] In the terminology I have been using, the content.

both logically and temporally prior to its shadow, and to imagine that a tree, as yet non-existent, can cast a shadow is an absurdity. It may be objected that this last sentence is so phrased that it begs the question. The point at issue is just whether the future is 'nothing at all', or not, and to adopt, for instance, Broad's view would prejudge the question at once. At this stage it would be just as valid to hold, with Dunne, that there is no ontological difference between past, present and future: in which case the phrase "as yet non-existent" is highly misleading, and tends to throw suspicion on a perfectly reputable analogy. Nevertheless, I do not think that the objection is valid, for the contradiction stands even if it is phrased in terms of before and after, and not in terms of present and future.

I would suggest that the attempt to relate precognitions to events by means of causality—whether expressed by shadow-analogies, or not—is based upon a fundamental confusion. The sponsors of this are trying to have it both ways: they insist on the temporal priority of the precognition, and yet pretend to explain it by a relation which holds only between earlier and later. The question does not merely concern a few stray dreams or visions—had it been that only, nobody would object much—but involves the whole validity of the causal relationship. Those who have held this view have rarely seen the subversive consequences it entails. (I do not mean to suggest that the notion of causality is so firmly entrenched that it is beyond suspicion, or that it is completely understood by us, but I do suggest that it is not to be lightly overthrown, if any other explanation, not involving the denial of the unidirectionality of causality, is feasible.) The easiest way, perhaps, to understand the situation, is to consider the question: If the relation is one of causality, which is the cause and which the effect? Does the dream cause the event, or vice versa?

It is not impossible to imagine a case in which the dream might be at least a part-cause of the event. Suppose, for instance, that a man dreamt that he visited a certain small town to which he did not often go. Shortly afterwards, a friend with a new car that he was anxious to try out called unexpectedly, and offered to take him out, giving him the choice of direction. The mere fact that the name of the town was fresh in his memory, even if unconsciously, might lead him to choose it. There is no particular difficulty in such a causal connection. But, very evidently, there is no precognition in any proper sense of the word. On the other hand, if the event causes the dream, we can only ask, "How?" For such causation would be of a fundamentally different kind from what is usually called causation: so different, indeed, that it would be dangerous to call both notions by the same name, because of the risk of confusion. I suggest that the masquerade of this second notion under the name of the first serves no purpose except to obscure our minds to its changeling origin, and to make us believe that we understand it, when in fact we do not.

There is, however, one way in which an explanation of fulfilled predictions might be given in causal terms. Suppose that I had reason to think it possible, though not to be certain, that C would happen, and that my reasons were sound. If certain events at t_1 caused C to happen at t_3, is it not also possible that they caused D a (dream of C) in the intervening time—at, say, t_2? Thus neither C nor D is a cause of the other, but they are linked by causation, for both are effects of a prior event or events. Such an explanation, though possible and even plausible to account for the undoubted 'belonging togetherness' of prediction and real event (otherwise very hard to explain), is certainly opposed to precognition. For it involves that there is no special relevance to the fulfilment in the 'prediction', other than as a collateral effect of the same causes, and it postulates nothing more than normal unidirectional causation. It may be objected that the similarity of D and C may be due to coincidence—but that objection is not likely to be made by a supporter of precognition, nor would it help him if it were, since coincidence is his own worst enemy. Causation, then, cannot be the relation involved in prediction.

A second suggestion offers identity as the solution. Now it is agreed that D (the dream) and E (the event which is its fulfilment) have the same content—this is, indeed, one premise on which the notion of prediction was based, since otherwise there would be endless arguments as to whether D referred to E or to some other similar event. But alone this is not sufficient—we have to explain how such identity is possible. To go too far in this, and to deny the *possibility* of the same content at different times, would be to endanger memory and planning, and to create unnecessary difficulties. The main point which distinguishes the carrying out of a plan and the fulfilment of a prediction is that in the former (though the *psychological* emphasis is admittedly on the future) the *logical* emphasis is on the past, while in the latter it is on the future. Identity is not itself a temporal relationship. Hence when it is applied to things in time, I will not say it loses part of its force, but rather that it is marked by the queer lopsidedness of time. Identity is perfectly symmetrical: time is not. It would, of course, be an absurdity to suggest that identities become not quite identical, and this is not what is meant: an example may make the meaning clearer. Two events (such that they would be commonly spoken of as 'the same thing happening again') are not identical, for they have different temporal characteristics such as date. The two contents, considered in abstraction from time, *are* identical: but the two events as a whole (as events in time), are subject to time. Hence, to carry over into our dealings with events notions of identity that apply only in abstraction from date is a mistake: and it is *not* absurd to talk of 'difference of emphasis' between two events which have identical contents.[1] In a perfectly conceived plan, the plan and the execution have the same content, but though the planner emphasizes what he hopes *will* happen, the *logical* emphasis is on the plan, which has both logical and temporal priority over the execution. I have been at some pains to show that sameness of content is not incompatible with such emphasis: it is perfectly consistent, therefore, to hold *both* identity of content between plan and result, *and* that the emphasis throughout is from plan to result. The same thing holds also in the case of memory. In prediction, though there may be identity of content, the emphasis is always from later to earlier: the prediction is considered as having no importance independently of the event which is its fulfilment. Logically, the later is considered as conditioning the earlier, which is a return to the first suggestion, that has already been discussed: the notion of identity has no particular relevance, except to bamboozle us into believing that no difference in the status of prediction and fulfilment is required. But this is the abstract, mathematical view of identity. It is only as a result of confusion that we can apply

[1] The 'difference of emphasis' is not, of course, the work of identity, but of time (if the hypostatizing language be permitted for a moment). Identity is 'all that it ever was', and the irregularities are not sins of omission on its part, but of commission by time.

to temporal events notions of identity which are appropriate only in abstraction from time. The postulation of identity, then, leaves essential points unexplained, and cannot rationalize prediction.

There remain as possibilities only coincidence, miracles, and a new relation, not reducible to either identity or causality, but resembling them in certain respects: and these need not be discussed at length. Coincidence is, of course, anathema to the believer in precognition: nor would 'miracle' satisfy him, especially if, like Dunne, he believed precognition to be common and normal. As regards the new relation, until we are given positive grounds for recognizing it, there can be no harm in heeding Occam's maxim.

By its failure, then, to give a satisfactory explanation of the relation subsisting between prediction and fulfilment such that the former can rightly be called a prediction 'of' the latter, must precognition be judged, and condemned.

II

Yet accurate forecastings have been known. How is this to be rendered consistent with the conclusions that have just been reached? In the first place, there are plannings—but I have tried to show that these are quite distinct from predictions proper. Secondly, there is guesswork—but that also is not prediction. Thirdly, and most important, there are the so-called predictions[1] of science. It is with them that this section will be chiefly concerned.

Recently, there was an account in the newspaper of an eclipse of the moon which will take place on a given date. Beginning at 4.28 p.m. the eclipse will be total for 23 minutes, and partial for 3 hours 23 minutes, and for a period of $5\frac{3}{4}$ hours the moon will be in the penumbra. The moon when eclipsed will be copper-coloured, and, lastly, we are promised that the eclipse will be visible from all over the British Isles and France—the only condition being that the sky must be clear! There are here no less

[1] I use 'prediction' and 'precognition' indifferently. To distinguish between them is useful, since the former term is entrenched in science, and there certainly *are* predictions as science uses the word: but in the long run, the familiar sense betrays us—and we assert 'prediction' in that sense also. It seems to me that to say scientific 'predictions' are not real predictions is the lesser evil.

than five positive—not vague—statements. Three concern the duration of the event and the time of commencement: one mentions the places at which it will occur, and one describes what it will look like. A prediction that was not firmly believed would never be made in such precise terms. This example shows scientific prediction at its most confident level. It is perhaps better to start with a simpler one. Many of the statements in science are causal ones, and it is not too much to say that the first great step in scientific investigation is taken when a number of occurrences, hitherto regarded as fortuitously connected, are exhibited as causally connected. What exactly this involves is by no means clear, but at least it involves that like causes are followed by like events. "Arsenic causes death" means *at least* "All men who have swallowed x grains of arsenic, granted certain circumstances (state of health, etc., and absence of counteracting circumstances), have died", *and* "if A, in similar circumstances, swallows x grains of arsenic, *he will die*".[1] This latter statement is a prediction about what will happen. It is derived from the general causal principle, "same cause, same effect"—but what is meant by the "same cause"? It was said, in the first section of this chapter, that two events are never 'the same', and that what is meant is merely that their contents are the same. The 'sameness' of causes is a sameness of content, and to that extent causation abstracts from events: yet, because content by itself is nothing unless it is the content of an event, this abstraction can never become complete. This double characteristic of partial abstraction from, and yet essential reference to, events is fundamental to causality. Hence what causality predicts is not a future event, but that at some future date there will be an actualization of a given content. This distinction may seem trifling, but it shows how the predictions of causation can be made consistent with the common-sense difference between the present and the future. It may be helpful to state the position simply at first, and later re-shape it. If my predictions are so exhaustive that they include 'the event' as well as its content, then this event is in all

[1] As I am not specially concerned with causation, I do not go into the question of the validity of induction. Neither do I attempt to amplify the 'certain circumstances', as long as it is realized that they are not left as vague as that, but are stated, as far as they are known. In theory, they can be exhaustively tabulated: whether this is so is another question.

strictness a present event, and the distinction between present and future has vanished. This I believe to be impossible. For, however accurate our predictions may be, there is always *something* that is lacking about them—a tiny corner missing, so to speak, that is only added *when the event actually happens.* It would, however, be a mistake to take the analogy of a jigsaw to which the last piece is added too seriously, for that would suggest, erroneously, that 'content' abstracted from events is as material as the whole jigsaw minus that one piece! Used with discretion, though, the analogy need not be harmful. Expressed in slightly more technical language, the position I am advocating is that the 'happening' of events is ultimate, indefinable, and unpredictable, though 'that E will happen' can in some cases be rendered very highly probable. This is merely a re-statement of a very familiar position. On the one hand, "don't count your chickens before they are hatched", and "there's many a slip 'twixt cup and lip", are the plain man's way of expressing, in a considerably less roundabout manner than the philosopher, the insecurity and uncertainty of the future. On the other hand, it would be foolish to deny the 'connectedness' of happenings, and that certain happenings tend to be followed or accompanied by certain others, so that from one we are led to expect, not altogether irrationally, others.[1] To deny that events are predictable with certainty is not to deny all connectedness. A very simple example can be taken to show that the two aspects are consistent. A child knits a scarf, which she gives as a birthday present to her brother. It is sufficiently obvious that the scarf could not have been given on the birthday had not its appearance been provided for by something that took place *before* the birthday —the act of knitting the scarf. Unless the scarf had been knitted, it could not be given as a present, and in knitting it the child was making it increasingly probable that it would be given. But at no time previous to the actual happening of the event 'child giving scarf to brother' could anyone be *sure* it would happen. Until it was finished, there was always the possibility that it would never be done in time, that the wool might be impossible to match, that she would be ill, and so on. Even when finished it might be lost, or mauled by the kitten, or accidentally unwound, or the brother might die, or disappear, or quarrel with his family.

[1] This is, of course, a minimum statement.

The present makes the future: does it also ensure it? That is the crucial question. A better mode of expression would be, perhaps, that events are admittedly to a certain extent (whether wholly, is another matter) determined by earlier events, and that we unquestionably believe that events, which as yet are future, will when they happen also be coherent with their predecessors. The second half of the question then becomes: Do present events ensure future ones? If the notion of causality is taken at all seriously, it is evident that in one sense the answer is "Yes": I want to show that in another, no less legitimate sense, the answer is "No".

In the scarf example, it will soon be objected that if the present is not given—that is, if the expected C is never actualized—it is not because there is real discontinuity between present and future, but because between E_1 (the event of finishing the scarf, which makes its presentation highly probable) and E_3 (the event of giving the brother a book) *something else* has occurred, for instance, the accidental burning of the scarf. Looking back on the sequence of events, the determinist could exhibit them as belonging to neat causal series: and he would find no discontinuity of any kind.[1] But this is not an objection to the view here put forward, and the whole argument can be granted, quite consistently. It may be further urged, however, that with complete determinism it is theoretically possible, at the time of E_1, to see that E_2 (the burning of the scarf) is 'going to happen'. But this is exactly on all fours with saying that the giving of the scarf 'will happen': and by that I do not merely mean that further intervention, such as removing the scarf from danger, is possible, but that no prediction is certain until it is actualized.[2] If you prefer to add, "because something might happen to stop it", you may—but you will lay yourself open to refutation by the advocate of complete determinism, besides missing what seems to me the more essential point, of the fundamentality of the *happening* of events. (In addition, it is no longer necessary to debate the question of complete or partial determinism, since in any case there is no determinism except in

[1] It might be difficult, in practice, to show *why* the book was chosen at one shop rather than another, and the determinist usually contents himself with saying, "*If* we knew all the circumstances, we could exhibit everything as determined", without claiming that he *does* know all the circumstances!
[2] Compare *Space, Time and Deity*, ii, 327–8.

abstraction from the temporal characteristics of events.) The present may be ensured by the past: perhaps, if this held good on many occasions, we should, by induction, think it probable that what is now future, when it becomes present, will likewise be ensured by its past, our present.[1] But there can be no presumption from that to the *different* statement: "While it is still future, it is ensured by the present", without committing the fallacy, rightly censured by Bergson, of confusing time passing with time passed. The present may be, as the determinists assert, the making of the future: it is never the future as made.

Causality, however, is based on induction, and the logical validity of this process is very often impugned. (The same thing is true of statistical investigations, to which the remarks above also apply.) It may be said that the uncertainty of its predictions is to be explained in terms of this imperfect logical process rather than in terms of its reference to events. The simplest and most relevant way to discover whether this is so is not to embark on a discussion of induction, but to refer to predictions in which the inferences are logically unexceptionable. Examples of these are trains of mathematical reasoning, simple no less than complex ones. Given that the sides AB and AC of a triangle are equal, *it follows* that the angles ABC and ACB are also equal, and this can be strictly demonstrated.[2] What is meant by 'follows'? It is above all important to see that this is a logical, *not a temporal*, 'follows', and that the notion is that of entailment, not of sequence. True, since we are creatures of time, the demonstration is worked out in time by the schoolboy (and so becomes subject to "The thousand natural shocks that flesh is heir to!"), but the reasoning itself is completely logical. Strictly, it is nonsense to say that the end of the demonstration is 'future' to the beginning, and it only gains a meaning in reference to the boy whose working through it 'takes time'. In other words, unlike causality, there is no essential reference to events in the inferences themselves, and there is no uncertainty.

Mathematical and logical relations, then, have no past, present,

[1] 'Ensured' is used, intentionally, non-committally. In passing, it may be remarked that the conjunction of 'think it probable' and 'will' is perhaps interesting. See the remarks made on prediction by Laird in chapter iii of his *Study in Realism*.

[2] Granted certain postulates, which do not affect the argument here.

and future, and consequently, there is no 'prediction' in the literal meaning of the word. But, it will be said, they have a logical order of precedence: cannot we say that one stage in the argument is 'before' another stage? In a sense, yes—but that is in its exposition by us. The easiest way to see that geometry—and still more, algebra—is not a matter of *linear* inference is not to think of 'steps' in the 'process' (both question-begging terms) but to consider data and conclusion. Since geometry is man-made, and so brings in other, properly non-mathematical, factors, we may *learn* more than we knew at the beginning. That is not the point. The point is, that the angles ABC and ACB have been equal 'all the time', as well as the lines AB and AC. They have undergone no change during the process which is our perception of their equality. If we must use temporal language to express non-temporal notions, rather than say that the equality of sides 'comes before' the equality of angles, let us say that both are contemporaneous. That disposes of the objection that there is any real logical precedence. There is no precedence in logic: if there is 'more in' the conclusion than in the premises, it is not completely logical, for, as Russell puts it, logic and mathematics are tautologies. A better way of expressing the point than by saying that the equality of AB and AC and the equality of ABC and ACB are contemporaneous, is to say that they hold good together. This is evident in the example given; it is not so evident in more complicated examples (such as that $[\frac{195}{60} + 3 \times \frac{1}{6} + (225 - 195) \div 40 + 5 \times \frac{1}{12}]$ equals $4\frac{11}{12}$) until the 'intervening' 'stages' have been worked out. But 'evidence' is not a matter of logic but of psychology.

Now comes the question of the interpretation of all this, and of the result in everyday life of the application to it of sets of inferences that are completely logical and, hence, certain.

A train leaves M for O, 225 miles distant. Until it reaches N, 195 miles from M, it travels at 60 m.p.h., but afterwards it slows down to 40 m.p.h. It stops at N, and two stations before it, for ten minutes at each: after leaving N it stops five more times for five minutes each. How long does it take the train to go from M to O? As far as the figures are concerned, the answer is, so to speak, contained in themselves, and all we have to do, it seems, is to call the $4\frac{11}{12}$ 'hours', and there we have a certain prediction. But not so fast. Is it equally certain that the figures apply to the actual running times of the train? Unless that can be established we have no right to claim that the prediction is certain. True, it would be a genuine prediction, if justified, which the mere cyphering of ($\frac{195}{60} + \ldots$) to $4\frac{11}{12}$ never would be. But *is* it justified? I suggest that it is not, and that once the results of mathematics are applied to events in time, they are in the same position as causal or statistical predictions, and liable to be upset. If it be said, "The train was seven minutes late to-day, I admit. But three minutes were lost because of a signal check; we had to wait six minutes at N for the train from the west, which was delayed by fog, and made up time by only staying four minutes at P and Q instead of five", the answer is the same as to the corresponding objection of the complete determinist. "You cannot tell what will happen until it happens."

The uncertainty is not, however, in the calculations themselves, but in the exactness of their application to events. It may be objected that the continual implied distinction between mathematics as it is and *our* use of it is unwarranted: the most effective reply to this is to ask what then is meant when we say that somebody's calculation is 'wrong'!

There are, then, two distinguishable elements involved when we say of a train travelling at 60 m.p.h. that it will take two hours to go 120 miles. The first is mathematical and certain: the second is the application of the mathematical results to the concrete position, and it is this last which 'infects' (in Bradley's phrase) the resultant prediction with its own uncertainty.

It is now possible to deal with the case of the eclipse. The earth is a body which moves, with very little aberration, in an orbit whose equation is known. Similarly with the moon and sun. The other known facts are their velocities relative to each other. Granted this information, and given an initial position of the bodies (such as that gained by telescopic observation of their positions relatively to the fixed stars on, say, February 15, 1831, at 2 p.m.), it is possible to calculate (1) their relative positions at any given time,[1] (2) the times when they will appear in a particular relative position, such as sun, earth, and moon in a straight line. The second of these is

[1] Compare Jules Verne's story of the detachment of part of the earth, and its projection through space. The mathematician on the fragment ascertained that its path was elliptic, and predicted its return to the earth.

involved in the present case. The six times given in the account (of the moon's entering and leaving the penumbra, of the beginning and end of total and partial eclipse), and the information regarding what part of the earth's surface will be turned towards the moon (that is, where the area of visibility is) are all calculable, and only the appearance is described from induction. The assumptions upon which the calculations are based are, first, that the equations that give the path of the bodies are correct, and *that they will not vary over the interval for which the calculations are made.* This is an assumption that is not *mathematical*, but concerned with the *applicability* of mathematics: it would not be self-destructive to doubt it, and so there is an element of uncertainty. Secondly, it is assumed that the variables of the calculation are applicable to experience, and in particular that the 't' of physics can be interpreted without comment as 'time'.

Essentially, the procedure taken is one of abstracting from events, manipulating mathematical expressions (in which, remember, there is no past and no future, and 'predictability', in any proper sense of the word, vanishes) until a satisfactory one appears, and finally reinterpreting in terms of events. And with this reinterpreting, the contingency, which is, essentially, the expression of the difference between an event as talked about, expected, hoped for, willed, and the event as *happening*, reappears. Unless you are prepared to admit the contingency of the future in this precise sense—that it is fundamentally different from the present in that it has not happened—you will find it extremely difficult to explain what you mean by saying that the event you predict is future, since there will be, to all intents and purposes, no difference between the event as you predict it now and as it happens in the future. Predictions approximate to certainty: but when they reach it they cease to be predictions, but are the realization.[1]

It remains now to distinguish between the various contexts in which the word 'prediction' has been used.

In the first place, as has already been said, mere guessing must be distinguished from prediction proper. Secondly, it is just as

[1] "The notion of perfect prediction is self-contradictory ... if we could forecast to-morrow's experiences in their utter fullness, to-morrow would be indistinguishable from the present, and prediction loses its meaning" (Weber, *Monist*, 1927, p. 526).

important that we should not fall into the opposite error of confusing what I propose to call 'intellectual foresight' with prediction. Lastly, the relation between prediction and certainty must be discussed.

There is a type of foresight which it would be a mistake to call prediction—unless 'prediction' were being used in a wide sense. Two men, A and B, are playing chess. At any moment, A perceives that certain combinations of moves are theoretically possible. By one of these, he could mate B in three moves—but only if B met him half-way by making fantastically bad moves. He does not seriously consider it as a possibility, and it would be very unnatural to say that his purely intellectual foresight of this particular end-situation was a prediction. Not merely, it should be noted, because of its *improbability*, but because the mere seeing of situation N as deducible from situation K (in accordance with the rules determining the game of chess) is in its essence *logical* and has, as it stands, no reference to the future. Suppose now that situation S (another mating position) is also deducible from K, and has the advantage that it does not postulate self-immolation on B's part, A may decide to try to bring it about. He is then regarding S, not merely contemplatively, but as a goal, and to its realization he sets himself.

Prediction, then, is distinct both from guessing and from purely intellectual contemplation: from the former, because it claims certainty; from the latter, because it essentially refers to future *actualizations* and not merely to logical possibilities.[1] It may be said that many predictions do not claim certainty. This is, of course, to some extent a matter of words: but it is advisable to keep to the stricter use. Admittedly, in ordinary language, 'prediction' is used both for more or less probable forecasts, and for claims of certainty, but this practice is not to be recommended. And, of the two alternatives, the latter is the interesting one, for the former raises no special philosophic problems. Granted, then, that predictions, strictly so-called, are certain, can there be any predictions?

---

[1] There is a widespread view that the future is the total of all possibilities, one of which is to be actualized. This is a plausible view, which needs discussion, but it cannot be adopted as yet. It is difficult to avoid misleading language which imputes premature conclusions on this fundamental question of the status of the future.

I think that the answer is No, and the reason is that prediction attempts to reconcile two incompatible notions: the notion of certainty, and the notion of happenings in time. A last illustration from chess. Mate is inevitable in three moves, those which B makes being forced each time. Is it not certain that B will be mated? The mating position can be deduced from the position of the pieces on the board, and the problem becomes akin to one of mathematics: there is no loophole anywhere. Beginning and end are compacted together. But in the actual playing out of the end they are spread out in time: they become events, separated by a finite duration. And in that finite duration the unexpected might happen—A might lose his head, or a very urgent visitor might arrive, or a careless movement might upset the table, or somebody might have a heart attack—and the mating of B by A would not occur. However unlikely is not the point: it is *possible*. An element of uncertainty has entered in with the spreading out of beginning and end in time. Logically, the end is given in the beginning, but this is never so in time, unless the 'happening' of events is degraded to nothingness. The certainty of logical and mathematical implications cannot survive their application to events, and prediction must be rejected as impossible.

It cannot but be evident that this chapter can have no cogency to one who rejects the assumptions and unsupported assertions on which it is based. Where fundamental metaphysical differences are reached, no further argument is possible. Certain assertions, however, need to be further amplified, and so the following chapters will be taken up with an attempt to analyse what is meant by the irreversibility and the 'becoming' of time.

CHAPTER X

IRREVERSIBILITY

THE conscious devisers of paradoxes can find little that is more amusing to them than the denial of the irreversibility of time; so strongly is it implicitly affirmed by common sense. Time is 'the subtle thief of youth', and its

> '... Moving Finger writes; and, having writ,
> Moves on: nor all your Piety nor Wit
> Shall lure it back to cancel half a Line,
> Nor all your Tears wash out a Word of it.'

In more homely language, the plain man subscribes unhesitatingly to the view of time as an ever-rolling stream bearing its sons always in one direction.

Nevertheless, in spite of, or because of, the easy obviousness of the irreversibility of time in experience, its denial, at least as an interesting hypothesis, has had a certain attraction to many. Thus in physics we hear of speeds greater than light as leading to a reversal in the order of events: the notion of eternity owes part of its attractiveness to the escape it offers from the flux of time: and the success of the plain man in repairing a blunder, so that it is as if, to common sense at least, it had never been, makes it seem that some actions can be reversed, and that "what's done cannot be undone" is false. All these tendencies have had repercussions in philosophy, and have given rise to recognizably distinct methods of denying the irreversibility of time.

First, those who emphasize the notion of eternity. They are concerned, not so much to deny that time is irreversible—indeed, they often emphasize this imperfectly logical character in order to throw doubts upon the consistency of the notion of time—as to hold that eternity is the true reality, and that time, even if it is not unreal, is at best defective in the view of reality that it gives. Hence irreversibility, which is a temporal characteristic, is slighted: though it is not denied to apply to time, it is denied to have any ultimate significance in a world where only the eternal is truly real. But since we have not at present to decide whether time is 'unreal', but are concerned only with the question whether the irreversibility commonly attributed to time is rightly so attributed (a question which idealists rarely raise), its further discussion can be deferred.

Physicists themselves are not as a rule concerned to make definite pronouncements regarding the irreversibility of time. Their statements are usually in the form of an "if-then", without inquiring too closely whether the hypothesis does in fact hold. It is one thing to say that *if* a man attained a velocity greater than that of light, he would see events in reverse order: it is quite another to assert that such reversibility is possible, and to do them justice, physicists have usually avoided this further statement. Unwary philosophizing from the results of physics is to be blamed for the worst excesses in this direction. What physics proves is not that the order of events is reversible, but that under certain circumstances it would be, for a given observer. But it affords not the slightest hope that these circumstances are realized, and in so far as physics is definite on this point, there would seem to be a presumption *against* their realization, as being contrary to its primary assumptions regarding light. This point will be returned to after the 'paradox' has been summarized.

Five events, A, B, C, D, E, 'happen' on the earth at regular intervals of one minute. Immediately C occurs, a traveller X leaves the earth at a high speed which is yet less than that of light. He sees D, not at the end of a minute, but after a (very slightly) longer interval; after double that interval, he sees E. Compared with the graph that Y (stationary on the earth) makes, X's is different, though similar, with the interval between C and D, and D and E, $1 + m$ minutes (where m depends on X's speed) instead of 1 minute. The second case is where X's speed is the speed of light: consequently he sees C all the time. The third case is where X's speed is greater than light: leaving the earth as C happens he quickly outstrips the rays of light from C, and where he is C has 'not yet happened'. If he is travelling fast enough he may see B, and then, outstripping that, see A. The four graphs of X and Y can quickly be compared.

$$
\begin{array}{ccccc}
A & B & C & D & E \\
A & B & C & \underset{m}{D} & \underset{2m}{E} \\
A & B & C & C & C \\
A & B & C & \underset{m}{B} & \underset{2m}{A}
\end{array}
$$

(In each case, X starts his journey at the time when C happens.)

As it stands, it is evident that all that is proved is that X *would see* A, B and C happen in reverse order: it does not prove anything about the reversed happening of A, B and C. On the contrary, it is taken as a premise that A, B and C do happen in that order, since only if they do can X's experience of C, B and A be accounted for. The distinction between what X sees, and what really is, is, however, very far from being a satisfactory dismissal of the problem. It is easy to say, "X, from the time he leaves the earth, *sees* events in reverse order, but they do not really happen in that order": it is less easy to explain what constitutes motion and rest. Ultimately, we have no knowledge of the order of events except through *seeing* that they occur in that order: and any argument which casts doubts on this must go too far. In such an extreme case it seems quite certain to us that X is wrong: nevertheless any attempt to tamper with his beliefs leads to disastrous results.

All the same, there is redress. For we have no reason to believe in the existence of X, nor, further, in his possibility. For physics, while it takes light signals as the means of determining questions of simultaneity and order, is *ipso facto* ruling out the possibility of there being speeds greater than light. The paradox is in direct contradiction to relativity physics in that it involves the addition and subtraction of light as an ordinary velocity,[1] as well as a speed

---

[1] In Cases I and II. Even if it is attempted to escape this objection, by saying that m in Case I is 0, in Case II it still remains. The plausibility of the 'stellar traveller' reversibility lies in the extension of the analogy from Case I and Case II to Case III. But, as Eddington showed, the traveller would "never know what a close race he was making of it", and for him the velocity of light would be what it always had been. The doubt thus cast upon Cases I and II makes Case III even less plausible.

greater than that of light. In other words, the paradox, though suggested by physics, rests upon assumptions which physics rejects.

Thirdly, though light signals are used as criteria in physics for determining the order of events, it does not follow that the behaviour of light has any extra-physical relevance to that order. The movements of an observer in space affect his perception of events, especially if he follows an agreed convention regarding the transmission of signals, but they do not affect the happening of the events. The point is put very clearly by Maritain with reference to simultaneity. We must not, he says, confuse "simultaneity itself and the sensible standard by which we are aware of it. We cannot appreciate simultaneity at a great distance without introducing certain conventions. . . . But simultaneity itself is totally independent of these conventions."[1] What holds of simultaneity holds also of temporal order in general, and to prove that the order of events is reversible we must do more than prove that, granted certain conventions, the order of events appears from a great distance the reverse of the real order. This is, in essence, the first objection to the 'paradox', restated to avoid the criticisms to which it was open. If the word 'real' is objected to, it can be replaced in the phrase by "the order in which events happen", beyond which no further definition is possible. To put the point in another way, observers may fail to agree as to whether A and B are or are not simultaneous: indeed, in special cases it may be impossible to determine this by physical means. Nevertheless, objectively, it must be true either that they are simultaneous or that one did in fact happen before the other, and it is this "happening" which is absolute and fundamental—and which is entirely unaffected by any hypothetical stellar traveller, whether accredited, or an impostor as this one is.

The third method of approach to the denial of the irreversibility of time is the most fundamental, even though it is the way of the despised plain man. He says, in effect: "You say that nothing that is done can be undone. That seems to me a hard saying, and an untrue one. My wife can unravel her knitting if she makes a

[1] Essay on "The Mathematical Attenuation of Time" in the volume entitled (in the English translation) *The Freedom of the Intellect*, p. 92. See also his criticisms on the well-known aviator example, in an article in the *Revue Universelle* (April 1924).

mistake in it. My children quarrel, but make it up, and all is as before. I, as a Communist, once placed a time-bomb in the City Museum, but on hearing X (a politician) broadcast, I was overcome with horror and repentance, and hastily removed it before it exploded. Surely these and other acts of undoing are familiar enough? Yet, according to you, the past is irreparable." The plain man takes up the position that the consequences of an act can be wiped out so that it is as if it had never been—in other words, that reversion to the initial state is possible. Whether this is so is the crucial question to determine: for irreparability involves irreversibility, and even if the contrary does not hold with certainty, the denial of irreparability at the very least weakens the claim of irreversibility.

It is unfortunate, if not surprising, that the plain man is not a very consistent guide in this matter. Common sense affirms, unhesitatingly, that the effects of a spider's crawl over a room in the Tower on January 1, 1600, have long since ceased to be felt, and that nothing in the world now would be different if the spider had never crawled at all that day. On the other hand, it also holds that certain events, small in themselves, like Cæsar's crossing the Rubicon, have a profound effect on the course of history, and that even to-day our lives would have been different had they not occurred. Once the two different views have been taken, the way is easy to showing that both examples are in much the same position. After all, a spider's crawl—though at a different time and place—was once responsible for important historical events; and in the heat death of the universe, Cæsar's conquests will no longer matter. Once we admit that, we are bound to agree that there is no logical halting-place between two extreme conceptions. One is, that whatever we do—our most important decisions equally with the mechanical avoidance of an obstacle—makes no real difference: it will all be the same a hundred thousand years hence. The other says that everything matters, and that, however trifling the occurrence, the world never is as if it had not been. If I had not avoided the obstacle, but, in falling, had cut my leg on a rusty iron, developed blood-poisoning, and died, the world in a hundred thousand years would have been different in not having my descendants to gladden it. And so on.

Both alternatives are unpalatable and savour of morbidness,

IRREVERSIBILITY

and there is something to say for the plain man's rejection of both, in their extreme form. But they are so horribly logical: once we quit the shelter of one, we are driven on without a halt until we reach the other, and if we rebel at, 'Nor all your tears wash out a word of it', we must espouse 'Tout passe, tout casse, tout lasse'. Is this really so, though? Would it not be possible to hold that, though nothing can ever alter the fact (if it is a fact) that a spider *did* perambulate a room in the Tower on January 1, 1600, nevertheless all effects have long since died away? Or, on the other hand, that, though much is transitory in its effects, some lasting differences may abide?

Take the former case first. There is something about the "irrevocable past", in its extreme view, that seems to me to savour of an old familiar confusion regarding the truth of propositions about the past. It was said earlier that "The Battle of Hastings was in 1066 is always true" is liable to lead to confusions: and not the least of these is that which causes us to imagine that when we say "That it has happened is true" we are saying anything in particular about the *present*. Certainly, if there had been no Battle of Hastings, we could not now truly say, "The Battle of Hastings was in 1066", and to that extent the past 'affects' the present—if we wish to put it in that misleading way. But it does *not* follow from that that it affects it in any other way. Not all our tears and regrets can alter the fact that the Battle of Hastings was in 1066—that goes without saying. It is, however, an unfortunate way of expression, for it sounds as if we can never reach a state of equilibrium in which all effects of that battle will have died away. In the case of the Battle of Hastings, of course, it is perfectly easy to claim that the whole course of English history has been, and still is, influenced by it: so perhaps the spider example is the better. We can never alter the fact of the spider's crawl: but there is no logical compulsion to pass to the *different* statement that the world to-day is different from what it would have been had the spider not crawled.

A pendulum, set in motion by an outside agent, swings in ever-decreasing arcs, and finally comes to rest. Where the initial impulse is great, it will swing for a longer time than it would for a slight impulse, and, similarly, some events have more important repercussions than others. It is not contradictory—on the contrary, it is the plainest common sense—to say both: "The slight impulse I gave has now ceased" *and* "At 2.15 on January 10, 1936, I touched the pendulum." For the latter statement to be true it is not necessary to deny the former, and where this has been done, it is only as the result of confusion. Agreed, that it *may* be true that the effects of *A* never really die out, as the determinists assert, yet it must be clearly seen that this is a *further* position, and one which it is not logically necessary to hold.

The second case is less important for our purpose. It seems to me that to say, "Because the effects of *A* and *B* and *C* have died out in time, everything finally dies out", is no stronger than any other induction from 'some' to 'all'. It is and remains an illegitimate extension from the point of view of logic. This does not mean that it may not be highly probable on its own merits: but that its claim to infallibility is unsound.

It should be evident by now that there are two fundamentally distinct senses in which the word 'reparability' is used. The first may be called reparability of things, and has no particular relevance to time, except in so far as everything is 'in' time. If I drop a book, I can pick it up again: if I lose it, I can go to the Lost Property Office and recover it. But not everything is reparable in this way —dolls break, clothes wear out, and electric bulbs fuse. It is interesting to note the mixture of reparability and irreparability in an ordinary conversation—"Don't cry, darling. I'll buy you a new one"—"No, please don't apologize. It really doesn't matter, for it can easily be replaced"—and so on. Although there is an irreparable element—the cup, once broken, cannot be repaired—the total situation is taken as reparable when replacement is easy. As usual, the plain man has a practical, not a logical, criterion of what is reparable and what is irreparable, and the child, who begins by being strictly logical, soon conforms to conventional behaviour, and finds comfort in another doll. Moreover, common sense alters its views on reparability with the passage of time—a clumsy breaking of a treasured possession seems unforgivable at the time, but after a year it matters less. In this connection comes the phrase, "time the healer"—but it should be clearly seen that it is not *time* that is either reparable or irreparable in such cases. What is really meant is that the effects are getting less, the swings of the pendulum shorter. Time enters in because the pendulum swing 'takes time', not, as the phrase suggests, as itself an agency making for equilibrium.[1] Lastly, it should be remembered that 'reparability' is here used in a general sense to include both annihilation of gain as well as overcoming of loss. The vandals whose wars destroy picture-galleries and cathedrals and who threaten to make Europe revert to its primitive savagery equally with seekers of lost property show that 'reparability' can be either positive or negative.

The so-called irreparability of time is quite distinct from all this. I drop my book, and immediately pick it up. Yet I *did* drop it, and nothing can alter this: what can be altered is the position of my book on the floor.[2] The notion of reparation applies, not to time, but to the content of time. Something can be done about "My book is on the floor", but nothing can be done about "At 2.15 on January 11, 1936, my book fell on the floor"—it just *is*. And it is tremendously important to realize that the 'is' in the last sentence is a *timeless* 'is'. True, it can be interpreted in a temporal manner; I can, for instance, truthfully say the next day that it had fallen. But if we confine ourselves to this interpretation, we shall have a very stunted view of the problem, and be likely to fall into one of the fallacies mentioned earlier.

Secondly, for the second statement to be true it is not necessary that the book should be on the floor at the time when I make the statement. The truth of a statement about the past is independent of any reparability in the things concerned: consequently, so far as logic goes, it is consistent with a state of affairs (at the time of the statement) in which all trace of the past event has disappeared.

(This is, of course, a restatement of the earlier position: in terms of the analogy then used, 'that there was an impulse' is compatible with any length of swing now or with none at all.) But, it may be said, if this is so, how can I *know* that I am speaking the truth? The book really did drop, but now it is back in its place; how am I to convince somebody coming in now that it did drop? This is quite evidently a separate question: and whether we hold that "what really happened" is discoverable in principle (that is, that

[1] It is beside the point to bring in here questions of entropy. Even if time cannot be defined in physical terms without reference to entropy, we are not here concerned with physics.

[2] Weber takes the example of a physicist who, in an experiment with a pendulum, loses count: "So far as the experiment is concerned, he may 'repeat' time by setting the pendulum swinging again, but he has 'lost' some time which he can never repeat" (*Monist*, 1927, p. 530).

traces are left, and that *things* are not reparable—determinism) or whether we hold that perfect reparation is possible in things, does not affect what did, in fact, happen. What is meant by the irreparability of time is merely and simply that what happened *did* happen.

But this simple view, it may be said, is open to the grave objection that it depends on an over-glorification of date. If all that is meant by irreparability as applied to time, the critic urges, is this emphasis on the date at which an event happens, the irreparability may be granted straight away, but it is worth very little, for it is admitted that all that it comes to is the tautologous assertion that X happened when it did happen.

There is some truth in this, but the last word has not been said upon the subject. It does not seem to me merely a tautology, but the statement of a very important principle to say that if the 'happening' of an event is taken as ultimate, two consequences follow—first, that there is temporal irreparability in the sense given above, and secondly that propositions about that event are logically independent of the time at which they are made (this is often known as the "timelessness of truths"). I believe that this view is fundamental and that it is presupposed whether we deny or assert what I have called, not very clearly, the reparability of *things*. An example to make this clearer: when Housman says,

> "To-day the Roman and his trouble
> Are ashes under Uricon",

he is referring to the transience of human activities, until it is as if they had never been. The determinist, complete or partial, steps forward and objects that some effects of Roman occupation still remain, and that the obliteration is not yet, perhaps never will be, complete. But both alike assume that *once* the Romans were there and *also* that this fact (that they were once there) does not alter with the passage of time. I do not know whether a spider crawled round a room in the Tower on January 1, 1600, and I do not expect ever to know. But it either did or did not happen that a spider so crawled: whatever the case was, one of these alternatives happened, and that is the ultimate fact, beyond which no more can be said.[1]

[1] Of course, as historians are not omniscient, more *evidence* may come to light: and historians of successive epochs might say: "It is true that a

IRREVERSIBILITY

It is often held that each happening is a 'fact' which is 'timelessly true'—another way of expressing it is that once a thing has taken its place in the time-series, the passage of time can make no difference to it.

But what about the reparability of *events*? So far, it has been said that the content of an event may or may not be reparable (the determinists and their opponents are still engaged in controversy about this)—and that date is not reparable. Had this alone been stressed, the criticism of hypostatization would have been justified, for 'date' by itself is an undesirable substantialization. But, with the best will in the world, I found it impossible to commit this fallacy (with the intention, of course, of treating 'content' and 'date' separately, and then inquiring what holds for their union in events). Hence the last few pages, while dealing professedly with 'date', have, through the failure of complete abstraction, application also to events. Events, as regards their content, may be reparable: as regards their date, they cannot be—and the event as a whole, since it is 'infected' by its date, is irreparable, in the strict sense that it *has* happened at a certain time. True, this sense may be perfectly trivial: it sounds unnecessarily pedantic to say that when I drop a book on the floor, the *event* is irreparable because it *has* happened. Nevertheless, it seems to me the only logical position to take up, in spite of the superficial consistency of those who hold either that nothing matters or that everything matters. But it goes without saying that this usage of irreparable is not the common one, and that it is a *minimum* usage—when we have said that an event is irreparable in this sense we have said very little.

All this is supposed to have cleared the way for, and led up to, a discussion of the irreversibility of time. Yet it cannot but be evident that much of the latter part depends on certain postulates about time, and this may seem to be a begging of the question. "Events, as regards their content, may be reparable—*as regards their date, they cannot be.*" Why not? unless we are already covertly introducing the notion of irreversibility. But the fallacy, if it be a fallacy, cannot be avoided: the notions of irreparability and irreversibility are essentially connected. Much of what follows will be

spider crawled," and "It is true that a spider did not crawl." But that does not affect *what happened* (whatever it was); only our *knowledge* of what happened.

unsupported assertion—unsupported, because it seems to me basic —and any disagreement will therefore be ultimate.

Reversibility is a notion with which we are all familiar, yet it is one for which it is very difficult to find a definition that does not either mislead or beg the question. Perhaps the most harmless form—if not the most enlightening—is this: "A series A, B, C, D, E is reversible if its terms may indifferently be taken in the order A, B, C, D, E or in the order E, D, C, B, A. It is irreversible if this cannot be done." This definition says nothing about the nature of the terms—they may be the properties of a circle or a row of cabbages numbered from left to right or right to left, or events in time.

Secondly, it should be noted that asymmetry is not the same as irreversibility, for though the latter involves the former, the former does not necessarily involve the latter. If A is greater than B, B is not greater than A—the relations of 'greater than' and 'less than' are not symmetrical. But it does not follow, and it is not in fact the case, that irreversibility is involved, for it is indifferent whether we say, 'A is greater than B' or 'B is less than A'. Either method of statement is equally correct.

Thirdly, it is nonsense to talk of the reversibility or irreversibility of single things. An event is neither reversible nor irreversible —it is only of an order that reversibility can be predicated.

Lastly, if not nonsensical, it is at least elliptic to talk of 'time' as being irreversible. The view which hypostatizes 'Time' into a big blank absolute, a singular subject of pious generalizations, thereby makes it impossible for itself to ascribe any meaning to the statement that time is reversible or irreversible. (Unfortunately, since "nothing's impossible to faith" this attempt has often been made!) It is only if time is modestly conceived as the order of a series of events, not as a hypostatized absolute, that the question whether it is reversible or no can be asked.

To say that the order of events is irreversible means that a series of events cannot *indifferently* be taken in the order A, B, C, D, E or in the order E, D, C, B, A. This is easy enough, but it is much harder to explain *why* the order is not indifferent, without presupposing temporal characteristics.

I am inclined to think that it is more fundamental to explain irreversibility in terms of the happening of events than to explain the happening of events in terms of irreversibility. For in the latter case we are still faced with the question *why* the order is irreversible, and to answer this by "because they happen in that order" is to return to the starting-point. Granted that we must start from what is ultimate and indefinable, we must yet beware of choosing the wrong starting-point.

If we say that A and B are two events, and that B follows A, what is involved by this? Firstly, it is quite evident that if B follows A, A does not follow B. Yet, it may be objected, supposing B's and A's were arranged alternately, like black and white beads on a string, it would be quite true to say both that black follows white and that white follows black. That, however, is not the point. We are not saying that *a* white bead cannot follow a black one: what we are saying is that *the* white bead (call it Matthew) that precedes Mark, a black bead, cannot also follow it. This is the plainest common sense, and the strictest logic: a *similar* bead to Matthew may follow Mark, but the *same* Matthew cannot both precede and follow Mark.

So far, however, we have only got asymmetry, not irreversibility. Counting from left to right, we may say, "Matthew precedes Mark", and because the relation of precedence is asymmetrical, we cannot, *as long as we count in the same order*, say that Mark precedes Matthew. But we can reverse the order of counting, and go from right to left equally well. In this case we can say "Mark precedes Matthew", and we cannot say that Matthew precedes Mark. It is indifferent which order we decide to use.[1] The question is, whether this bead-analogy is properly applicable to events in time. Certainly, if we look upon events as 'strung out' in a hypostatized time, we have no reason for doubting it. But it would seem, at least at first sight, that it is altogether misleading to think of events as objectively 'there', and of our passing from one to another as akin to the process of counting beads. After all, we are ourselves 'in' time, and it is only by an effort of thought of doubtful validity that we can put ourselves 'outside' time, and announce triumphantly that 'objec-

---

[1] It may become conventional to use one rather than the other. All English reading depends on the agreement that the letter nearer the left is 'before', the letter nearer the right 'after'. It is remarkable, when one comes to think of it, how easily we "understand" the spelling rule—"I *before* E, except *after* C"! The Chinaman reading English would get this wrong.

tively' the beads can be counted in either direction. (Exact significance of the words in inverted commas unknown!) But this seems to me to beg the question. If, *per impossibile*, we could put ourselves 'outside' time, we probably *should* find things very different in that specious Utopia, but that is not the point. The question at issue is whether, *as things are*, events can be counted in either direction. If so, and the bead analogy is a permissible one, the time-order will be asymmetrical, but it will not be irreversible. There is *nothing* in the bead analogy to give irreversibility. Is there, then, any meaning, and if so, what meaning, in saying that the order of events is irreversible?

It is, first, necessary to distinguish between two different senses in which 'irreversibility' is used. First, there is 'irrevers*ibility*' proper, used only of an order which *cannot* be reversed. Secondly, the word is often also used for what would better be called 'unreversed', of an order which is not, in fact, reversed. A one-way street is an example of unreversed order, since all cars do, in fact, proceed in one direction only. But it is not impossible that a car should go the other way, and so the order is not irreversible. Irreversibility involves unreversedness,[1] but not vice versa.

If A and B are two events, and B follows A, A *does not* follow B. Nobody would dispute this. But it is a different position, and one which is not logically involved by the former, to say that A *cannot* follow B. We must distinguish between the irreversibility of law and the unreversedness of fact. *Why* 'cannot' A follow B? Because, it may be answered, of something in the nature of A and B. *This, however, has nothing to do with temporal order as such.* I am not concerned to deny that, in causality for instance, there may be something more than mere temporal priority which marks A out as the cause of B, some causal bond (of various degrees of stringency, according to different writers) between their natures. But I *am* concerned to deny that this is temporal. On the contrary, it is opposed to time, and is the result of abstraction from the temporal element, for the word 'cannot' has no place in time.

The only temporal part is A *and then* B—and the whole point of time is in that "and then", which is not further analysable, for the happening of events is ultimate.

I am inclined to think that the question of irrevers*ibility* is in

[1] I apologize for the uncouth expression.

a sense almost irrelevant to time, and that what we mean by the unidirectionality of time is not a matter of 'musts' and 'cannots' but just a matter of fact. It just happens so.

This is not, of course, equivalent to asserting that time is reversible, which seems to me nonsense, and misleading nonsense at that. It may or may not be the case that contents could conceivably have been actualized in a different order, and that B might have preceded A—that is a question that concerns causality. But they have not, in fact, happened thus, and A *did* precede B—and that is all that matters for time. Put differently, the order in which contents are actualized may or may not be reversible: but *time*-order is, strictly, neither reversible nor irreversible, though the latter mode of statement is less harmful than the former.

It may be objected that the position rests on an undesirable abstraction of time from content and of both from events. Undoubtedly, this abstraction is undesirable if carried too far, but up to a point it is both legitimate and useful, and I cannot see that it is carrying it too far to say that something which can be predicated of the order in which contents are actualized (reversibility or irreversibility) cannot be predicated of time-order. On the contrary, it is the opposite view, that time-order, which is a mere cumulative 'and then', can be called 'irrevers*ible*' or 'revers*ible*' which is the real hypostatization of time. Only with the aid of this distinction are we enabled to take the very simple, and, I think, correct view that the 'happening' of events is ultimate, and transcends any talk of reversibility. As far as *time*-order is concerned, it seems to me unmeaning to ask if it could be 'reversed'. Time-order is 'irreversible' only in the loose sense of unreversedness, that it has happened so, and not otherwise; but if we say of events that their order is irreversible, we are referring not only to purely temporal characteristics, but also to content. It is only where the notion of content enters that reversibility or irreversibility can be properly predicated.

Those who affirm reversibility do so usually with their eyes fixed on content, and they adduce cases of 'reparability of things' in their favour. On the other hand, many opponents of reversibility have said how ridiculous it would be if things were reversed, and how ludicrous it would be to see the cow jumping backwards over the moon. But both, opponents and defenders alike, seem to me to emphasize the wrong thing. I am not here concerned to go into details about whether scientific 'laws' can go backward, which in essence is what these people are arguing about, because whatever the result, *time* has not in any sense been made to 'go backward'. It is conceivable that *A might* succeed *B*, but that is a difference in the order in which the contents are actualized in events: it has no bearing whatever on time as such. Whether it is '*A* and then *B*' or '*B* and then *A*' is irrelevant to time, for all that time is, is the 'and then' of the *happening* of events.

It may be objected that we can only know (for instance) causal relations as in time: how then have we any right to say that the irrevers*ibility* is in these (with their talk of the 'natures' of *A* and *B*) and not in time? The answer is, that we can never prove our position, and that nobody can be forced to agree on this matter, for disagreement if there be any is ultimate. But it is a strong point in favour of this view that with a simple distinction (one which is constantly made in other contexts, and which need not be carried to the point when it becomes vicious) much verbal complexity and difficulty can be cleared away. The problem of irreversibility is in great part a pseudo one: and its genuine difficulties are great enough without adding to them.

Can, then, the order of *events* be reversed? This question can be taken in three senses, two of which are not fundamental.

Firstly, comes the excessive preoccupation with the temporal order of events to the exclusion of content. Can events, in so far as they are temporal, be reversed? This question has no meaning,[1] on the suppositions I have been making.

Secondly, there is the opposite extreme of emphasizing content and neglecting date. This error seems to me on all fours with that of saying that the bead Matthew can both precede and follow Mark, when what is meant is that *another* white bead, qualitatively exactly like Matthew, follows Mark. It is to confuse qualitative similarity with numerical identity. Those who lay too much stress on the possibility of "reparability of things" and who fail to see that it is totally irrelevant to the question of irreversibility, seem to me to

[1] That is, unless we are prepared to interpret temporal order in terms of irreversibility, instead of vice versa. This seems to me a much clumsier way, as happening' is more fundamental. This is a dogmatic statement for which no proof can be given or required, but I believe it to be justified.

IRREVERSIBILITY

commit this fallacy. When all frills have been removed, any doctrine of "cycles of events" ultimately depends on this notion. What this comes to is that the 'same' event can recur over and over again. This is rubbish. The same *content* may or may not recur—that is a different question—but each time it happens, it has a different date, and is a different event. This is implicit in the very word 'recur'.[1] It may be objected that when the two events are exactly the same in every particular except date, it is mere pedantry to insist on calling them 'two', and that they are 'really' identical. This is to a certain extent a matter of language. I do not deny that this difference of date is in many cases supremely unimportant, and that for practical purposes we often refer to them as one thing, and not as two. This substitution of 'thing' for 'event' is not a slip of the pen, and it seems to me very important. Even if it *is* only a matter of language it might as well be clear language and consistent language. If we are going to use the word 'event' as having an essential reference to date, there must be no hedging over it—especially as such hedging is totally unnecessary, while we possess the word 'thing' for the other notion. Secondly, it is quite different to talk of cycles of things and to talk of cycles of events, and we cannot pass from one to the other. Even if the same content does recur, that proves nothing about the reparability of time—and what is more, the denial of the latter does not rule out of court the possibility of the reparability of things. (This point has been even more overlooked than the other.)

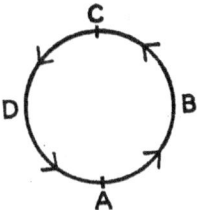

A brief example to clear the matter up. Suppose (after the fashion of Herbert Spencer) that from an initial point A, the course of events could be regarded as a steady evolution until a culminating point of complexity was reached at C, and that then the opposite process of devolving began, until the primitive simplicity of

[1] See also on this point, Lotze, *Metaphysics*, pp. 315 ff.

A was again reached, after which the whole process began again, exactly the same points (B, C, D) being reached as before. It is not nonsense to say that it is a repetition of the same process in time, and that the event of passing B the first time is a different event from that of passing B the nth time. It is not nonsense: and it is the only logical position to take, since any alternative, however it defends itself by counter-attacks of 'pedantry' and 'merely verbal consistency', commits the fallacy exposed above. However trivial the difference between the two events, and however difficult it be for me to avoid at least the appearance of hypostatizing time,[1] we *must* admit that there is a difference, or ruin any hope of attaining a satisfactory theory of time, on a wretched muddling hedging about 'identical' and 'exactly similar'.

Thirdly, can events, sanely conceived as having both content and date, occur in reverse order? It is evident that there are two questions here, and the whole of this chapter has been an attempt to show that, though they cannot, without fallacies, be treated in complete isolation, yet they are logically separable, and that to see this is to avoid some of the worst confusions that have made the problem of irreversibility a byword. The whole purpose of the distinctions made in this chapter is not to divide the indivisible—to chop up 'events' into slices neatly labelled 'Date' and 'Content' like sandwiches at a party—but to attempt to get clear what properly belongs to what, in the belief that only so can we get clear on the more fundamental notion of 'event'.

The first question is the one on which nine-tenths of the ink shed over "irreversibility" has been lavished. Granted the notion of causality, can the normal sequence of cause and effect be reversed? "Everything unfolds in a certain direction, and if, by chance, we saw something produced in the opposite direction we should be immediately struck by it as by something contrary to the course of nature. We need not, as a matter of fact, have here recourse to imaginations such as those of Wells: we can *see* this reversed world. To do this we have only to provide ourselves with a cinematograph and to insert within it a reel of pictures representing moving phenomena—such as the jumping or the falling of a horse, a drop

[1] And certainly the argument could not be worse chosen for the plausibility of my view. I think that the supposition is a thoroughly bad one. Compare Bergson's remarks, *Creative Evolution*, p. 385.

of water dripping into a pond, the descent of a mass of stones or of sand—and to turn the crank in the opposite direction. It is impossible to describe the strangeness of the impression which comes from the aspect of these pictures. It is not sorcery; but is something more or less like it: it is a world manifestly absurd, which presents no analogy with the one we know."[1] Meyerson's remarks can be paralleled from any of a dozen writers, without any difficulty, and there is no need to enlarge on the point, as it is immediately evident.

One last warning may, it is hoped, reinforce the effect of previous reiterations. In dealing with causal relations, there is need for the greatest care; for causality, as well as abstracting from, has essential reference to particular events in time, and it would be useless to imagine that the question of the 'before' and 'after' of cause and effect (to mention only one temporal element) could be excluded altogether. Nevertheless, with the exception of the regularity view of causation, it is generally thought that there is 'more in' causality than mere temporal sequence, and though that 'more' is extraordinarily difficult to render explicit, it is usually such as to justify (in however slack a use is not the point), some reference to 'law'. It is the appearance of the notion of 'law' that I wish to discuss here, and in so far as it is possible to separate off the purely temporal element and examine the other without particular reference to time, this will be done. The warning is against believing that this separation can be final.

When a scientist says, "Acids turn litmus paper red", he is asserting a general correlation between two different kinds of things. These 'kinds' are the result of his selection of certain aspects in which he is interested from situations that may be different: thus what he calls 'acids' differ in many ways, and agree only in the one property which he, thinking it important, calls 'acidity'. The assertion of 'law' (in however vague a sense this is interpreted[2]) implies abstraction, more or less arbitrary, from particulars of date, place, secondary qualities, and so on. To a certain extent, then, all causality

[1] Meyerson, *Identity and Reality*, p. 217. See also Breton, article on reversibility in *Les Mondes* (December 1875); Fechner, *Vier Paradoxa*; and Karl Pearson, *Grammar of Science*, p. 394.
[2] I have no wish to prejudge the question of 'law' in causality, and use both terms in a very wide sense, since the minimum that can be said is sufficient for my purpose.

involves reparability of things, since it postulates that the 'same' cause can occur over and over again. ('Same', of course, is used relatively, even so far as content is concerned, for, as Whitehead showed in his Principle of Convergence to Simplicity with Diminution of Extent, it is only by taking smaller and smaller pieces, and treating them as isolated systems, that we can get exact qualitative similarity.) The dipping of litmus paper in carbolic acid by A at time t_1 is compatible with the dipping of litmus paper in sulphuric acid by B at time t_2. What causality asserts is not so much the exact repetition of a whole situation, as the repetition of certain generalized elements—and content, no less than date, is abstracted from. Nobody would deny reparability of things in this *schematized* form, though there might be more doubt as to whether an exact replica of a given complex scene would ever occur. But there is no need to reopen the question of reparability of things: the conclusions formerly reached should be recalled, that, theoretically, reparability of things is possible, but that the probability of exact repetitions varies from high, in simple cases like dropping a book, to low in complex situations. But this alone does not give reversibility. All that reparability asserts is that a content *can* recur: but reversibility involves the *further* position that the intervening stages between the

$$\overline{A \; K \; R \; A \; M \; A \; Z \; Y}$$

initial and final positions (A and L) can be retraced in reverse order.

$$\overline{A \; B \; S \; L \; S \; B \; A}$$

Here again it is a matter of plausibility. In the case of simple movements, for instance, it seems easy to 'go backwards', and retrace one's steps, like the famous Duke of York and his ten thousand men, whereas complicated situations are much more difficult.

But is this so? Motion in mechanics is reversible, but is it in even the simplest situations in practice? I move forward two paces, and back again immediately—but energy has been used in the process, and *the energy used is more than the work done in moving me forward and back again*, for heat has been generated which is lost beyond recall. It is wrong to murmur that entropy and time are bound up together, and that here, where we are attempting to ignore temporal characteristics, entropy should also be overlooked: for that would be to beg the question. I do not here intend to go into the physical question, which has been excellently discussed by Meyerson[1]—but it seems to me significant that physics should attempt to relate to each other two sources of departure from the ideals of rational mechanics that are, at least at first sight, very different from each other, loss of heat and time-order. Secondly, as well as the phenomena of loss, there are also those of gain. As was pointed out in a former chapter, there is some empirical evidence for the view that novelties do occur, and it is simpler in the long run to admit them than to indulge in the endless and unsatisfactory task of attempting to explain them away in terms of postulated elements. Thirdly, as the laws of chance make it extremely improbable that a complex situation should ever recur in all its details, it is only in very simple cases that recurrence need be considered as a practical possibility.

It would seem, then, that even as regards content, there is not a great deal of evidence in favour of reparability, except in very simple situations, and there is still less in favour of reversibility.

As applied to time-order, the notion of reversibility is unmeaning, and its use depends upon a bad blunder, which would lead to an infinite regress. If we think of time as moving, it is a very easy step to the view that its course is 'laid out' as it were behind it, and then to the view that this course can be retraced like movements in space.

As Dunne quite correctly pointed out, such a movement would itself 'take time', and thus the first step of his regress is taken. But the movement of time is so different from ordinary movement that it is a misnomer to call it movement: where I differ from Dunne is not in the consequences to which such a view would lead, but in thinking it, not a self-evident starting-point, but a fallacy. The unidirectionality of time is fundamental, and is not to be analysed away in terms of notions of irreversibility which themselves derive from it.

[1] *Identity and Reality*, passim; and in particular the very clear summary on p. 199 of the first volume of *De l'explication dans les Sciences*.

Events, then, must mediate between the bare 'happening' of time which transcends reversibility, and the *possibility* of reversibility which generalization of content affords. Yet even if that latter possibility were more than a possibility, the order of events could never be reversible. In so far as events have an essential reference to time, to that degree they are infected by the peculiarities of time. The sum of odd and even is always odd, and similarly the clash of (theoretically) reversible, and unreversed series must always result in the victory of the latter. In this is the true Triumph of Time.

CHAPTER XI

"BECOMING"

IT is unfortunate that what is probably the most celebrated definition of time should also be one of the worst. Aristotle's name has given countenance to it, and it reappears with maddening iteration for centuries, in such unlikely places as theological treatises, and works on literary criticism, as well as in all histories of philosophy. The unsatisfactoriness of the definition of time in terms of motion is not in anything that can be definitely controverted, but in its onesidedness, and in the stunted view of time to which it gives rise.

No one would deny that we cannot distinguish the passage of time without counting movements, but that alone does not mean that time itself is *nothing but* "movement in so far as it admits of enumeration".[1] Aristotle himself saw that the before-and-after relation (the *B* series) is not specifically temporal, but that, on the other hand, *unless* we apprehend a before and after relation (and this involves movement) we cannot apprehend the *passage* of time. But Aristotle wrongly omitted 'passage', and this meant that the conditions of our apprehension of duration were considered by him to be the very characteristics of the nature of time. To say that "time is a kind of number" is, from one point of view, true, but it is curiously insufficient. If it were nothing more, it would not be what we mean by 'time', for there is nothing in this view to account for the asymmetry which is the most important characteristic of time, and this is the main defect in Aristotle's view. It seems to me that of the two notions, time and movement, the former is much the more fundamental. Even if (ignoring 'becoming' for the present) we attempt to analyse time in terms of motion, we can only proceed with the help of the notion of change, and *by*

[1] *Metaphysics*, IV, 11. For Plotinus' criticisms of Aristotle's and similar theories, see *Enneads* (translated Guthrie), pp. 986 ff.

discounting the spatial aspect of movement. This is much more complicated than the opposite process of analysing motion in terms of change or time, and space, and describing it, for instance, as "change generated in space".[1] But, secondly, there is a heavier count against the definition of time in terms of movement. Even if we agreed to perform the complicated process of analysing duration by motion, the further difficulty remains of the 'becoming' of time. This cannot be analysed as motion, except in a specialized and (I think) a thoroughly bad sense. For such 'movement' (of the 'now', of the 'present' 'into' 'the future') is not motion through space, which is the only motion we can understand *unless we are already presupposing time and becoming*; and everything is as inexplicable as ever, for the explanation is only verbal. *What* is it through which becoming, if it is analysed as motion, 'becomes'? The question is unanswerable, for it is nonsensical, and rests upon a vicious conception of time and change—a conception which leads straight to an infinite regress. Nevertheless, since the 'becoming' of time as ultimate and irreducible is far from being universally accepted, and is indeed what is in question in this chapter, it would be a mistake to rely too much upon this argument at the present stage. It is included here as an added reason, to some philosophers, for rejecting any definition of time in terms of motion: for the others, that it is cumbrous and complicated, should be sufficient.

What, then, of change? Can time be completely analysed in terms of change? and can we deny, as McTaggart does, that there could be time in a changeless universe? It is certainly psychologically inconceivable, as has been pointed out over and over again, that there should be consciousness of time without change, for we can only apprehend duration against a background of change. Yet, it may be said, it is all the same logically possible that there should be time, even though we could never be conscious of it. It is not impossible that the universe should be a static, changeless whole, like a child's rubber ball lying lost and forgotten, and that time should nevertheless 'go on', as it does while the ball lies untouched, unchanging, among the nettles.

This is a thoroughly undesirable view, and depends on a shocking

[1] The opposite view is taken by W. K. Clifford (*Lectures and Essays*, I, p. 262).

hypostatization of time into a thing in itself, apart from the universe of events. Time is not an abstract metronome placed snugly outside the universe, and measuring mundane events by its ticking: it is not something that is logically independent of the universe: if it were, the universe would not be 'all that is', and so would not be the universe. We are back at the dubious equivocations of Kant's First Antinomy.

The supposition, then, is false: if *nothing* changed, not only would there be no consciousness of time, there would be no time. Change involves time, but equally, time involves change: the two are co-implicant. Are they, then, equivalent? Ultimately, perhaps, yes: but we find it useful to use the two words to show that different aspects are being stressed. 'Change' is used when we want to emphasize the content, the 'what': 'Time' is used when we are dealing with the medium, the 'in which' of change. I use the word 'medium' quite deliberately though aware of the dangers to which its misuse is open: like the ether, time is liable to have substantial qualities attributed to it, and to become, in Maritain's pleasant phrase, a place where we put all our blackest contradictions out to pasture! Nevertheless, it seems to me vital to take a very simple view of time as that in which events happen, risking the possible misuse of 'in which', rather than blurring its usefulness by a too-facile identification with change. Time and change, then, though ultimately inseparable, emphasize different aspects. Is it sensible to ask which aspect is the more fundamental, and if, for instance, time can be analysed, other than methodologically, in terms of change? I doubt it.

This is where the importance of the question of 'becoming', with which the rest of this chapter will be concerned, enters in. If we were to assert a fundamental and irreducible becoming, we should commit ourselves to the view that qualitative change (what Broad calls 'changes in time') is insufficient as a correlate to what we mean by 'time', and that a fundamentally different type of change is also required.

'Becoming' is commonly used in two senses, which, though connected, are not the same. Besides its normal use in everyday life, it is also used by Bergson and Broad in a semi-technical sense. When Broad, for instance, asserts that the future "is nothing at all" there is a sense in which this is so obviously true as to seem trivial.[1] Quite evidently, part of what we mean by an event's being future (is) that it does not exist now. Nobody denies the non-existence of the future in this sense: what many have denied is that there is any more to it than that.

On the other hand, we might interpret the statement "the future is nothing at all", in another way, and this is the interesting one. In the less exciting sense above, the past, equally with the future is "nothing"—for it follows from the definition of past and future that they are distinct from the present—but in this new sense, past and future are not admitted to be on the same plane.

In all this discussion it is extraordinarily hard to keep clear in our minds what is mere tautology, what is due to our subjective limitations, and what is genuinely important, and yet it is vital that these differences should be kept in mind. Arguments from 'subjective limitations', for example, cut both ways: we have no reason to suppose that the world really is what we inevitably believe it to be, or that there 'must' be an ontological difference between past and future because we have knowledge of the one in a way in which we have not knowledge of the other; but, on the other hand, it is intellectual suicide to begin doubting our only means of knowledge. Granted that metaphysics may be vitiated by the egocentric predicament: I yet fail to see that there is any sense whatsoever in dreaming of Metaphysics as an ideal Thing-in-itself. Hence, in the absence of evidence to the contrary, that our cognitive relations to past and future are different is prima facie evidence to the distinction's between them being a genuine one. And that our cognitive relations *are* different, very few, if any, have ever attempted to deny.

Becoming, in the interesting sense, is conceived of as analogous to growth. Of course this is a bad statement, for strictly growth is an example of becoming, and to reverse the two is to put the cart before the horse. But that just illustrates the difficulty which we are in: the conceptions with which we are dealing are, it is claimed, so fundamental that any analogy is bound to be circular. All the same, something has to be done, and circularity is not necessarily vicious: the upholders of such a view are bound to start somewhere, and

---

[1] A definition, for instance, like "The future is reality which is not made and is not yet being made" (!) gets nowhere (Fawcett, *Divine Imagining*, p. 150).

growth has the advantage that it is immediately familiar to all, even though, on more sophisticated levels, as physicists and biologists, we ignore it or explain it away in terms of a postulated conservation theory. On Monday, a shoot of green is visible above the soil. On Tuesday, it is an inch above the ground, on Wednesday, two inches. (We are supposing it to be of the mushroom family!) We say of this shoot that it has *grown*. Now there is no need to go again here into the question, partially discussed in an earlier chapter, how far it is plausible to suppose that what we call its 'development'[1] is implicit in its past state, and not a real 'development' in any proper sense of the word: instead, I shall make three brief remarks. Firstly, *our belief in growth is original*, and the attempt to reduce everything to a sum in simple addition and subtraction is a later device *that may have no more than methodological utility*. It is the product of too much learning. Secondly, although for simplicity the example considers only the growth of one green shoot as measured in space, growth is not confined to mere elongation of the already given, like the American's chewing gum. In time,[2] a flower will come. Growth is essentially connected with novelty. Thirdly, even if the present state is implicit in the past, that proves *nothing at all* about a future state, unless we prejudge the very question at issue, which is the legitimacy of the identification of 'passing' with 'passed'.

On the other hand, however, it must not be forgotten that the analogy halts and fails in some respects. It is evident that if we took it seriously, we should be committed to holding that past and present have the same footing, in opposition to the future, just as Monday's inch of green is as much 'there' as what is 'now' being added, in contradistinction to what is 'not yet' there. If upholders of 'becoming' are bound to take this substantialized view of the past, it will be a serious objection against the plausibility of 'becoming'. Nevertheless, there is a sense, easier perhaps to see than to express, in which it is justifiable to talk of the past as 'there' in a way in which the future is not 'there'.[3] I use the vague expression 'there'

[1] Not always realizing what that implies.
[2] This harmless phrase seems to me very significant.
[3] "Future and past alike are not, but the manner of their not-being is not the same" (Lotze, *Metaphysics*, p. 325). Inge (*Philosophy of Plotinus*) relates the difference to different attitudes of will to past and future.

to avoid 'existing', or 'present', or 'is', all of which invoke ideas of grammar which are irrelevant to the question, but which, if used, would lead to difficulties of tense, and confuse the issue. It is vital to see that we are not concerned now with the mere 'tautologous' use of tense-expressions: were that the case, it would be self-contradictory to talk of past events as *existing* in some sense, just as it would be perfectly trivial to assert 'becoming'. Put briefly, the point is that the sense in which the past "exists" is in no way reducible to any statement about what at present *is*. (The denial of this leads to the difficulties of the Ontological Argument.) It may be asserted, or denied, that this sense is worth bothering about. If it be denied, *cadit quaestio*. If it be asserted, as I think it may very well be, then half of what the supporters of 'becoming' maintain has been granted. As for the other half, that the future 'is' not *in the sense*[1] *in which the past 'is'*, the arguments in its favour are, from the very nature of the case, probability ones only. Firstly, there is the common-sense belief in the difference between past and future, and in the absence of proof to the contrary, it offers a presumption that there *is* such a difference. Secondly, unless you allow becoming, there appears to be very little point in insisting upon the unreversedness of time. Is succession alone enough to constitute time? In other words, is the *A* series, with its asymmetry and curious unidirectionality, merely the contribution of our own busy brains, and is, 'objectively' (whatever that may mean!) the *B* series sufficient to time? That, of course, raises the difficult and possibly meaningless problem as to whether there would still be time in a mindless universe, and the (at the least) unprofitable speculation as to how and why such 'time' would differ from what we poor egocentric mortals call time! You are committed to this unless you admit 'becoming'. Thirdly, 'irrational' as such becoming is, there is much in the world that is irrational. The postulation of self-contained mechanical systems, of machines of perfect efficiency, where, so to speak, an exact balance sheet can be drawn up that checks exactly, is a harmless little game which hurts nobody, and

---

[1] The point is so important and so often confused that reiteration may be forgiven. The 'is' is not the ordinary temporal 'is' of present time: and to say that the future 'is' not in this easy sense is, so far from being an argument for asserting 'becoming' in any important sense, totally irrelevant to it.

which can give much æsthetic pleasure. But, apart from our æsthetic and ethical feelings, which, as Russell has assured us, are quite irrelevant, there is no particular reason why we should expect the universe to conform to our ideal of the Perfect Balance Sheet. It seems to me that rather than admit unknown x's by the back door at the last minute to make our accounts tally,[1] we should do well to admit them at the beginning. If there is irrationality, it may as well be admitted first as last: for philosophy is not science, and though there is some justification for the scientist who unswervingly seeks for the ideal of a completely 'rational' explanation, there is none for the metaphysician. Fourthly, when all is said and done, we do use the notion of becoming, and feel that we know what we mean by it (until we become over-critical and sophisticated). It is difficult to see why there should be so ready an acceptance of, and familiarity with, an entirely ungrounded notion, on the part of the plain man.[2]

Admitting, then, an irreducible 'becoming', what is the result on the status of the future? Firstly, such a view results, in an essential asymmetry between past and future: there is a continual instability in the time-series in the direction of the future. This instability Alexander conceives as a *nisus* towards deity: Bergson thinks of it as a continual process of creation, ever evolving new forms. But this instability, as well as urging onwards to ever new and higher forms, is also destructive, as is witnessed by the common view that links time with a transience that is too often pitiful—"All flesh is grass, and the goodliness thereof is as the flower of the field. The grass withereth, the flower fadeth. . . ." There is nothing in either of these views that is in conflict with common sense: on the contrary, the plain man would readily agree both that time passes and that 'in time' (in that very significant little phrase that was noticed earlier) new things are created. The instability of time, and the essential difference between the status of past and future, cannot rightly be ignored. Secondly, it makes more plausible,

[1] As I, when a child, 'balanced' my accounts by "Lost, 7½d.", or "Unaccountably gained, 5d." There is some candour in the 'unaccountably' that is absent from too many philosophies!

[2] As Lotze put it, we must either admit Becoming or explain the becoming of an unreal appearance of Becoming! (*Metaphysics*, p. 105). The law of Identity, he insists, only says that a thing is what it is, not that it must always remain so.

though it does not, I think, absolutely necessitate, a view such as Broad's, who holds that the future is 'nothing at all'—in a sense which is very far from being trivial. Proof of this position, from the nature of the case, is impossible, and when all the evidence for and against has been summarized, it must be just accepted or rejected, for an ultimate disagreement will have been reached.

The first objection that naturally comes to mind when told that the future is 'nothing at all', is: "How, then, is it that we can and do make judgments about the future?" As Broad clearly saw, it is no answer to this to deny that our judgments may be certain ones, and to say that prediction is impossible: "Our question is not whether we can have *certain* knowledge about the future, but is the prior question: What are we really *talking about* when we profess to make judgments about the future, and what do we *mean* by the truth or falsity of such judgments?"[1]

Broad deals with this very important question at length, and successfully on the whole. Briefly, his argument is, that statements may have meaning even though the object 'about' which they are made does not exist. We can give *meaning* to the statement "Puck has turned the milk", even though Puck does not exist and has never existed. Similarly, Broad argues, we can attach meaning to the statement "It may rain to-morrow", without having to attribute to to-morrow some obscure kind of 'existence' at the time when I make the judgment. Secondly, Broad distinguishes between what a judgment is *about*, and the *fact* to which the judgment *refers*. The distinguishing characteristic of judgments 'about' the future (and that which distinguishes them from judgments 'about' imaginary entities, which do refer to a fact, even if it is a negative one[2]), is that there is no fact to which they refer at the time when they are made. "They are therefore at that time neither true nor false. They will become true or false when there is a fact for them to refer to: and after this they will remain true or false, as the case may be, for ever and ever. . . . 'Judgments' which profess to be about the future are not genuine judgments when they are made, but

[1] *Scientific Thought*, p. 70.
[2] This doctrine of negative facts is not universally accepted. But it is probable that by a re-statement of what is, after all, not vital to his main position, Broad could avoid criticism on this score. The same applies to some rather queer language at the top of p. 72, with a dubious use of 'real'.

merely enjoy a courtesy title by anticipation, like the eldest sons of the higher nobility during the lifetime of their fathers."[1] It should be noticed that the temporal language in this passage is not, as it might seem at first sight, a defect, since Broad's whole point is that the reference to the future is ultimate and irreducible. So far, except for minor dubieties of statement that do not affect the main argument, he has made out a good case for himself. But when he goes on to analyse "It has rained", "It is raining now" and "It will rain", with a view to showing that the tense-reference in the latter is irreducible, I cannot think that he has proved his point, for reasons which were explained in an earlier chapter. Nevertheless, it would be foolish to attach too much importance to this. Admittedly, it would be a useful short cut for Broad if he could show that even our formulations cannot wholly eliminate a reference to the future. But even if that is not so, the essentials of his view are very far from being disproved, since, as he himself pointed out earlier, verbal juggling is easy. "Much of the trouble about Time and Change comes from our obstinate attempts to reduce such judgments to the characterizing form. Any judgment can be *verbally* reduced to this form. We can reduce "S is" to "S is existent". But the reduction is purely verbal, and those who take it seriously land in the sloughs of the Ontological Argument. Similarly, "S is future" is verbally a judgment that ascribes a characteristic to an event S. But, if we are right, this must be a mistake."[2] Broad's view seems to me impossible to prove by such a short cut as this would be, for, as was suggested in the earlier chapter, it is doubtful whether it is ever possible to prove a *metaphysical* theory of *time* by the use of strict *logical* tenseless language—but that is no argument against it.

A more important question is how, on his theory, we can assert glibly that my statement "It will rain to-morrow" will be confirmed or refuted by what happens to-morrow. It would seem that this is itself a proposition about the future, and that there is danger of an infinite regress. Broad's answer to this is satisfactory: "With *any* judgment we can tell what *kind* of fact will verify or refute it, as soon as we know what the judgment is about and what kind of assertion it makes. But no amount of inspection of a judgment

[1] Op. cit., p. 73. See also McTaggart's criticisms of Broad (*Nature of Existence*, Sec. 334 et seq.).   [2] Op. cit., pp. 68–9.

itself will show us *the particular fact* which makes it true if it is true and false if it is false. There is therefore no inconsistency between the statement that we can know at once what *kind of fact* would verify a judgment about the future, and the statement that such judgments do not refer to any fact when made."[1]

This exposition of Broad can suitably be ended with the advantages which he believes he gains by his theory. Firstly, he claims that the differences of our cognitive attitudes to past and future, otherwise very hard to explain, are accounted for on his principles. "It is commonly held that there can be no certain knowledge about the future, but that all judgments which profess to be about it consist of more or less probable conjectures made by analogy with the past. Now we do not always recognize how odd our certainty about this is on the assumption that the future really is something that has "future existence" as the past really is something that has "past existence".... If the future exist, and be just that part of the existent which succeeds the present, it is difficult to see why a present act of cognition might not know an event which is later than itself, just as it can know some events which are earlier than itself."[2] It would, of course, be a mistake to suppose that this is an *argument* for his view, except very indirectly.

Secondly, Broad claims that he can avoid the vicious infinite regress criticized by McTaggart: "Is there anything contradictory in the fact that Queen Anne's death has been present and is now past? There very well might be if we had to take the change of an event in respect to the characteristics of presentness and pastness as analogous to the change of a signal lamp in respect to the characteristics of red and green. But we have seen that that cannot be done, and that the second kind of change depends on the first.... What happens when Lord Bolingbroke swears is not that something which was false of Anne's death becomes true of it, but that something becomes true of Anne's death which was before neither true nor false of it."[3] It seems to me that Broad has justified his claim to have demolished the need for a regress, and that there is much to be said, both metaphysically and from the standpoint of common sense, for the view that the future is nothing at all. The rest of the chapter will be taken up with a discussion of two points. The first is the analysis of propositions that would commonly be

[1] Op. cit., p. 74. [2] Op. cit., p. 78. [3] Op. cit., p. 81.

said to be 'about' the future.[1] The second is—What are we going to do about *other* theories of the future?

A proposition such as "Either he will come or he will not come" need not detain us long. It is evident that this is a purely logical disjunction, and we do not need to have knowledge of the future in any sense whatever to attach meaning to this.[2]

"Either he will come or he will write to explain." This, again, it may be said is not a proposition about the future but a logical alternative, the assertion of whose actualization brings in the reference to the future. It is implicitly assumed that the disjunction is exhaustive, and if this is so, the proposition can, it is claimed, be exhibited in a completely logical form. Suppose, however, that neither alternative was realized, the alternatives could not have been exhaustive, and this was because our knowledge at the time when we made the statement was incomplete. If I say, "He will come either on the train or on the bus", and I am right, in that he *does* come on one, that does not mean that I 'knew' the future. What it does mean is that my judgment has approximated to an exhaustive logical disjunction, in which the reference to the future is at a minimum, that is, zero. If I am wrong, and he misses both train and bus, and has to telegraph, the disjunction was evidently not an exhaustive one.

But it should be evident by now, that if the analysis stops here, it is very far from being satisfactory. It is perfectly correct that in so far as I can reduce propositions 'about' the future to a logical form, I am to that extent *eliminating* the future. But that is only half the story, and a misleading half at that, since it leads us to attach emphasis to the wrong end. The other half is, that *such a reduction can never be completed, though it may approximate very closely to the logical ideal*. It is perfectly correct to say that *if* the disjunction is exhaustive, "Either he will come or he will write to explain" becomes a logical alternative, but then the whole question is given away by the apparently innocent remark about "the

[1] In view of Broad's excellent treatment of this topic, the remarks here are to be regarded only as supplementary to his.

[2] Compare the examples given by McTaggart in his criticism of Broad (*Nature of Existence*, ii, pp. 23–6). McTaggart is mistaken in supposing that logical disjunctions referring to the future can be adduced as an argument against Broad.

assertion of whose actualization brings in the reference to the future". *Above and beyond the logical alternative there always remains outstanding the question of actualization.* This seems to me much more important than Broad's attempt (even if it had been successful) to show that a *verbal* reference to the future must always remain outstanding. Again, the attempt to say that incomplete alternatives are to be attributed to our inadequate knowledge is a return to the old view that differences between past and future are merely cognitive. It should be emphasized that it is quite possible to hold this view; what I am objecting to is not this view as such, but the type of analysis of propositions 'about' the future which covertly begs the question.

In so far, then, as there is a *genuine* reference to the future in propositions such as "He will come on the train or on the bus", it is not merely a question of the alternatives being not exhaustive *in fact*, but it is *in principle* impossible that they could be logically tabulated and completely set out.

It is essential that we should be clear on the difference between 'knowing that X is red' (or 'that E will happen') and between *knowing what is meant by* the statement that X is red, or that E will happen. Part of the value of Broad's exposition is that he is definite on this point. The former is a question of prediction:[1] the latter, as Broad points out, is the prior one of *understanding* what it is that a proposition asserts. It is not a contradiction, and it is only by ignoring this distinction that it could be thought to be one, that we can say *both* that we know what is meant by "E will happen", and that we do *not* know that E will happen. Expressed differently, the denial of the proposition "E will happen" is itself an implicit assertion that we know what is meant by the proposition which we are denying. As Broad put it, "There is no inconsistency between the statement that we can know at once what *kind of fact* would verify a judgment about the future, and the statement that such judgments do not refer to any fact when made."[2] All this may seem elementary logic, but it is fatally easy to get confused, and to

---

[1] I am ignoring the 'X is red' type and concentrating on the 'E will happen' type. The former was only adduced to show that the distinction between 'knowing that' and 'knowing what is meant by' is not peculiar to propositions 'about' the future.

[2] Op. cit., p. 74.

produce shallow and ungrounded arguments in consequence both for and against 'becoming'.

How, then, are we to analyse "X will die"? It is irrelevant, even if true, to say that this statement, though probable, is not certain, since it rests on the validity of induction . . . and so forth. The trouble is, that this irrelevance is not always seen at once, since 'will' is ambiguous, implying both the mere reference to the future and an assertion that at some future date the event '*will*' certainly happen. But even if we deny that "X will die" is certain, what we are denying is the assertive connotation of 'will', not that it essentially contains a reference to tense. In his analysis of how it is that we can attach meaning to statements that refer to the future, when the future is nothing at all, Broad is very sound, and there is no need to go into it further here. Granted the initial act of faith—and Broad never convinces me that it is anything other than an act of faith, though none the worse on that account, since we have got to begin somewhere—he has rendered the statement of his theory very plausible.[1]

The second topic to be discussed was what other views of the future are held, what their degree of plausibility is, and how far it would be possible to make them consistent with the view that becoming is fundamental.

There is, first, the familiar view, still flourishing, like the green bay tree, that all events from 'past' to 'future' exist in a fixed order which is timeless, and that all we mean by 'time' is given by the notion of a single point along that fixed row of events. 'Becoming', then, which is the movement of the 'now', is fundamental to *time*: but neither it nor time are of any real importance. On the one hand, we have idealists such as Bradley and McTaggart asserting that such a view of time is obscure and contradictory, and that the true Reality is to be found in a static, changeless realm where time has been transcended. On the other, Dunne urges that if we grasp the nettle of infinite regresses boldly, we can thereby explain the mysteries of the Cosmos. Both views—though this is not so obvious in the case of Dunne—rest ultimately upon a belittlement and denial of time, and a dismissal of all genuine temporal problems as being 'mere appearances', even if, as in the case of Bradley, there

[1] For a criticism of Broad from a totally different point of view, see the article by R. M. Blake in *Mind*, 1925.

is hedging to the extent of admitting these to be *really* appearances! Such a view of the future, as being in some sense 'really there' all the time, seems to me a very unfortunate one, and one can sympathize with those idealists who found that it led straight to contradictions. The objections against it are fourfold. It is contradictory to, or at the very least, in no way supported by experience: it is based on a hypostatization of 'past', 'future', and the 'now': it leads to endless antinomies: it is through and through spatialized. Besides this, it is to me an added objection that, in emphasizing duration, it not only ignores but denies 'Becoming' to be fundamental. It should have been scrapped long ago.

But we have not to choose between the two extremes of this view and Broad's. There is a third view, mediating between these, which has much to recommend it. In Bosanquet's words: "In going on, time not merely expresses, but is, the movement of the real, that is to say, of the universe. It may be conceived, indeed, not as a mathematical abstraction, but as a concrete super-intellectual experience, a creative growth. . . . Divergence, novelty, free originativeness, and a certain degree of indetermination are the principal laws of things. And this is the very source of our freedom and inspiration. The open gates of the future make the interest and excitement of life. . . . There is nothing fixed. *Tout est donné* is the principle most abhorred. Our destiny and that of the universe is really and effectively in our own hands, with no reservation except that the universe has many other members besides us. Time, in the sense of duration, is at the very heart of things."[1] This third view, exemplified by Bergson, differs but slightly from that of Broad. But there are passages, especially in *Creative Evolution*, where Bergson abandons the view of a pure becoming and talks as if the *élan vital* 'chose' one of several alternatives open to it. As has already been said, if this language is more than metaphorical, Bergson lays himself open to the criticisms that he had himself put forward in *Time and Free Will* against a too-spatialized conception of choice, which sullies the splendour of pure durée. Nevertheless, I think that sympathetic interpretation of this kind of view (not necessarily of Bergson's own statements) might yield a meaning which is not only possible but highly plausible.

Many people boggle at Broad's view because it goes too far.

[1] *Value and Destiny of the Individual*, pp. 292-3.

They would agree with him not merely that the future 'is nothing at all' in the tautologous sense, but that in the more important sense that 'becoming' really is fundamental the future is non-existent: nevertheless, at risk of self-contradiction, they cannot wholly agree with him. On the other hand, the dubious method of conceiving of several 'pathways' open to the *élan vital* is even more disagreeable, and with reason.

Is it possible to modify the pathway view into something less blatant, and consistently to hold this modified view together with the view that 'becoming' is fundamental? I believe that it is.

It is attractive to think of the future as the realm of possibilities[1] —and not the least part of its attraction lies in its readiness to admit almost any interpretation. First, of course, there is the very concrete interpretation of these possibilities as 'pathways', branching and intersecting and altogether behaving in a delightfully geometrical way. The too-enthusiastic acceptance of this view, and the prompt recapitulation by its opponents of the objections to which it is very evidently open, have combined to bring into disrepute the notion of a realm of possibilities. This is unfortunate, for it is possible to make a quite different interpretation, which escapes the criticisms brought against a too naïve 'pathways' interpretation.

Of course, the phrase 'a realm of possibilities' is itself very unfortunate, as leading to notions of the 'universe of discourse' type—a substantialized home of hypotheses and might-have-beens. We might substitute for the much-abused word 'realm' that of 'total', but that is open to the opposite danger that it may lead us to suppose that all possibilities are of the same type, and that their 'sum' is something 'objective'—which is nonsense. It should be clearly realized that what is meant by 'total' or 'realm'—whichever word we select as least misleading—is not a mathematical sum, nor a universe of discourse, but is merely a shorthand expression for a conception which is perfectly legitimate, though apt to be misused.

Secondly, there are many usages of 'possible' and confusion is easy. Their disentanglement will be attempted in the next chapter: here it is sufficient to say that 'possible' is being used in the very wide

[1] "The real future is the possible as distinct from the actual" (Macmurray in Symposium on *Time and Change*, Aristotelian Supplement VIII, p. 160).

sense in which anything is called possible that is neither logically necessary nor logically impossible. This logical possibility must be distinguished from the subjective uncertainties, and ignorance which leads us to say, "It may possibly be so", where "I do not know" is implied. It is not the place here to discuss the view which has been held (notably by Spinoza) that all possibility is merely our ignorance, and it will be assumed for the present that they are distinct.

"It will rain to-day three weeks", "It will not rain to-day three weeks". Together these propositions exhaust the possibilities, and I can assert with certainty that one of them will come true. In like manner I can make an infinite number of statements about to-day three weeks, arranged in pairs such that one of each pair contradicts the other,[1] as for instance: "London Bridge will fall down", "London Bridge will not fall down": "There will be more than five crocuses out in the park", "There will not be more than five crocuses out in the park"; "It will be cold in London", "It will not be cold in London", and so on. Given infinite patience, it would be possible in theory to compile a list such that nothing, however trivial, which happened on the chosen day in London should be omitted from the list. And by extending the list, every event anywhere, at any time, could be included. We never dream, of course, of making such a complete list: but we often do think in an analogous fashion about certain events in which we are particularly interested. The boy who very much hopes that he will be given white mice on his birthday thinks the night before, 'Shall I or shall I not be the possessor of white mice to-morrow night?" A man in danger on a sinking ship wonders if he will ever see his home again. It is, then, not particularly strange that it should have been thought possible to extend this conception of the future as a store-house of alternatives, and it is a perfectly logical extension. If it is permissible to think of the future as holding in its lap exciting alternatives, such as life or death, happiness or misery, fame or penury, it is

---

[1] I say 'in pairs' for simplicity's sake, but this is not necessary, as long as the alternatives are exhaustive, thus: "I shall wear black", I shall wear brown", "I shall not wear either black or brown", and so on. In practice, we can rarely make both specific and exhaustive disjunctions: whether this is merely factual, due to our ignorance, or is a matter of principle, is another question.

equally permissible to think of the future as an infinitely long list of alternatives, not all of them exciting. The question is, *Is* such a view admissible? To which I think the answer is, "Yes, *within limits*." And these limits are the limits of hypostatization: as soon as we begin to talk about 'the future' as possessing 'a lap' we are getting dangerously near the borderline.

The plain man turns up his nose at the complete list. It is, as he rightly remarks, trivial: who cares whether there is, or is not, a portion of a day old *Daily Mail* containing a banana-skin in a wastepaper-basket at Marble Arch to-day three weeks? What is more, we cannot even tell from the list whether this supremely uninteresting event does occur: it is just put down as a possibility, along with its contradictory. And that, I think, is the whole point. The list *is* trivial: it gets us no further: it is just the bald statement of disjunctions. If it *does* go further than this, it is fallacious, as claiming a power to predict which we have seen to be impossible. All that the list can tell us is the trite and undoubted statement that either such and such a content (and here follows a list of 'contents', most of them uninteresting) will be actualized or that it will not.[1] It gives no hint whatsoever as to which contents will be actualized and which will not: *the question of actualization is a totally different one*. To get rid of the rather clumsy symbolism of the last few pages: the list of possibilities is purely and strictly logical, and it affords no clue at all to what will, in fact, happen. We have learnt nothing more about 'becoming' with all our efforts: wrapped up in a static logic, all our adducing of possibilities has got us no further.

This, then, is a purely logical conception of future events and *it is concerned, not with futurity as such, but with the abstract relations of equivalence and contradiction, in so far as they are exemplified in the content of these events*. It is vitally important to realize that the sense in which we say, for instance—"There is a possibility that . . ." has emphatically not anything to do with existence. "There *is* a possibility that" must not be interpreted temporally. It is pos-

[1] McTaggart seems to hold (*Nature of Existence*, Vol. II, pp. 23-5) that this is inconsistent with Broad's view. I cannot agree. He says: "It seems to me quite certain that '*It will rain to-morrow*' is either true or false", but it does *not* follow from that, as he imagines, that "England will be a republic in 1920" was false in *1919*.

sible that a banana-skin wrapped in a newspaper will actually be deposited at Marble Arch in three weeks' time: it is also possible that there will be no such deposition. But we are not to conceive of these possibilities as having a kind of bodiless existence,[1] or as waiting to come and be actualized—where actualization is thought of merely as adding a kind of social *cachet* to the proceedings, comparable to W. S. Gilbert's rhyme of the two men cast away on a desert island who found themselves unable to enter into conversation until they had been properly introduced! That is the nemesis that awaits all those that traffic in possibilities—the danger of hypostatizing these possibilities into something having existence, though not an actual existence. Even Leibniz himself has not wholly escaped this criticism.

It is extremely unfortunate that ordinary language should have emphasized this tendency. Whatever our metaphysical views, in unguarded moments (or moments of common sense, which ever you prefer), we revert to the language and beliefs of everyday life. This is in many ways a blessing, but it cannot be denied that it has its dangers, in the way of uncritical acceptance of dubious statements, which quickly find their way into our metaphysics. Whenever we say, as we do unthinkingly, "I wonder if I *shall have* a letter to-morrow", "I wish we had known what the end of this *would* be", "Do you think there *will* be war?" we are simply asking for trouble. This method of formulation is highly misleading, for it leads us to think of the possibilities of the future, not merely in the abstract logical way, which is the only legitimate one, but as being in some way concrete and 'positive'. The step is a short one from considering the possibilities 'having a letter to-morrow' and 'not having a letter to-morrow', to using 'positive' language which implies that we can attach a concrete interpretation *now* to to-morrow's receipt of a letter. That the implication is only half-realized makes it all the more dangerous. Similarly, "Do you think there will be war?" can be interpreted in one of two ways. The first, and duller, one is that we are considering the alternatives 'war' and 'not-war' with reference to some unspecified future date. This is perfectly legitimate. But it can also be interpreted positively, so that the answer 'Yes' would be taken to mean that war is waiting,

---

[1] Certainly, they exist as thoughts in my mind, but that is a totally different matter.

so to speak, round the corner—if we are now at B, war is waiting at C.  . This is a spatialized conception of time, and is illegitimate.[1] Again, Brutus might, looking back over past events on the night before Philippi, say to himself, "I wish that I had not murdered Cæsar; I did not anticipate *this* end", but as soon as he uses the expression "what the end *would be*",[2] it sounds as if the end was in some way predetermined, and could *in principle* have been known. It is vital to realize that this 'positive' language must not be taken as it stands, but that all we can logically say of the possibilities of the future[3] is the mere bare statement of disjunctions. Failing this, there will be constant confusion between temporal and non-temporal statements.

Yet, it may be objected, if I say, "I wonder if there will be a letter from X to-morrow", I can justify any temporal interpretation that the conjunction of 'will' and 'to-morrow' suggests, for after all it is either true or not true that a letter from X *now* lies in a mailbag on its way to me. But that is to give the whole case away. Certainly it is true that there either is or is not such a letter for me: this has never been denied. Neither is it denied that we can *now* give a *meaning* to such a statement as, "There will be a letter for me to-morrow." What is denied is that we can *now* assert the possibility, in any other than a logical and abstract sense, of something that has not yet happened. Possibility and actuality are distinct: if we wish to look upon the future as a sum of possibilities, we can do so, as long as we do not make this a stepping-stone to the different and definitely wrong view that these possibilities have some mythical existence of their own at this present moment.

It may be said that such a conception of future events is perfectly trivial and worthless, and that if this is all that our long search

[1] It does not alter matters if C is assigned no determinate place, but is vaguely said to be merely 'ahead': the fallacy remains the same.

[2] Compare John Gunther, *Inside Europe*, p. 379. "Almost everyone saw the remarkable film of the assassination. Its great quality of emotion came from the fact that the audience knew, from the time the King stepped off the boat, that he *would be* dead in ninety seconds. And the King did not know this." Italics mine.

[3] "The possibilities that the future holds in store" is a favourite and shockingly bad expression, which illustrates as well as anything the kind of view I am criticizing. Of course 'holds' is *timeless*.

has resulted in, we might as well fall back upon Broad's view and say that the future is nothing at all. But it seems to me that this conception allows for a very important point which otherwise is very difficult to explain—and that is, that the future is not merely a constant extraneous 'tacking on' but 'grows out of' the present.[1] Whether or not a complete deterministic scheme can, ultimately, be accepted, is a moot point—but at least it is not obviously silly to talk of causal connections and regular sequences. Nobody really doubts that diamonds cut glass, that night follows day, that water boils at 100° C. Events *are* connected in experience, and it would be a poor view of time which made their constant connection a miracle. Kant's insight was great when he saw that the time-series not only allows for, but requires, the connectivity of events.

To say that the future is nothing at all, is true, in a sense that is not merely tautological: but its over-emphasis may blind us to the importance of connectedness and continuity between past, present and future. Brutus, looking back, can discover a connection between his present state and his past decision to support Cassius: he can see how one event led up to another, and how each decision in turn excluded a number of alternatives, and made it more probable that the event, which is now actually happening, should occur.[2] Even on a minimum view, which refuses to postulate determinism, we are bound to admit that there is *some* connection between past and present, and that it is not entirely irrelevant to adduce, as at least a partial explanation for what is happening now, events that have occurred at some past date. We can and do attach a meaning to the statement that Brutus' decision to hear what the conspirators had to say was the first step on a road that led to Philippi. *On a road.* Looking back over past events, we spatialize them in a way which is illegitimate for future events. But, though the analogy cannot be exact, we can yet use it to a certain extent. *For, though the present is never the future as made, nevertheless it is the making of the future*, and must not be regarded as totally irrelevant to it. In the present alone we act, but our actions restrict and alter the possi-

[1] Compare the first dialogue in André Maurois' *Captains and Kings*.

[2] Though Tarde, in an interesting passage, says: "L'être n'est pas le connaître, et il est peu philosophique de voir dans le passé la source de l'être parce que le souvenir est la source de la connaissance" (*Revue de Métaphysique et de Morale*, 1901, p. 125). But this view is rarely held.

bilities of the future. It is possible that X will become Prime Minister, but if, at this moment, he is shot dead by an assassin, this possibility can never be actualized. Our actions are purposive and directed towards an end which is often other than immediate satisfaction: we work when we would rather be lazy, because by doing so we believe that we are making it more probable that an event which we consider desirable will occur. No sane view of time can neglect the importance of planning.

It is perfectly consistent to hold all this conjointly with the view that the future is nothing at all:[1] indeed, it is only on the latter assumption that we can give any effective meaning to any talk about 'possibilities'. (When Dunne, for instance, uses the notion of possibility, he is merely being inconsistent: on his view he has no right to use it.) But again it must be repeated that these possibilities are purely logical, and that to admit them is in no way to deny the ultimate and fundamental nature of becoming, but rather to emphasize it. The present is the making of the future, but it is never the future as made: there is always an ultimate residuum which is unpredictable, and which we call, very simply, the 'happening' of an event.

[1] The belief that it is inconsistent is a relic of the old view that 'possibilities' are not purely logical, but somehow 'exist'. This mistake vitiates McTaggart's criticism of Broad, previously referred to.

CHAPTER XII

CONTINGENCY

THE whole question of contingency is extremely complicated, but it is made unnecessarily so by the varying meanings which are attached to contingency and related conceptions, such as 'possibility' and 'necessity'. In the last chapter a rough explanation of how 'possibility' was being used was given: it is now time to analyse in greater detail the different conceptions involved, and to indicate in what senses the various words will be used in this chapter.[1]

Firstly, there is the strict sense in which 'impossible' is used to mean logical impossibility: it applies only to something which is self-contradictory. The logically necessary is that whose contradictory is impossible: the logically possible is that which is neither necessary nor impossible.

If that were all there was to it, there would be little difficulty, but there are looser meanings in common usage, which make for ambiguity and confusion. Logical impossibility and necessity must be clearly distinguished from what is impossible or necessary for all practical purposes. When a man says, "It is impossible that a thing should both be P and not-P", he is using 'impossible' in a different sense from his neighbour who says: "It is impossible for a man at Baker Street now to catch a Southbound train that leaves Waterloo in two minutes' time." The impracticability of the latter is extra-logical and could not be perceived without a knowledge of the relative positions of the two stations: it is not logically impossible that Waterloo might have been only a hundred yards from Baker Street, and then to go from one to the other

---

[1] Much of the material contained in this chapter has been taken from my Reitlinger Essay (1933), now in the University of London Library. For a fuller treatment of contingency, and from a somewhat different standpoint, reference may be made to this.

in two minutes would have been practicable. As it is, it is practically impossible to do this, but it is not logically impossible, since it is not excluded by logic. I shall call that 'impracticable' or 'practically impossible' which is not shown to be impossible by logic, but which is so very improbable that *in fact* it can always be neglected. Similarly with practical necessity as opposed to logical necessity.

This kind of impossibility and necessity is relative, and includes the looser usage of the plain man ("It is necessary for a man to be over twenty-one to have a vote"), as well as the more cautious use of the scientist: but the point is, that however probable a well-established induction may be, it must be distinguished from things that are logically necessary, and hence absolute. Thus it is practically and not logically necessary that water boils at 100° C., that all crows are black, and so on. In simple examples like this, it is easy to see the distinction: but the really harmful ambiguity occurs when people talk of well-established empirical rules as if they thought that they were logically necessary. That is false. Logic has nothing to say on the subject of particular concrete facts, nor on the generalizations based upon them, for it is entirely concerned with abstract relations. There are very few things which are logically necessary or impossible in themselves, but there are many more which are a logically necessary result, given certain conditions. Thus the premises of a valid syllogism, or non-syllogistic deductive argument, are quite correctly said to render the conclusion logically necessary. But the main point is that the conclusion alone is not necessary: it is only necessary as following from its premises. Obviously if the premises are dubious, the conclusion will be equally so: and we must have extra-logical knowledge about the truth of the premises, before we can assert the conclusion alone. To say, therefore, that X is logically necessary, is not the same as to say "*If A, B, C . . . then X* is logically necessary." X may be a logically necessary result of A, B, C, but until we are satisfied that A, B, C are themselves logically necessary (which, by the way, might involve an infinite regress), we cannot assert X alone to be logically necessary. Logically, therefore, even if we assume X to be entailed by $A, B, C \ldots X$ is *possible* but it is not necessary. This must be emphasized, for, unfortunately, entailment forms a very convenient stepping-stone between practical necessity and logical necessity: so that those who would draw the line at confusing the two latter directly have no objection to equating what is practically necessary with what is logically necessitated by its antecedents, and that with what is logically necessary.

It has been claimed that what we have called 'practical necessity', at least in its stricter usages by scientists, can be reduced to the logical relation of entailment. In other words, the content of events is logically (not simply *practically*) necessitated by the antecedents. Those who hold this view say that it is not simply our experience that all crows are black, but that the blackness of crows could be deduced from the whole state of the universe, if we had sufficient knowledge. This is a tenable view, and is implicit in all deterministic schemes, but here it is better to continue to distinguish between practical certainty and the relation of entailment than to beg the question by assuming that the former can be reduced to the latter. Still less is it desirable to assume that *events* themselves are logically necessitated by their antecedents, for reasons given earlier.

So far we have distinguished between logical and practical impossibility: logical and practical possibility: logical necessity, entailment and practical necessity. In the case of impossibility and necessity, the substitution of the logical for the practical kind narrows their applicability, but it is the opposite with possibility, for many things which common sense would say are impossible or necessary are not so on a stricter interpretation, but only very probable or improbable, and hence, logically possible. Although, for instance, the possibility of a coin's turning up heads in a hundred successive throws ($1 : 2^{100}$) is so slight as to be negligible, yet it is logically possible. Thus logical possibility is very much wider than practical possibility.

A third use of "possibility" must now be distinguished. We often say "It is possible that . . . " when what we mean is that we do not know. Such a use is subjective only, and is the result of insufficient knowledge. For example, we say: "It is possible that X will come on the 2 p.m. train to-day, or wait till 6 p.m.".: but if we had known that X's partner had been suddenly taken ill the night before, we should realize that X would be very busy that day, and that it would be practically impossible for him to leave on the earlier train. This is a very common use of 'possibility'; and it is often held that all possibility reduces to this—that what we call possibility is merely subjective and due to our incomplete knowledge. Spinoza, for example, held this view: using the terms in the strict logical sense, he says: "I call a thing impossible when its existence would imply a contradiction; necessary, when its non-existence would imply a contradiction; possible, when neither its existence nor its non-existence imply a contradiction, *but when the necessity or impossibility of its nature depend on causes unknown to us, while we feign that it exists.*"[1] He did not define the logically possible as that which *is* neither necessary nor impossible (since he believed that there was nothing corresponding to this), but as that which is not *known to be* necessary or impossible.

A second view looks to determinism to abolish possibility in any other than a subjective sense; but this is obviously not the case with partial determinism: if only physics is determined, it is not merely 'subjective' and due to 'finite limitations', when one man X talks of the possibility of a certain action on the part of another man Y. But even in the case of complete determinism,[2] some logical possibilities remain intact. Take, for example, the statement: "It is possible for X to walk twenty miles to-morrow." If the speaker did not know that X had sprained his ankle recently, the possibility could be shown to have existed only in his mind: but I do not see how it can ever be argued that the logical possibility is merely subjective in "It is possible for a man to walk twenty miles a day," because it is quite a different kind of statement from the former. What is more, the opponents of possibility cannot have it both ways: they can stigmatize it as being in one sense subjective, or in another, as denying determinism, but not as both at once. Thus if I say, "It is possible that this coin may come down heads or tails: I do not know", I am *not* asserting (1) that the result will be indeterminate, (2) anything either for or against the contention that the fall of the penny was determined by physical laws.

All this is not to be taken as implying that Spinoza was *wrong*

[1] *De Intellectus Emendatione* (*Selections*, edited Wild, p. 19). Italics mine.
[2] I am using 'complete determinism' for the doctrine that *everything* is determined: 'partial determinism' for the doctrine that only a part of the universe (for instance, that with which physics deals) is determined.

in believing that 'logically possible' is merely a courtesy title invented by our ignorance. But, until proof to the contrary is produced, we have at least prima facie grounds for rejecting his view, and for admitting, as the minimum interpretation, the possibility of the possible. In what follows, I shall be mainly concerned with logical possibility, and it will be assumed henceforth that this notion is not a merely subjective one.

What is the relation between the possible and the actual? between the bare coherence which is all that logic requires for 'possibility', and existence in time? and how does contingency enter into the world? It is in the work of Leibniz that these questions are most fully discussed, and it always seems paradoxical to me, that while Leibniz' explicit treatment of time is not very exciting, and could be easily paralleled among many philosophers without his genius, yet implicit in his work are suggestions that are of the highest importance—and all this without mentioning the word 'time'.

Briefly, Leibniz' position is as follows. Necessary propositions, as exemplified in logic and mathematics, are purely formal and abstract, and bear no essential reference to any actual state of affairs. There is some other element in any proposition which has an existential import, and this element can never be reduced to pure logic. Thus no existential proposition (except one dealing with the existence of God, which is itself logically necessary) can be justified in its entirety by logic—there must always remain an irreducible element. Hence what we call facts are contingent, for they cannot be deduced by reason alone—"Truths of reasoning are necessary, and their opposite is impossible: truths of fact are contingent, and their opposite is possible."[1] For all true statements there must be a sufficient reason why they are so, and not otherwise. Necessary truths, if not immediately self-evident, have a sufficient reason which can be discovered by analysis to be necessary: and contingent truths have their ultimate ground in the nature of God. Thus when Leibniz said that a particular truth was contingent, he did not mean that there was no reason for it, but that it depended on another principle besides the purely logical one. This principle is God's choice of the best. Let us imagine a collection of propositions (all of the subject-predicate form, for Leibniz thought that all propositions expressed the inherence of a

[1] *Monadology*, Sec. 33.

quality in a subject[1]). Some we can see are logically necessary, and others are impossible, but the great majority of them we should simply label 'true', or 'false'. Yet since there is not (to common sense at least) anything inherently impossible in the idea of a cow's being a rational animal, most of us would admit that it is logically possible (though incompatible with this world as it is) for it to be so. Hence, the logically possible includes both things that are actual and their contradictions, and as far as logic goes, there is nothing to choose between the propositions: "Camels have humps", and "Camels have not humps". But one of them, though possible in itself, is not compatible (or compossible) with what happens to be the actual world. This actual world is made up of a number of mutually compossible elements: but there are other possible worlds, all internally compossible, and the choice between them cannot be determined by logical principles alone, so why should *this* world and not the others, be actual? The reason is that God has chosen it instead of the other possible worlds because it is better than they are, and God necessarily but freely chooses the best. This is the real meaning of that much misunderstood phrase, "the best of all possible worlds"—it does not mean that *everything* in the world is better than any unrealized possibility, but that *taken as a whole*, the actual world is, literally, the best among the possible worlds. If the world were not better than any other, it could not have come into existence, for "When two things that cannot both happen are equally good; and neither in themselves nor in their combination with other things, has the one any advantage over the other, God will produce neither of them."[2]

All this can be summed up under three heads: firstly, everything is contingent which is not entailed or confuted by logic, and so all actual existence, except God's, is contingent. Secondly, the logically possible includes the false as well as the true; and thirdly, which of the possibilities should be actualized, is determined by an extra-logical, but necessary, principle, God's choice of the best. Leibniz' detailed working out of his metaphysics is open to several objections, of varying importance. It is said that this world is very far from being ideal, that he fallaciously hypostatized 'possibilities' and conceived God as choosing this world from all the

[1] But the value of his view is not limited to this artificial scheme.
[2] Quoted Russell, *Philosophy of Leibniz*, p. 210.

other possible worlds much as a child chooses the biggest and brightest balloon from a dozen in a shop-window, that his view of the logical structure of proposition was defective, that he got into difficulties with discrete monads, which could not possibly communicate with each other, and so on.

Of these the criticism of hypostatization is most important in the present connection. Leibniz cannot wholly escape this criticism; and, as was said in the last chapter, to regard possibilities as substantial is to give away the case entirely and to make useless the distinction between possible and actual. But because Leibniz failed to keep to the straight and narrow path does not mean that such a view is inevitably doomed to failure—on the contrary, it seems to me that as long as we are careful to remember that the possibilities are purely logical, and that in asserting "S is possible" we are not asserting that S is, in fact, *likely* to happen, the distinction is of the highest importance. It is vital, however, to realize that if we use the notion of 'existence' in connection with these logical possibilities, *it is not a temporal existence*. The sense in which possibilities 'exist' is so unlike ordinary existence in time, that the word is better avoided altogether as offering too great a temptation to confusion. 'Subsists' is almost as bad. On the whole it seems simpler to keep to the verb 'to be', as long as it is remembered that it is being used timelessly. When we say "S is possible", our statement is in no way analogous to "X is red", but is rather the assertion "S—possible". Whatever his occasional transgressions, Leibniz' view of possibility is essentially not a hypostatization—on the contrary, his distinction is one which, taken seriously, would banish hypostatization for ever.

Before going any further, it is advisable to get clear on what Leibniz meant and what he did not mean by contingency. The word 'contingency' has been used in three totally different senses, and it is important, in interpreting Leibniz, not to read into him a meaning which he never intended. First, there is Leibniz' use, *which is purely a logical one*. For him, as we have seen, everything that was not logically necessary was contingent, and since necessity was abstract, all particular existents were contingent. But this admission of contingency into the universe is not incompatible with determinism, and Leibniz could consistently have been a determinist. His contingency is logically irrelevant to determinism.

Secondly, there is the common-sense view. The plain man would agree with Leibniz that it is contingent in the morning whether it rains in the afternoon—because he doesn't know—but he would not say in the afternoon that the rain in the morning was contingent, because it was a 'fact'. To common sense facts are facts, and not contingent, but to Leibniz it was just because a thing *was* a fact that it was contingent. Common sense, in its distinction between the possible and the actual, would say that it is the former which is contingent: Leibniz would say the latter. Obviously there is a radical difference between the two conceptions. In this second sense, we call things contingent when we mean that we do not know what will happen,[1] and it is a purely subjective view.

The third sense of contingency is the most exciting one, and is the one which is usually involved when scientists and philosophers discuss whether there is "a contingent element in the universe." (As is usual with cosmic questions, it is extraordinarily difficult and not always profitable!) Nobody has ever doubted that certain things are contingent for us—but there have been many who have doubted that, objectively, there are events which are contingent, and that there is, not merely an uncalculated, but an incalculable element in the universe. It is in this third sense that contingency is the denial of determinism.

Of these three senses, it is the first with which we are mainly concerned, and which is to be understood unless the contrary is stated.

Contingent propositions, then, are those which involve reference to parts of time. This is implied in the statement that it is the actual, and not the possible, which is contingent. That was as far as Leibniz got, and he never worked out in detail the extremely interesting implications of this view with regard to time. The rest of this chapter will be taken up with an attempt further to extend this view of contingency and possibility, and to see how it concerns the problem of time.

Firstly, this view involves a sharp cleavage between the logical and the non-logical. Logic suffices only to give the compossibles (by weeding out what is blatantly self-contradictory through the

[1] Spinoza, of course, would have said that all contingency was of this kind. (Compare *Ethics*, I, 33, Sch. 1.)

Law of Non-Contradiction), and it in no way determines what is to become actual. Thus, from among a collection of possibilities[1] a few can be rejected out of hand: but the great majority remain, and there is no way of distinguishing between them *by logic alone*. Consequently, we call to our aid a factual criterion: we say that some of these possibilities, though legitimate for all that logic can tell us, do not *in fact* correspond to anything in actuality.[2] We say briefly and with an assurance that is almost pathetic, that they are 'false', and that others are 'true'. This is not the place to go into the controversy as to whether or not 'truth' is relative, as admitting of degrees, and that we merely call something 'true' when it is more true than false (in the words of Bradley's epigram: "Every truth is so true that any truth must be false").

Nevertheless, there is a sense in which it is correct to say that true and false are only relative distinctions, and that the decision and confidence with which we use these terms (except in comparatively rare borderline cases) may mislead us into believing them absolute. I do not mean to say that this is the only sense, nor that it is the most important one: the point that I am trying to make is that the distinction between true and false is not *wholly* to be explained in terms of logic. And this is not only because logic leaves indeterminate which of several possibilities are "true" and which "false": but *also* because a possibility which is actualized at one time (as, for instance, that *this* signal-lamp should be green) may not be actualized at another. Were the distinction a purely logical one it could never be said (in popular language) that what is true at one time is false at another time[3]. This latter point must be emphasized because the attempt has sometimes been made to show that logic does not leave indeterminate what possibilities are actualized, and that, if we only had sufficient data at our disposal, we could see that all alternatives but one are cut out *logically*. This is, of course, a return to the view that we have met before:

[1] To avoid the criticism of hypostatization, the possibilities can be regarded as *statements*. Some of these statements are ruled out at once as self-contradictory, but the rest are 'true' or 'false' in fact.

[2] Or that they are not coherent with the rest of the world.

[3] This is getting near the deep waters of the 'timelessness' of truths. Were the statement to be interpreted literally, it would be open to the objections raised earlier, but the immediately obvious sense is all that is required here.

that 'possibility' is merely a name for our ignorance, and that everything is *logically* necessary or impossible. (It should be noticed, too, that it is a mistake to think it necessary to hold this view as a corollary to determinism: this is an ultra-determinist view, and the determinist could perfectly well reject it.) Such a view is invulnerable, for it can never be disproved (at least until somebody is bold enough to assert that he *does* know everything), and in spite of its unplausibility in practice, it is logically quite tenable.

But the case is altered when, in support of what I am calling the 'relativist'[1] view of truth and falsity we can adduce, not only the element of contingency in which one among possible alternatives at a given time becomes actual, but also the undoubted fact that different things hold good at different times, and that what holds good at one time does not hold good at another. That cannot in any way be explained logically. The notion of change is essentially inexplicable to a purely static logic: to say that "A has x, and then A has not x" is not a contradiction because A has 'changed' (in the loop-hole afforded by that obliging 'and then'), is the mere postulation of a new word to designate what can never be genuinely explained by logic. Bradley was undoubtedly right when he insisted that change is not amenable to logic: where, it seems to me, he went wrong was in denying change to be real on that account—he would have done better to re-shape his views of 'rationality'.[2]

This imperfectly logical character cannot be got rid of in a way analogous to the former. Though in the former case it could be held that, if we knew everything, 'possibilities' would be reduced to impossibility or necessity, no such treatment avails here. The contradiction is much too blatant. It is no longer a case of discordant possibilities, but of discordant actualities, and the juggling which might save the former cannot save the latter: it is a brute (and to some tender logical susceptibilities, a brutal) fact that what is the case at a given time may not at another time

[1] Using this as a shorthand expression *only*.
[2] "It might seem that the successive presentation in time of various states is neither more nor less noteworthy a feature of the world of experience than the simultaneous presentation of a like variety" (A. E. Taylor, *Elements of Metaphysics*, p. 159).

be the case. And, in passing (the point will be returned to later on), it may be remarked that the use we make of time to mask the contradiction—not to mention the facility with which we persuade ourselves that there really is no contradiction at all—is highly significant.

The cleavage between logical and non-logical which this view involves is in no way paradoxical to hold. We constantly distinguish between the pleasant possibility that there may be a letter in the morning, and the somewhat uninspiring necessity exhibited in the disjunction "Either there will or there will not be a letter in the morning." Even if, by a rigid super-determinism, we attempt to show that the former is as necessary as the latter, *it is evident that this is not an original belief, but is the product of rationalization.* The *onus probandi* is on those who would assert it, and until then we are at liberty to hold that there is a genuine difference. Then, secondly, it is obvious that change involves an illogicality which no determinism can explain away, for however learnedly we delve into the 'causes' of the change, and however zealously we show that the change was determined and not 'contingent' (*in a different sense of 'contingent'*, please note), ultimately we have to face the fact of change and contradiction, and of something which the laws of logic can never explain. I hope, finally, to show that these two floutings of logic have the same root: but for the present it is sufficient to hope that enough has been said for us to take the cleavage between logical and non-logical for granted.

The second main point is that, granted this cleavage, the contingent element enters in with actuality. What do we mean by actuality? It would be foolish to expect an analytic definition, for this is one of the basic notions from which we start, and which must always be presupposed in our speculations. Still, it is evident that it contains some reference to time[1]—not that that is a very good way of expressing it, since it may mislead us into thinking of time and actuality as logically separable. Nevertheless, to say of something that it is actual is to connect it with the verb 'to

---

[1] Compare Schopenhauer, speaking of necessity, possibility, and actuality: "What keeps them apart is the limitation of our intellect through the form of time: for time is the mediator between possibility and actuality" (*World as Will and Idea*, English translation, ii, 73).

happen'—whether with any particular tense of that verb I do not here inquire, for that is a secondary question, which is logically dependent upon this very notion of actuality. Granted that, when from possibilities we pass to actuality, a contingent element enters in, *may not what we call 'time' be this contingent element?*

Certainly all our conclusions so far would seem to suggest that there is something peculiarly and essentially alogical about time. Its connection with change, and more particularly with that highly disreputable variety, Becoming: its fleetingness: its unreversedness —all these involve that, judged by the standards of a static logic, it is riddled with contradictions. Take, for example, the latter character. Can it be dealt with by logic? Not in the least. All that logic can do is to postulate that in rational mechanics (note the adjective!) all operations are reversible. Now nobody objects to the reversibility of operations in logic and pure mathematics: but the mathematician is not satisfied—*he seeks to apply his figures to the world about him.* That is a very laudable endeavour, and it meets with a considerable amount of success. The correspondence between his calculations and the actuality is near enough to encourage him to proceed. But, by the nature of mathematics, he cannot rest content with a general correspondence, but claims that it is exact, or failing that, that exactness is in theory possible and only not attained through experimental error. Logic is absolute, and nothing short of certainty can suffice: and in its application to the actual it postulates an equal certainty. In this it goes too far: the ideal of conservation is a chimerical one as applied to actuality. This last is a bold statement, but I think the *facts* justify it. No actual motion attains, though it may approximate to, the ideal of 'rational' mechanics. Take, for instance, a typical example in Dynamics, which invites the student, given initial speed, weight, and so on, to calculate the momentum of a train. In brackets, almost as an afterthought, comes the injunction: *Neglect friction!* But such cavalier treatment cannot always suffice, and sometimes among the data is a modest little note to the effect that the coefficient of friction is such and such. In such circumstances, it is claimed that an *actual* train, set running under those conditions, would in fact have the momentum calculated for it, which was not the case as long as 'friction' was neglected. Everybody is happy: the mathematician works out his problem, and the answer is checked in practice, amid universal admiration. Surely, then, it may be said, the ideal accuracy of mathematics has been found applicable to the physical world? A ball is set bouncing from a height of three feet. How long will it be, given certain particulars about the 'elasticity' of the ball, before the bouncing ceases? An answer can be quickly given to this problem. Nevertheless, *is it not obvious that something has happened which cannot be reversed?* The ball on the ground does not, *in fact*, start bouncing higher and higher back to the level from which it was originally dropped. That in itself should show us that here is something which a purely 'rational' mechanics can never fathom, and which is contradictory to the perfectly correct answers that the mathematician has been giving. The solution of the contradiction is, that it is the notion of friction, of diminishing elasticity, of dissipation of energy in the form of heat, which the mathematician cannot understand: once it is postulated that the 'friction' is so and so, he can continue his calculations in perfect peace. But the clarity of the notion of friction, judged in terms of a static logic, is purely verbal: friction is essentially incomprehensible on logical premises. It is, at bottom, only a word for the quantity of aberration from what is calculated: whether great or small, it *is* an aberration, and in admitting it, physics admits that the ideal of a purely mathematical description of the world has already broken down. The absolute has given place to the relative, and contingency has entered in.

While on this point, a few words can be said about entropy, a notion which is very much to the fore nowadays, and which has been linked by some physicists, notably Eddington, with that of time. "Without any mystic appeal to consciousness it is possible to find a direction of time on the four-dimensional map by a study of organization. Let us draw an arrow arbitrarily. If as we follow the arrow we find more and more of the random element in the state of the world, then the arrow is pointing to the future: if the random element decreases the arrow points to the past. That is the only distinction known to physics."[1] And, "The practical measure of the random element which can increase in the universe but can never decrease is called *entropy*. . . . The law that entropy always increases—the second law of thermodynamics—holds, I

[1] *Nature of the Physical World*, p. 69.

think, the supreme position among the laws of Nature."[1] The Second Law of thermodynamics is in essential opposition to 'balance-sheet' theories, in that it postulates a continual running-down of the universe, a constant degradation of energy into the form of heat. Time, too, is opposed to such theories: and it is no accident that physicists like Eddington should seek to relate the two notions of time and entropy. But where it is possible that Eddington may be wrong is in making the notion of time dependent on that of entropy. It is one thing to say that earlier and later *states* could not be *distinguished* in physical terms without making use of the conception of entropy: it is quite another to say that all that 'earlier' and 'later' *means* is more and less organized collections, as Eddington is inclined to do.[2] On the contrary, it is only in time that we can talk of a collection 'becoming' less organized, and the notion of time is essentially presupposed. Eddington may be right, that when entropy is at a maximum, we lose "time's arrow", meaning that there is no *physical* means of distinguishing between earlier and later states; but when he goes on to infer that in such a case, "time is still there, and retains its ordinary properties, but it has lost its arrow: like space it extends, but it does not 'go on,' "[3] he seems to be talking nonsense. Nevertheless, in spite of criticisms of detail, it is in the highest degree significant that there should be a strong tendency in modern physics to identify the passage of time with such an obviously alogical conception as that of constantly increasing entropy—a conception which is plainly opposed to the old ideals of strict conservation theories, and is not even in theory reducible to them. What is more, the linkage of time with the increase of a *random* element must not be overlooked. Theories such as Eddington's, however vulnerable on points of detail, yet emphasize the essential alogicality of time, in contrast to the spineless '*t*' of older physics, from which all specifically temporal

[1] *Nature of the Physical World*, p. 74. Compare the interesting comment of Milne: "Relativity suggests that the flux of time is meaningless, whilst thermodynamics suggests that it is highly significant" (Article on "The Philosophy of Physics", *Philosophy*, 1934, p. 24).

[2] But in his later book, *New Pathways in Science* (pp. 52–4), he avoids this criticism. See also the remarks of Braithwaite in his article on "Eddington's Gifford Lectures", *Mind*, 1929.

[3] *Nature of the Physical World*, p. 79.

qualities had been eliminated in the interests of a static ideal of explanation.

I have illustrated at length the essential alogicality involved in the characteristic unreversedness of time. The same holds good, too, of its 'becoming' and 'fleetingness', but it is not necessary to develop this in detail, or to add any more on this point to the conclusions reached in earlier chapters.

Thirdly, as opposed to the absoluteness of logical necessity, contingency is a relative notion. It is by no means synonymous with pure chance, and the advocate of contingency can perfectly consistently agree, for instance, that granted the notion of 'friction' and the departure from logical standards which it involves, the rest of a problem of dynamics may very well be susceptible of exact mathematical treatment. It is well to notice this, since to believe the contrary would be to judge this view unfairly, as it is perfectly obvious that mathematics *can* be applied to concrete things like bridges and railway engineering. The point that I am trying to make is not that the exact methods of logic and mathematics cannot be applied to the actual world, but that, with existence in time, another element besides the purely logical one enters in. Call it chance, or contingency, or what you will—but the fact remains that it can never be explained without residuum in terms of logic, and if we try to do so, we are forced *either* to recognize that time is riddled with contradictions, *or* to postulate unknown x's to correct our static balance sheet, and by merely verbal explanations to seek to hide from ourselves the limitations of our method. But if we frankly face the fact that with time, an essentially alogical element enters into the world (instead of, ostrich-like, hiding our heads from such unpleasant facts), some very important consequences follow.

Firstly, it is possible to see how it is that some sciences should be more advanced than others, so that it has seemed plausible to many to arrange them in a hierarchical order. Secondly, we can explain the fact—on any strict determinist or necessitarian view, a difficult one—that with diminution of extent there is greater simplicity (in the logical sense of being susceptible to mathematical calculations), so that in the limit, the ideal of *complete* explanation in logical terms is in theory possible. Thirdly,[1] it accounts for the

[1] This point is mentioned here for completeness: it is not discussed until the next chapter.

difficulties and perplexities that have accumulated round time and kindred topics such as causality, freewill, and change, when dealt with from a purely logical standpoint; and lastly, it suggests an important connection between time and induction.

Take the last point first. It is interesting to speculate whether the notorious difficulties that logicians experience in dealing with induction may not be related to the introduction of a temporal element. The attention of logicians has usually been restricted to the illegitimacy, from a strictly logical point of view, of the inference from 'some' to 'all': but it is no less important to realize *why* our information is restricted to some only of a class, and cannot embrace *all* the members of the class. The 'uncompletedness' which characterizes time involves that there is always the possibility that at some future date negative particulars may be found which upset our previous generalizations. (The discovery of black swans in Australia is the stock example.)

The topic is a familiar one, but I think that we rarely consider it from this aspect. The point that I wish to make is that when we are dealing with objects 'in' time we employ the methods of induction, since we can only consider 'some' instead of 'all' of the members of the class with which we are dealing. The 'spread-outness' of happenings in time involves that an inductive procedure is more often applicable than a deductive one—yet from a strictly logical standpoint, however probable the results of this procedure may be, they can never be certain. The questions of induction, and of the formal invalidity of causality, are, I suggest, closely connected with time.

Secondly, *How* is it that there should be convergence to simplicity with diminution of extent? for that there is, nobody doubts.

Science does not, in practice, seriously advocate the complete interdependence of everything in the universe. It does not assert that every time I move, I alter the centre of gravity of Mars, though it is true, and the amount could be computed. It says, rather, that for practical purposes the change is so very small as to be negligible. Again, it does not in fact assume that every event is bound up with every other: rather it makes assumptions that certain matters are irrelevant. Common sense agrees with the scientist when he says that a sneeze in Australia is irrelevant to the fertility of crops sown in England. Yet the scientist cannot *know* that it is irrelevant: he only thinks it infinitely probable that it is.

What is more, these judgments are not merely made to simplify calculations, but are *essential* to science. Perhaps the most obvious difference between science and common sense is that the former is selective. It selects those elements out of a total situation which are 'important', and neglects those which, though perhaps more striking on a superficial view, are 'unimportant'. For the very fact that science frames statements of invariable connection (such as that pressure varies inversely with the volume and directly with the temperature), shows that it regards the connection between pressure and volume and temperature as being more important than the connection between pressure and, for instance, the colour of the experimenter's hair. The assumption that some connections between events and substances are intrinsic, while others are extrinsic, is of the greatest value to science, and it is not too much to say that without it there could be no science. It is true, that science is based on the observation of uniformities, but what is often forgotten is that science is based equally as much on the observation of relevant *differences*, and on the assumption that parts of the universe, for certain purposes at least, can be regarded as isolated systems. Thus the scientist assumes that very little that is happening in his laboratory, and nothing outside it, has any effect on events within his test-tube. By simplifying his experiments, and excluding factors with which he is not immediately concerned, he hopes to discover the interrelation of the two or three factors in which he is interested, and to state that relation in the form of a mathematical function. For with diminution of extent, there is also diminution of the different qualities and properties which make his task so much more complicated. But, I suggest, that is not all: it is not merely a matter of reducing complications, but also of eliminating difficulties of a totally different order, which enter in with time. The complexities of a large expanse of space complicate the calculations: those of time are opposed to the possibility of such a calculation. Reasons have been given for supposing *certainty* of prediction to be logically impossible, and that necessary statements can only be made in abstraction from time: the position I am now advocating is, to put it crudely, that the measure of time is the measure of contingency, and that with the diminution of temporal extent to a minimum we can render our statements about the behaviour of physical objects indefinitely probable, so that *for practical purposes* they may be taken as certain. But the proviso 'for practical purposes' must not be disregarded: we are merely laying up trouble for ourselves, if, for our immediate convenience, we deny the relative nature of that certainty. Somewhere we have to pass from absolute to relative, and it might as well be done first as last, as soon as time enters in. In the words of Professor J. E. Boodin: "Time creeps into our world of description and negates it."[1] But what it is necessary to see is that it is not an absolute negation, as I think Boodin himself would agree, but admits of degrees. The discrepancy may be small or great, and still be a discrepancy. The aim of science is to reduce this discrepancy, this contingency, to a minimum, and so to approach asymptotically to its ideal of logically certain prediction—an ideal which depends on the elimination of time, and yet essentially involves time. Hence, the principle which Whitehead calls that of convergence to simplicity with diminution of extent is not the mere elimination of unnecessary complexities, which could theoretically (given sufficient knowledge) be treated as satisfactorily as the rest: it is also the elimination of the irrational and the alogical, of that which is essentially irreducible to the standards of explanation that logic and mathematics recognize. Expressed slightly differently, the point of Whitehead's principle is not only in the elimination of complicating same-order characteristics; it is also in the elimination of characters of a different order.

Again, if we take a very small part of the universe, say this test-tube, and treat it as isolated, we may find an apparent determinism.[2] But the more a given system is taken in detail the less is it susceptible of a complete deterministic explanation. Now this is really very queer from the view that such an explanation is in

[1] *Time and Reality* (Monograph Supplements to *Psychological Review*, 1904–5, p. 24).

[2] I use 'determinism' in a very strict sense, as "exhibiting correlations which can be exhaustively formulated by strictly logical means." I am aware that this is unusually rigid, and that Boutroux used "determinism" as distinct from necessity. But in any other sense the assertion of 'determinism' is *irrelevant* to my usage of 'contingency', *which can only be controverted by this exceedingly harsh sense.*

theory possible, for what it comes to is this strange statement: It is only on the assumption that the great majority of events in the universe are irrelevant to happenings within a small part (which is taken as a closed system) that there is any appearance of determinism: yet this assumption is fatal to complete determinism. But, it may be objected, this only proves that there is complexity: it does not prove that a factor which is *in principle* irreducible has entered in, and we could still very well hold that with sufficient knowledge, it would be theoretically possible to make a complete description in mathematical terms. The objection may be granted, that nothing has been (nor, we may add, can be) proved about irreducibility: nevertheless, it seems to me highly plausible to suppose that more than mere added complexity is involved when we deal with large spatio-temporal 'slices' instead of small.

This supposition receives added confirmation if we turn to the first point, that of a hierarchy of sciences arranged in order of increasing concreteness, beginning with mathematics and ending with sociology.[1] In Comte's words: "Step by step we at length ascertain the invariable hierarchy, both historical and dogmatical, both scientific and logical, of the six fundamental sciences Mathematics, Astronomy, Physics, Chemistry, Biology, Sociology. The first is the necessary and sole starting-point, the last is the one essential goal of the whole Positive Philosophy, which henceforth is to be regarded as, by its nature, forming a truly indivisible system."[2] This idea of a hierarchy is by no means confined to Comte. Emile Boutroux, for instance, endeavoured to show that the determinism of the physical sciences was not the same as logical necessity and was even incompatible with it. Logical necessity, as exemplified in mathematics, is completely formal and abstract, and there is no way in which we can reach the actual from logic and mathematics, except by the addition of elements that are not formally necessary and can never be justified by pure logic.[3] Thus, for instance, though many of the laws of physics contain mathematical elements, there remains a residuum irreducible to mathe-

---

[1] "Physics is but logic spoiled" (*Creative Evolution*, p. 338).
[2] *Discourse on the Positive Spirit*, Sec. 73 (Beesly's translation).
[3] Boutroux, like Leibniz before him, never related this irreducible element to time.

matics: chemical laws cannot be entirely reduced to physics: while when we come to psychological and sociological laws, the discrepancy is even more obvious. In other words, the discontinuity between the sciences is fundamental and irreducible: not even physics can claim the complete necessity that belongs only to pure logic. Necessity is abstract, determinism is asserted of concrete things, and they should be clearly distinguished: "Necessity expresses the impossibility of a thing's being different from what it is: determinism expresses the sum total of the conditions which ensure that the phenomenon is stated just as it is."[1] Since determinism is distinct from necessity, although it may be perfectly true that a phenomenon is determined by certain conditions, there is nothing to necessitate those conditions—"There is nothing to prove that the real support of so-called mechanical phenomena is itself mechanical and subject to determinism."[2] Boutroux also objected to the subordination of facts to laws, and he insisted that the former are logically prior: "Laws are the bed on which the torrent of facts flows; they have hollowed it out, although they follow it."[3] Laws have no constraining force, for they are not abstract, and therefore not necessary, but nevertheless if they succeed in synthesizing the facts they may yet be valid.

It should be noticed that Boutroux's distinction between determinism and necessity is by no means universally accepted: it is always open to the scientist to claim that the determinism is a necessary one, though that makes determinism correspondingly more difficult to hold. But it is vital that we should not quarrel about terminology here. The crux of Boutroux's argument is not merely that in passing from one science to another, from the more general to the less general, from the abstract to the concrete, we find ourselves faced with increasing complexity, but that there is a real discontinuity between the sciences, which are, so to speak, on different levels.[4] It is irrelevant to object to the distinction between determinism and necessity: what we are concerned with is not precisely where the line is drawn between probability and necessity,

[1] *Natural Law in Science and Philosophy* (English translation), p. 90.
[2] Ibid., p. 77.   [3] *De la Contingence des Lois de la Nature*, p. 39.
[4] Compare du Noüy, op. cit., p. 142: "Can all the very special phenomena which characterize living beings be assimilated to the phenomena of inorganized matter?"

as long as it is admitted that there *is* such a distinction, and that we pass from one to the other *somewhere* between logic and sociology. It is also irrelevant to object that there may not be a large number of irreducibly different levels, as Boutroux suggests: all that the view I am supporting requires is that there should be one clear-cut distinction between absolute and relative, between necessity and contingency, and this having been once admitted, all the rest may be a matter of degree. All I suggest is, that as soon as a temporal element enters in, however great the probability, certainty and logic are for ever banished: and that this contingency increases with the importance of the temporal element. In dynamics, our calculations are nearly right, and they can be corrected with a slight allowance for friction: but when we get to psychology, we have to reckon with free-will, mnemic causation, and the like: and as for history and sociology, where the temporal element is essential, the difficulties in the way of a logical treatment are overwhelming. Everybody agrees that physics is 'more advanced' than biology, and biology than sociology (even if they object to details of Comte or Boutroux), and that is sufficient for my purpose. I suggest that the admitted complexity of the more concrete branches of knowledge is due to the difficulty of eliminating time; and that time, judged by a static logic, cannot but appear irrational and contingent, and that it infects with its contingency whatever it has to do with. The denial of this view can only be accomplished by the assertion that all sciences, including sociology, deal with the 'necessary'—and this statement is obviously far-fetched. Of course, it may be objected, even granted that the sciences can be arranged in order of the probability of their statements, it has not been proved that time can be related to this. This is so: and I hasten to add, that on my own principles, no such logical proof is possible. Nevertheless, it seems to me very probable that the connection between the temporal element and the failure to reach logical necessity in the sciences is by no means accidental, and that it is not going too far to say that time is the contingent element which, in the phrase of Boodin's to which Gunn took such a violent objection, creeps into our world of description and negates it. After all, time is usually and rightly considered to be bound up with change, and when Boodin said,[1] "Time is that property which makes incom-

[1] Op. cit., p. 28.

patible judgments necessary," he was but slightly over-stating the essential incomprehensibility of time and change to logic. The possible, the general, the abstract: all these are subject to logical determinations—but, as Leibniz so strangely saw and yet did not see, when we pass from possibility to actuality, when we come to events happening in time, we have left that ideal realm of logic, and have introduced a radical contingency into the universe.

CHAPTER XIII

REALITY

THE denial of 'reality' to this or that apparent character of our experience, though it has been a common pastime among a considerable section of philosophers, has not always been accompanied by a corresponding clarity in what exactly this denial is supposed to involve. It is evident that Reality is a fundamental concept which everyone must assume, whatever his metaphysical position: and just as metaphysical positions are numerous, so there are irreconcilable and ultimate differences, all the more dangerous because they can never be explicitly stated, between different people's ideas of what Reality is. The same divergence appears in different views of God—as the prime mover of Aristotle, the Demiourgos of Plato, Jeans' pure mathematician, Leibniz' highest monad, Alexander's nisus to perfection, the Word which "was made Flesh, and dwelt among us". The question what Reality is, receives as many answers as the question what God is. It would, then, be a hopeless task to attempt to assess all the different conceptions of Reality by reference to which time has been judged and, as often as not, found wanting. Nevertheless, there are two very different notions that appear in uneasy partnership under the word 'real', and their distinction may perhaps be a consolation for our inability to make a more fundamental analysis. These two notions are those of existence and value.

It has rarely, if ever, been denied that time is real in the sense that it is an element—whether a necessary one or not, is not here the point—of our experience. Kant insisted that time was empirically real, and an indispensable factor in our experience, while Bradley, though asserting that time is only an appearance, admitted that it is *"really* an appearance". Plato said that it was only the "moving image" of Eternity, but never denied that it *was* an image: and McTaggart rejected the *A* series and hence time as contradictory, but said that though time is only a phenomenon, it is at least a "phenomenon *bene fundatum*". To say, then, that time is unreal is not to say that it is a mere hallucination, and that we have no grounds for believing that we perceive things as in time: what is often denied is that this way of perceiving things has any ultimate significance. I think that this is the right way to put it.

This brings us to the second and much more important sense in which reality is linked with value, and it is this sense which is the debatable one. To some, it is self-evident that Reality is such that time is merely an appearance: to others, it is equally self-evident that Reality is an inclusive Whole, which includes time, albeit in an inferior position. Still others have no immediate intuitions on the matter, but announce as a result of thought, that time can or cannot be real, in accordance with premises which are to them beyond question. We are back at the old disagreements: all the same, the various views held reduce to two, between which there is fundamental opposition. These two views are respectively the assertion and the denial that time is 'real' in a sense closely connected with values.[1] It should be noticed that this distinction does not correspond to the general one between idealists and realists, since many who would be called realists affirm merely the empirical reality of time, and are either indifferent to the question of values and ultimate significances and what-nots, or agree with the idealists that time is in some sense, in Russell's words: "An unimportant and superficial characteristic of reality. . . . A certain emancipation from slavery to time is essential to philosophic thought. . . . To realize the unimportance of time is the gate of wisdom."[2] As against this, Alexander retorts: "I should say that the importance of any particular time is rather practical than theoretical, and to realize the importance of time as such is the gate of wisdom."[3] On the other hand, idealists such as Croce and Gentile insist on the importance of history and the time-process. On the whole, though, idealists are much more solidly against the ultimate reality of time than

---

[1] This vague statement is all that can be said—"ultimate significance" is just as vague. The whole notion, or rather notions, is indefinable. Compare Inge, *God and the Astronomers*, p. 175, who holds that value and reality are ultimately identical.
[2] *Knowledge of the External World*, pp. 166–7.
[3] *Space, Time and Deity*, i, 36 n.

realists are for it, and the quarrel becomes one between them, and a section who, for want of a better name, can be called evolutionists. These latter assert an ideal of progress through time, and hold that time is indispensable to the realization of the highest goods. Bergson goes even farther: for him, time is not only the medium of evolution, but it is, in some sense at least, its force. Time is itself creative: its part is not passive—the mere realization 'in time' of values—on the contrary, the *élan vital*, which is conceived as somehow connected with time, directs the course which evolution shall take. Again, Alexander conceives of a continual nisus or striving of the world towards Deity, and of time as being, "that principle of impermanence which is the real creator",[1] and in which values are produced.

The various views have been well brought out by Bosanquet, from whom the following quotations are taken:[2] "These are the two extremist views, both representing prima facie demands of human nature. Let time be the most real of realities, and give us a fighting chance of making over the universe into something nearer to what we take to be our heart's desire. Or let time be a minor incident or phenomenon in a whole, planned with certainty to bring us in the end to our heart's desire, whether on earth or in heaven." To Bosanquet, both doctrines alike rest on a rather facile and shallow reliance on the future—"Both of them use it as a counterbalance which they can rely on to turn the scales against any conceivable amount of past and present evil"—and he rejects them both. His own opinion is: "We consider time as an appearance only, a position which the former doctrine denies, but in opposition to the latter doctrine, as an appearance inseparable from the membership of finiteness in infinity, and therefore from the self-revelation of a reality which as a whole is timeless. We have thus to assign a place to progress within such a whole, and as its manifestation. The test of philosophy in dealing with progress is . . . to reconcile the sense of creative achievement in the self as promotion of the good cause, with its recognition and acceptance of a perfection which is not won by its own finite activity, though represented in it." And . . . "What is left that our probably limited future . . . can do for us, when we discard what I call miraculous expectations, is to increase our grasp of the whole, both

[1] Op. cit., ii, 48.   [2] *Value and Destiny of the Individual*, pp. 294–6.

in practice and theory, and more especially, in consequence of this fuller grasp and also as a contribution to it, to aid us in a very profound and considerable transmutation of values."[1] The main question at issue seems to be whether values are absolute, and so opposed to time which is incomplete, or whether the gradual realization of values by an asymptotic approach not only allows for, but even involves, a time-process.

Such, then, are some of the positions that it is possible to take up on this question of the ultimate significance of time. But before we can attempt to decide between them there is very evidently a prior question which must be faced, and this question is *"What is time?"* To this question, we, the children and the captives of time, can give no final answer. As long as we are in time, it masters us, and its limitations are ours as well, so that we cannot be sure what to attribute to time, and what to the spinnings of our own busy brains. As long as we live, time is with us, and only in death is there freedom from it. Whatever answer we give must be provisional, must be the result of a partial and necessarily egocentric standpoint, must halt and fail. A thousand years ago Augustine said, "What, then, is time? If nobody asks me, I know . . . but if I try to explain it to one who asks me, I do not know."[2] To-day Whitehead says: "It is impossible to meditate on time and the creative passage of nature without an overwhelming emotion at the limitations of human intelligence."[3]

But, there are *two* senses in which these quotations can be interpreted. The first is, that time is inexplicable because inseparable by us from our experience: the second is that time is inexplicable because of certain difficulties which are peculiar to it. These two senses are *not* the same, and it is extremely unfortunate that they should ever have been thought to be so. The first view looks on time as fundamental, as something of which we necessarily have but a partial and subjective view,[4] the second view decries time by implication, and insinuates that there is something peculiarly irrational about it. I am far from denying the latter alternative, but my point is, that it is dangerous to assume that the (agreed)

[1] Op. cit., p. 310. But, "To think of work as already done, or as still to be done, is equally to place the eternal in time" (Hallett, *Aeternitas*, p. 324).
[2] *Confessions*, XI, 14.   [3] *Concept of Nature*, p. 73.
[4] Since, in Kant's language, all our experience is under the form of time.

inexplicability is to be attributed wholly to time rather than to us. To proceed thus would be to imply that we can make neat little divisions into 'time' and 'us', which seems to me highly undesirable since we ourselves are in time. This, and all that follows, is only opinion, and cannot be supported by arguments: but it does seem to me that the former interpretation is preferable, in so far as we have to choose between them. (This does not involve that we cannot also hold that there is something 'irrational' about time: what is rejected is merely the second view as a basis for decrying the first.)

Again, it is extremely significant that Augustine said, "What, then, is time? *When nobody asks me, I know.*" The notion of time is immediately familiar to us all: *it is 'inexplicable' as being the ultimate datum from which we must start, not as being a contradiction which an evil genius, such as Descartes' mocking spirit, designed to dog our path.* Time is fundamental: if it is a contradiction, judged in terms of logic, then, in Broad's vigorous phrase, so much the worse for the laws of logic! But that is a different point, to be raised later.

These preliminaries have been directed towards establishing that the notion of time is fundamental in our experience, so fundamental that it cannot be separated from our experience, and hence, our analysis of it must always be incomplete. On the one hand is the danger of attributing our subjective limitations to it: on the other hand is the opposite and worse danger of hypostatizing time into something having an independent existence. All metaphysics must risk this danger, and Alexander was quite right when he said:[1] "To consider Space and Time by themselves, abstract and difficult as it is, is not an illegitimate abstraction, but is in fact nothing but the consideration of things and events in their simplest and most elementary character." Strictly, even to speak of 'time' is a substantialization, in however slight a degree,[2] but we are bound by the exigencies of language to do it: the important thing is to avoid going too far.

Granted, then, that time is (in Dr. Oakeley's phrase) an essential nerve of our experience, we cannot hope to give a finally satisfactory answer to the question "What is time?" We are bound, I think, to take time as an ultimate datum, and to take a very simple

[1] *Space, Time and Deity*, i, 39.
[2] I am only too well aware how often, recently, time has been referred to as "it".

view of it as being the name we give to the happening of events. *A* happens, and then *B* happens: and both 'happening' and 'and then' are to be regarded as ultimate. For this view, many of the problems which have become associated with the notion of time are pseudo ones, and arise from our tendency to substantialize this very simple and fundamental characteristic of happeningness into an all-pervading medium, a serial order stretching from the infinite Past to the infinite Future. A great deal of harm has been done by failure to see that whether or no time is real in the sense of ultimately significant it is certainly empirically real, and by consequent disinclination to take it as a given in experience. Instead of starting from the simple common-sense view of happenings, as we should do, we ignore it, and begin from a sophisticated and substantialized view of time—and then triumphantly proclaim that, as we had thought all along, time is through and through contradictory! We find it easy to detect and laugh at the fallacy of those who rioted when the calendar was changed, and who clamoured, "Give us back our eleven days," but this fallacy, in a more insidious form, is still rampant. It is useless to pay lip-service to the notion of time, while we hold a view that deprives it of any real meaning, and an excessive glorification that makes of time an hypostatized absolute, is as undesirable as its neglect. Only a very simple view can be genuinely satisfactory.

But all this, though asserting that time is inexplicable, because it is basic, is not to deny that time is also 'inexplicable' in the sense of being irreducible to pure logic. Time, however simply it be regarded as a "this, and then that", cannot get away from the notion of "and then". Logic might admit time if all that it meant was happening and existence, but there is also the "and then", and this a purely static logic can never understand. Consequently, time is fundamentally alogical—not illogical, but alogical in the sense that there is something essentially incomprehensible to logic in the notion of time. With it, and its disreputable associates, change, causation, entropy, novelty, contingency, chance enters into the world. It is hardly too much to say that all chance is temporal, and that, as Boodin insists, wherever there is real process, there is chance. To identify time with chance might be misleading, but the alogical element in the notion of time does seem to me fundamental. It is this queer lopsidedness of time, this stretching-forth to ever-new forms, and also this toppling over into ruin and death, that relates it more especially to the living. Bergson was fond of contrasting 'living' time with the dead matter of space: and in Alexander, too, time is conceived as akin to mind (or perhaps the converse would be the better statement), which infuses discrimination into the bare blankness of space. I am not saying that these remarks are to be interpreted literally—indeed, the function of a certain type of speculative philosophy[1] is to express in myth and metaphor intuitions which are so penetrating that the language in which they are set is only a fingerpost pointing beyond the bounds of reason. But it is significant that time should have been considered, by two of the most eminent of modern philosophers, as analogous to activity, to life, to mind, and in virtue of that very asymmetry and instability which is associated with life.

Again, chemical compounds are usually divided into organic and inorganic matter: and the peculiarity of the former seems to be in its asymmetry. Natural synthesis is asymmetrical, for the living plant apparently produces optically active substances without their optical antipodes, directly from inactive materials: whereas synthetic products are always racemic substances or externally compensated mixtures. It is true that doubt has been cast on the absoluteness of the distinction between natural and artificial synthesis, and that at some future date improved methods may show it to be unfounded:[2] nevertheless, as long as too much *metaphysical* weight is not attached to an essentially scientific view, it is interesting to see how living matter is conceived of as differentiated from dead matter by its asymmetry. Instability is a characteristic alike of life and of time: and although life ends at last in death, and time passes, it would yet be a mistake to emphasize this aspect only, and to forget the creativeness of life in time.[3] But whichever of these we stress, whether the transience of time or its inventiveness, in either case time remains fundamentally alogical. If I were to attempt to answer in a single sentence the question, "What is time?" the answer would be, "The alogical

---

[1] Plato is the supreme example.

[2] See, for instance, Jaeger, *Lectures on the Principle of Symmetry*, especially the last chapter, from which this account is taken.

[3] Alexander particularly insists on this point (*Space, Time and Deity*, ii, 48).

element in the universe", whether that element is manifested under the form of change, of chance, or of life. Boodin's remark, that "time is that property which makes incompatible judgments necessary",[1] may be a little too strong, but he is right when he says: "The time-character involves precisely the relativity or falsifying of any description which tries to exhaust the real subject-object. Time *creeps into* our world of description and negates it."[2]

Granted this fundamental alogicality, what is to be done about it? One way is to start from logic and discover that time is irreducible, and then look with horror on it as something 'inexplicable'. The alternatives seem from this view to be: *Either* time must be rejected because of its inexplicability, *or* it must somehow be shown (by the generous use of optimistic postulates and spatializing language) that after all time is amenable to logic—in much the same way as a crippled and paralysed man is amenable to the behests of his doctors! All this is, surely, a rather silly procedure? To begin with abstract consistency and to attempt to pass to time is sheer defeatism: it is to begin at the wrong end. The only sensible procedure is to consider if, *in fact*, we have any experience of time; and if so, to accept that fact. True, it is perfectly open to us to attempt to explain away temporal characteristics as 'appearances' and not 'real'[3]—but that is passing on to the second question, of the *ultimacy* of time. I suggest that, on the level of experience, no attempt to eliminate time or to reduce it to abstract consistency has succeeded, and that apparent successes,[4] on closer inspection, surreptitiously make use of notions that are essentially temporal to bridge the gap from concrete to abstract. That being so, it seems to me infinitely preferable to start from the other end, to accept time as an ultimate datum, and to postulate it in the very simple sense of 'happeningness'. When this is done, we can go on to consider its relation to what we call, for short, 'logic': but to start from logic and then to condemn time out of hand is blatantly to beg the question. Of course, it will be said, it is just as bad to

[1] *Time and Reality*, p. 28. Compare Schopenhauer: "We may define time as the possibility of opposite states in one and the same thing" (*On the Fourfold Root of the Principle of Sufficient Reason*, Bohn's translation, p. 32).
[2] Ibid., p. 24.   [3] As McTaggart did.
[4] Among which I would class, for example, Russell's theory of time as expounded in the *Monist* of 1915, which deals with the unessential throughout.

begin with time and then to reject logic. This may be so (though I doubt it, since logic is not as familiar in our experience, especially in everyday life, as time is!) but there is no need to take the extreme view. All that is here maintained is that logic, in the sense of abstract consistency, is seriously insufficient by reason of its exclusion of time. "So much the worse for logic",[1] says Broad, if it does not allow for time, and his challenge may be echoed here. If Logic—in the sense of a particular branch of study—can evolve a new organon of thought[2] which can deal with 'becoming' as well as with 'being', with time as well as with the logic that is abstract consistency, it will make a new and great step forward, and such a step is long overdue.

I do not think that this is an entirely chimerical notion, though it may well be long before it is realized: after all, the kindred study of mathematics has evolved a technical dodge by which rate of change can be expressed in mathematical terms. But, it may be objected, the Differential Calculus depends on the neglecting of very small quantities, and in so doing it forgoes the absoluteness of pure logic. Granted. But nobody denies that, despite the relinquishment of this Absolute Perfection, mathematics has made astonishing progress since its introduction, and that the old "Method of Fluxions" has grown into an instrument of great power and flexibility. Similarly, Logic would not be what we mean by Logic—it would not even be 'logical' in the sense of necessary[3] —but it might nevertheless be of more importance.[4] To an extension of this kind a sane view of time is essential, one which treats 'becoming' as ultimate and simple, neither making it a miracle, nor overlooking what it involves, nor, feeling that the whole affair

[1] *Scientific Thought*, p. 83.

[2] The cumbrous phrase is used deliberately, to avoid repeating one word in so many different senses.

[3] It may be as well to reiterate that that is the sense that has been used here throughout—up to now. The 'branch of study' sense is put in capitals. It is a commentary on the present state of this branch of study that the adjective derived from it should unquestioningly be taken as synonymous with 'necessity'.

[4] As admitting, for instance, that scandal of the orthodox, induction. All induction presupposes time. As suggested earlier, it may very well be the 'uncompletedness' which this dependence on time involves that makes it irreducible to logic.

is really indefensible, deciding to be hung for a sheep as well as for a lamb, and furtively substituting a solid hypostatized Time for the 'and then' of events. To continue the metaphor, it is no wonder if this prove too tough even for the digestion of metaphysicians!

This is, however, a speculation: and a Logic that is not logical and allows for time may be only a dream. All the same, Logic as it is at present understood, completely fails to deal with time at all, and though we accept time as really given to experience, we cannot accept it as 'rational'.

The second question to be asked concerns the reality of time, where 'reality' is used in an axiological sense. What is the relation of time to values? Is the time-process essential to the realization of values? or is it a mere episode, and an unimportant one at that, in comparison with the full glories of its transcendence in eternity? As Gunn puts it, expounding Von Hügel, "We may retain the Reality of Time, but doubt its ultimacy. It is not the last word about reality. However much we stress the *Devenire*, the Becoming, it must be remembered that our life has value and significance only because, and so far as, it realizes in fact values which transcend Time and Becoming, and are true at any time and for all time. Ultimately, perhaps, only Beauty, Goodness, Truth, Justice and Love are real."[1] On the other hand, Tennyson asks for virtue only "the glory of going on, and still to be".

It is generally admitted that the existence of a valuable object is better than the mere imagining of it, or, as Moore puts it, in a somewhat questionable form, "We do think that the emotional contemplation of a natural scene, supposing its qualities equally beautiful, is in some way a better state of things than that of a painted landscape: we think that the world would be improved if we could substitute for the best works of representative art *real* objects equally beautiful."[2] Again, it is not nonsense to talk of values where there is no question of human existence, and we can and do, as Moore points out, compare two wholes in respect of value even if neither of them can ever be contemplated by men. "Let us imagine one world exceedingly beautiful. Imagine it as beautiful as you can: put into it whatever on this earth you most

[1] *Problem of Time*, pp. 363–4. Compare also Inge, *God and the Astronomers*, pp. 72 and 91; Urban, *The Intelligible World*, especially chapter vii.
[2] *Principia Ethica*, p. 195.

admire—mountains, rivers, the sea; trees, and sunsets, stars and moon. Imagine these all combined in the most exquisite proportions, so that no one thing jars against another, but each contributes to increase the beauty of the whole. And then imagine the ugliest world you can possibly conceive. Imagine it simply one heap of filth, containing everything that is most disgusting to us, for whatever reason, and the whole, as far as may be, without one redeeming feature. . . . The only thing we are not entitled to imagine is that any human being ever has, or ever, by any possibility, *can*, live in either, can ever see and enjoy the beauty of the one or hate the foulness of the other. Well, even so, supposing them quite apart from any possible contemplation by human beings: still, is it irrational to hold that it is better that the beautiful world should exist than one which is ugly? . . . I admit, of course, that our beautiful world would be better still, if there were human beings in it to contemplate and enjoy its beauty. But that admission makes nothing against my point. If it be once admitted that the beautiful world *in itself* is better than the ugly, then it follows, that however many beings may enjoy it, and however much better their enjoyment may be than it is itself, yet its mere existence adds *something* to the goodness of the whole: it is not only a means to our end, but also itself a part thereof."[1] Existence, then, according to Moore, has itself some value, and this should, I think, be remembered when we attempt to assign to time its ultimate place in the scheme of things. Differently expressed, the Ideal Forms may be non-temporal, but a particular object which exemplifies the Idea of Beauty has an additional value in that it exists. But to say no more would be to beg the question, for, after all, is 'existence' necessarily existence in time? It is the chief point of idealists and mystics—a large proportion of men—that existence in time is limited, and that there is a fuller, truer, existence that transcends time. True, Moore's example concerned existence in time, and many would agree with him that an additional value, however slight, is given by such existence, but it is still open to the critic to object that temporal existence is not ultimate. And this is the important question to discuss.

I am inclined to think that some of the difficulties that appear in this controversy are the result of verbal obscurities: the combatants first raise a dust, and then complain that they cannot see. First of

[1] *Principia Ethica*, pp. 83–5.

all, it is in the highest degree unfortunate that 'time' has so often been used as the opposite of 'eternity', with a consequent depreciation of temporal existence by those who believe in the absoluteness and eternity of values. Being and Becoming are too often regarded as the original Kilkenny cats, engaged in a life-and-death struggle. This is a very stupid view. I have tried to show that the notion of time includes both 'happening' and 'and then'. (Of course, 'includes' is an unfortunate word, since it suggests the very disparity and two-ness which I am trying to eliminate.) What the view I am criticizing amounts to is an attempt to separate the 'happening' from the 'and then', the being from the becoming. The former is called eternity, the latter time, and not unnaturally, their relation is found to present certain difficulties. But in any fundamental view of time, both time and eternity—in the narrower sense—can be regarded as 'in time'. This is a paradox: we are accustomed to hear that eternity transcends time, but not that time transcends eternity. Nevertheless, it is not such a queer doctrine as it sounds. What it asserts is merely that Being and Becoming are co-implicant, and that together they form a whole,[1] which, whether it be called Time or Eternity, is much more fundamental than either considered in abstraction from the other. There is very little to quarrel about between this view and that of those who, rightly feeling the instability and imperfection of Becoming, postulated a perfect whole in which this would be transcended—and called it Eternity. The verbal difference is not of significance except in so far as the holders of this second view tended to debase time to the subordinate position of Becoming,[2] and to dignify Being—eternal in the narrower sense—to the position which belongs only to the union of Being and Becoming, whether this be called Time or Eternity. Neither usage is wholly satisfactory, since we are so accustomed to considering 'time' and 'eternity' in their narrower, antipathetic senses: but 'Reality' would be worse, as neglecting other characteristics that have nothing to do with time, which can justly claim to be a part of reality. On the whole, it seems better to keep to the word 'time' here, as long as it is realized that it is used in a sense that includes both 'being' and 'becoming'.

Before passing on to consider whether time, so conceived, is

[1] I apologize for the language.
[2] Just as Bergson glorified Becoming at the expense of Being.

ultimate, it will be as well briefly to defend the view that becoming and being are co-implicant, and to show that it is one which it is plausible to hold.

Firstly, when all is said and done, this connection of Being and Becoming, so inexplicable if it is not taken as ultimate, is immediately given to experience in the specious present. We not only see a black object, but we see the black object as actually moving. This was dealt with in Chapter I, and here it is sufficient to remind ourselves that at every moment of our lives we have empirical confirmation of the connection between Being and Becoming.

Secondly, there is the logical problem of identity and difference. How are we to explain this, without presupposing the notion of becoming? Among the many important hints in the first book of *Space, Time and Deity*, is the following: "The elements of the one reality which is Space-Time, and not either Space or Time alone, owe their distinctness in either kind to the complementary element. We have not yet arrived at an examination of the notions of identity and diversity. But using these terms in their common sense, either of the two we may regard as playing the part of identity to the other's part of diversity."[1] This hint is further developed later, and same-and-other is related to Being. "Existence is the union of identity and difference. But this designation of union must be received with caution. It is not properly a blending or mixture of identity and difference; nor, on the other hand, are identity and difference to be regarded as in reality one. The splendid image of the *Timaeus* in which the Demiurge is represented as pouring the Same and the Other into a bowl and creating Being (Ousia) from their mixture is not by us to be understood literally, if it was so understood by Timaeus. . . . Being is not something new made up of the two, but is the same taken along with its relation of otherness."[2] It is extremely significant that the problem of identity and difference should be connected in this way with the question of time and its relation to space. Alexander has, of course, a special metaphysical doctrine to maintain, but nevertheless his general position is of interest in this connection, and his treatment of the question is much more satisfactory than that of those who attempt to reduce everything to bare identities—a mistake analogous to that of neglecting Becoming and over-emphasizing Being.

[1] Op. cit., i, 60. [2] Op. cit., i, 197–8.

The third example I shall take concerns a favourite metaphysical puzzle, which Leibniz and Clarke, for instance, set each other. Could God have created the world any sooner than He did? If so, why didn't He? If not, how is this consistent with His omnipotence? Leibniz said: "To suppose that the universe could have had at first another position of time and place, than that which it actually had: and yet that all the parts of the universe should have had the same situation among themselves, as that which they actually had: such a supposition is an improbable fiction."[1] Improbable or not, the question stands, but Leibniz was on firmer ground when he added, "Once it has been shown that the beginning, *whenever* it was, is always the same thing, the question why it was not otherwise ordained, becomes needless and insignificant."[2] Yet it was not until the Fifth Letter that Leibniz found the best answer: "To talk about creating the world sooner, is making time a thing absolute, independent of God, whereas time only coexists with creatures, and is only conceived by the order and quantity of their changes."[3] (After this, it was curious that he admitted it possible to *conceive* of an earlier creation, and said that if it had been reasonable God would have created the world sooner.) There is no need to adopt the particular metaphysical position that Leibniz was upholding against Clarke to see the sound sense of the last statement. To affirm or to deny that the world could have been created earlier is to think of time as a hypostatized absolute, abstracted from the world of events, and as somehow 'going on', even in a vacuum. It is to think of Becoming apart from anything which becomes, and apart from Being—which, in spite of Bergson, seems to me an undesirable conception.

Fourthly, the adoption of this view of time as involving both 'happening' and 'and then' gets rid of the rather superficial view which contrasts time and eternity, and which, seeing in time only becoming, either glorifies it by some evolutionary theory or else tries to get rid of it altogether as imperfect. Of the two, it must be admitted that the 'and then' of becoming is more fundamental to

---

[1] Letter IV to Clarke, p. 95 (*Correspondence of Leibniz and Clarke*, London, 1717). [2] Ibid., p. 101.
[3] Letter V, p. 217. Compare also Augustine's answer to the question: "What was God doing before He created the world? Preparing Hell, for those that pry into such mysteries!" (*Confessions*, XI, 12).

time than the 'happening' of existence,[1] since the latter can so easily degenerate into a static passivity that is the denial of time. Nevertheless, it is important that we should realize that happeningness (or 'is present', or actuality), also pertains to time, and that it would be a mutilated view which ignored it and concentrated only on the, admittedly important, creativity and transience of time.[2]

What, then, of values in relation to time so conceived? This, a part of a single chapter, is not the place to embark upon a discussion of what value is—a vast topic which has fully occupied many large books. It would be foolish to ask how many ultimate values there are—truth, goodness, beauty, and perhaps knowledge—to canvass the claims of the last-mentioned, to inquire whether evil and ugliness are positive dis-values or are essentially negative, to ask whether or not truth and the rest may not all be reducible to a general concept of Value. Here it can only be assumed that there are, in fact, situations about which we make judgments of value (using value as a general term to include æsthetic and ethical judgments). Are such judgments absolute? or is what we call (for example) 'beauty' only a name for our subjective predispositions? —as meaning, when all frills have been removed, "This is what I like"? A highly respectable set of supporters can be found for each of the opposed views (sometimes for both!). The relativist points out the great divergences in æsthetic and moral judgments between different races, creeds, social orders, and civilizations, and argues that ethical beliefs are *completely* conditioned by environment and by pragmatic considerations. There is much to be said in his favour. Nevertheless, it is always open to the critic to object that absolute standards are presupposed throughout, and that we do, in fact, judge that one set of beliefs is 'better' or 'worse' than another set. Mr. I. A. Richards, for instance,[3] scorns "wish-fulfilment" literature, and takes it for granted that a preference for Shakespeare is in some way more worthy than one for Miss Wilcox. I am far from impugning his taste, but I really do not see how, *on his prin-*

---

[1] And, of course, the alogicality of becoming remains.

[2] This language, which suggests that there are two 'aspects', is apt to be misleading—my whole point is that time, as simple 'happenings', transcends both.

[3] *Principles of Literary Criticism* (especially chapters vi and vii), and *Practical Criticism*.

ciples, he knows that it is 'better' than that of the Girl in the Bus. Without in the least intending to shield "mystical entities", it does seem to me a common-sense view to take, that we do, in fact, assume that certain things just *are* better or worse than others. Nobody doubts that our judgments are fallible, and subjective, and biassed by our upbringing—but it is a further step, and one that it is not logically necessary to take, to say that there is *nothing* more to it than that. After all, we *do* say, "He meant well, but he made a mistake", or "Children have very crude tastes, but they improve somewhat as they grow up", and we do correct subjective and fallible estimations by judgments which claim a greater degree of objectivity. Of course, it will be said, our corrections are themselves subjective: what seemed to me a mistake may to someone else with fuller information about the results seem a brilliant strategy, and so on. All this, however, is only to say that we are not infallible and that our judgments are necessarily personal. It is plausible to hold that however far we push back our inquiries, in the end we accept an absolute standard of value.

Belief in the absoluteness of values is usually held to involve that values are, in some sense, 'eternal'. If, it is argued, values[1] change with changing times, they cannot be absolute: conversely, if they are absolute, they cannot alter with time. Values so regarded are properly non-temporal and not subject to change: though the standards of value may vary between different individuals, nations, and eras. From this point of view, particular standards of value are merely copies, more or less imperfect, of the true and ideal Forms, which transcend our incomplete temporal existence, but which nevertheless give point and meaning to it. The Elizabethan, mourning extravagantly for his dead lady, swore that in her death Nature had lost the "one perfect mould", which could never again be attained—a queer perversion of Plato, whose whole point was that the Ideas were distinct from particular copies of them, and were immune from the change and death that ends temporal existence. Thus, though the lady dies, beauty lives on: though jesting Pilate asks, "What is truth?" it remains to confound him: and goodness

[1] Not, of course, standards of value. Nobody doubts that these are different at different epochs: but to say that *values* change involves the further position that the standards of value of different ages cannot be compared with respect to their 'value'.

is more than all the sophistries of Protagoras. Such a view is open to obvious objections that it conceives of Values as having a queer mystical subsistence along with the Ideas of beds, mud, and hair, and as being mere hypostatized figments, illegitimately separated from particular examples of goodness, truth, beauty. We are back at the old question of the relation between universal and particular. It may be granted that these criticisms are to some extent justified, and also that cheapened imitations of this view, which erect theories of æsthetics on the basis of a plentiful supply of vague generalizations and a generous use of capital letters (Art, Poetry, Tragedy, and so on), are peculiarly irritating. Nevertheless, difficult as it is to formulate, and easy as it is to debase with sentimental popularizations, there is an important truth in the doctrine that values are eternal—a truth that is partly obscured by misunderstandings over the word 'eternal'. To say that beauty, for instance, is 'eternal', does not mean that particular beautiful things are eternal. Quite obviously they are not: statues are broken, pictures fade and the countryside is covered with bungalows and arterial roads. Nor does it mean that there are always beautiful things—that when one picture fades, another, equally beautiful, is painted—and that the amount of beauty in the world is constant. Nor, to avoid these obviously silly alternatives, is it necessary to rush to the opposite extreme of hypostatization, and completely to ignore particular beauties in the postulation of an ideal Beauty. For, to say of values that they are eternal, is not to say that they endure throughout unending time, but that they transcend time, in the narrower sense of flux.

But what of time, in the wider sense of uniting Being and Becoming? What is its relation to the ultimate values? On the one hand, its essential incompleteness, no less than its impermanence and transience, are opposed to their realization. On the other hand, even if we imagined a perfect world, in which all values were completely realized, what could the passage of time add further? Nothing. What need, then, would there be for the becoming of time? "Give her the glory of going on", Tennyson asked for virtue. But that glory is in an imperfect world: what glory could it add to a perfect one? It would be irrelevant and trivial. Faust, if asked, would prefer an hour of bliss to a minute of bliss, because he knows that both must end and be followed by torment: but absolute perfection—that fears no to-morrow's anti-climax—is heedless of duration. Alexander said that the nisus towards Deity was not the mere turning of a squirrel in a cage: neither is Deity itself, could it be achieved, the static hibernation of the squirrel through a blank and featureless duration—a torpor that is hardly distinguishable from death. "The world . . . was made to enjoy rather than to last",[1] said Samuel Butler, and duration is of little account in comparison with value. That it is of any account at all is a mark of an imperfect state of things, which attributes value to a prolongation of happiness in the teeth of instability, and even, negatively, to the cutting short of unhappiness.

All this may be true: but however cavalierly we treat duration, we cannot neglect Being. Granted the existence of a perfect state, duration may be ignored[2]—but such a state must first exist. It is often said that such a state is timeless because it ignores duration, that its existence is not temporal existence, but this again is largely a matter of words. If we take time as involving Being as well as Becoming, then in so far as it involves happening, existence, actuality, to that extent it partakes of value. Time is in tangential contact with Reality, the point of contact being that instant which we call the present. In this point that alone *is*, we can glimpse, though fleetingly, the stability and completeness that we seek. It was no accident that led Boethius to talk of "the never-failing now", and though the Being that is this present moment is, by comparison, transitory, it yet *is* and is the opportunity for the actualization of value.

But it does not last, for time is also Becoming. The colours in the sky fade, and the night comes, and memory, instead of consoling, may make the contrast with what has been still more bitter.

> "Beauty vanishes—Beauty passes
> However rare, rare it be."

The transience of time makes it appear inimical to values, and McTaggart voices the opinion of many when he says that it is the last enemy to be overcome. Some, following Plato, deny that time has any power over beauty itself, and that though particular beauti-

[1] *Notebook*, p. 17.
[2] As in the story of the old monk, who, transported by a lark's song, was unaware of the passage of the centuries.

ful things vanish and pass, beauty remains and is eternal. But the question still remains—What, then, are we to say of the threat of transience lowering over the particular? Beauty is timeless: but as soon as it is actualized in time it becomes subject to time. Though time is in the end powerless against Value, it can infect particular values with its own instability and imperfection, and the relation between the universal Idea of Beauty and individual objects that are beautiful reduces to the relation between Being and Becoming. Again, there is another way in which imperfection is evident, and this concerns the frequent conflicts of values which we experience. The controversy over what is usually called "Art for Art's sake" exemplifies this, for whatever the side we take, whether that of 'art' or 'morality', the other must be flouted. It is tempting to suppose that this conflict is a sign of our incomplete view of value —an incompleteness which, since we are creatures of time, will necessarily persist.

So much for the debit side of Becoming. It would, however, be a mistake to stress this too much, to the exclusion of the credit side. Though Becoming falls short of absolute perfection, so does this present world of Being, and Becoming has still a useful part to play in that it makes progress possible. Social reformers may dream of Utopias which are impossibly perfect, but they need, as well as a vision of the ultimate ideal, the comforting assurance that change and progress can be made, and for this Becoming is necessary. What transcends Becoming can never be reached by Becoming, but an asymptotic approach to it may be made, and the nisus towards producing ever higher and higher forms, though it can never rest content with itself, is not on that account to be despised. On the other hand, there may be no progress, but degeneration—but this possibility rather increases than detracts from the practical importance of Becoming. Where the potentialities for good or evil are great, there is more likely to be active effort. Becoming, then, though it must fall short of attaining absolute values, yet allows for their progressive actualization in increasingly adequate forms in a way[1] which a static world could never do.

To those who reject the notion of absolute values, of course, this imperfection is no imperfection, and the question falls at once;

[1] Von Hügel says that time is not a barrier against Eternal Life, but the means by which we apprehend life (*Eternal Life*, p. 383).

so that the fundamental thing is of unceasing progress in time, and time is regarded as an integral part of reality. But any other view has to take into account the twofold character of Becoming, its creativeness as well as its transience. I would urge, too, that we have to consider that time involves 'happening' as well as 'and then', and must not blindly be cut off from all participation in Being.

What, then, is time, when all these factors are remembered? The answer must be, imperfect. The sum of even and odd is always odd, and though the present moment of actuality has the value which existence has, yet the instability and inherent restlessness of Becoming infects all time with its imperfection. Time passes: the young grow old, and the old die: the hour of "splendour in the grass" can never be brought back: poets and social reformers and martyrs live and die for a new world, and find it swarming with demagogues and refrigerators. Shakespeare, who watched the tide cover up his lady's name written on the sand, and who defied Time and Fate to erase the imperishable glory which that name gained through his poetry, saw in time a pitiless enemy, the destroyer of values—yet powerless in the end against Value. But, though Newton is dead, we have Einstein, and time is creative as well as destructive. A truer view than the defeatism of "Tout passe, toute casse, tout lasse", truer than that which looks upon the Eternal Values as a medicine-chest from which to repair the ravages of old Father Time (who is portrayed as looking, in baffled disgust, at a sonnet in which his name is disrespectfully mentioned!)—is that which, frankly accepting the dynamic nature of time, sees in it an opportunity for active attempts to approach ever nearer to the ideal. As McTaggart put it, eternity is in the future; or, in Meister Eckhart's words: "I charge you that ye give thanks to God while ye are still in time, for having made you out of naught aught, and unite yourselves with his divine nature. *Once out of time and your chance is gone.*"[1] Becoming is creation as well as transience, and only through it is there a chance that this present actuality of Being can be transformed into something more worthy of Plato's vision of ideal Being.

[1] *Works* (translated Evans), I, p. 352. Italics mine.

BIBLIOGRAPHY

NOTE.—While there are very few books expressly on time, nearly every book that has ever been written contains some reference to it. It is therefore to a great extent a matter of luck which references should seem interesting to which people, and very often a grain of wheat is accompanied by a bushel of chaff. On the one hand, a bibliography on such a vast subject cannot but be seriously incomplete: on the other hand, there is the opposite danger of including works which are largely irrelevant. To avoid the latter, where only a small portion of a work is relevant, I have indicated the important chapter. Since many writers are concerned mainly or wholly with the physical or psychological aspects of the subject, I have considered it desirable to list these separately from the main bibliography. Not all of the books and articles mentioned here are of equal value: the authors of the most important works have been set in small capitals. Where an article has been later reprinted in a book, I have usually referred only to the latter, to avoid unnecessary duplication.

I. PSYCHOLOGICAL

(Experimental work is marked *)

H. L. Bergson	Mind Energy, chapter v.
J. M. Bramwell	Hypnotism.
E. A. BURTT	"Real v. Abstract Evolution", *Proceedings of the Sixth International Congress of Philosophy*.
H. W. CARR	Theory of Monads, chapter vi.
*E. von Cyon	L'Oreille.
*B. Edgell	"On Time Judgments", *Amer. J. of Psychology*, 1903.
C. Flammarion	Before Death.
A. FOUILLÉE	Psychologie des Idées-Forces, Vol. II.
J. M. GUYAU	Génèse de l'Idée de Temps.
S. Hodgson	Metaphysic of Experience, I, 3.
W. JAMES	Principles of Psychology, chapter xv.

Paul Janet	"Une Illusion d'Optique Interne", *Rev. Phil.*, III.
Pierre Janet	L'Evolution de la Mémoire et de la Notion du Temps.
I. Mackenzie	"Biological Basis of the Sense of Time," *Aris. Suppl. V.*
T. W. Mitchell	Medical Psychology and Psychical Research, chapter i.
*H. Münsterberg	Beiträge zur experimentellen Psychologie.
*L. du Noüy	Biological Time.
E. Osty	Supernormal Faculties in Man.
M. Roberts	Time and Thomas Waring (fiction).
*F. Schumann	Articles on time-perception in the *Zeitschrift für Psychologie* for 1893 and 1898 (Vols. IV, XVII and XVIII).
*W. L. Stern	"Psychische Prasenzzeit", *Z. für Psych.*, 1897, Vol. XIII.
*L. T. Stevens	"Time Sense", *Mind*, 1886.
G. F. Stout	Manual of Psychology.
C. A. Strong	Second article on "The Genesis of Appearances," *Mind*, 1926.
*M. Sturt	Psychology of Time.
W. von Tschisch	"Warum sind Raum und Zeit-anschauungen beständig und unentbehrlich?" *Z. für Psych.*, 1898, Vol. XVII.
*C. Vierordt	Der Zeitsinn.
J. Ward	Psychological Principles.
A. Wohlgemuth	Note on "Paramnesia", *Mind*, 1924.
*W. Wundt (Editor)	Philosophische Studien. Contains experimental work by: J. Kollert (B. I), V. Estel (B. II), M. Mehner (B. II), R. Glass (B. IV), E. Meumann (B. IX and XII), F. S. Wrinch (B. XVIII).

II. PHYSICAL

C. Benedicks	Space and Time.
H. L. Bergson	Durée et Simultanéité.
L. Bolton	Time Measurement.
L. Bolton	Introduction to the Theory of Relativity.
C. D. Broad	"Euclid, Newton, and Einstein", *Hibbert Journal*, 1920.

BIBLIOGRAPHY

E. Cassirer	Substance and Function, and Einstein's Theory of Relativity.
F. Cunningham	The Principle of Relativity.
H. H. Cunynghame	Time and Clocks.
A. S. Eddington	Space, Time, and Gravitation.
A. S. Eddington	Nature of the Physical World.
A. S. Eddington	New Pathways in Science.
A. S. Eddington	Science and the Unseen World.
A. S. Eddington	The Theory of Relativity and its Influence on Scientific Thought.
A. Einstein	The Meaning of Relativity.
A. Einstein and others	The Principle of Relativity. (Contains papers by Einstein, H. A. Lorentz, H. Minkowski, and H. Weyl.)
C. H. Hinton	What is the Fourth Dimension?
P. Langevin	La Physique depuis Vingt Ans, chapters v and vi.
J. Maritain	The Freedom of the Intellect (Essay on "The Mathematical Attenuation of Time").
J. Maritain	"Nouveaux Débats Einsteiniens", *Rev. Universelle*, 1924.
A. A. Merrill	"The t of Physics", *J. of Phil.*, 1922.
A. A. Merrill	"Is Time Relative?" *J. of Phil.*, 1934.
I. Newton	Principia (Third Latin Edition, pp. 12–18).
M. P. Nilsson	Primitive Time-Reckoning.
C. Nordmann	Einstein and the Universe.
C. Nordmann	The Tyranny of Time.
K. Pearson	Grammar of Science.
H. Poincaré	La Valeur de la Science.
H. Reichenbach	Atom and Cosmos.
E. H. Rhodes	"Measurement of Time", *Mind*, 1885.
J. Rice	Relativity.
A. D. Ritchie	Scientific Method, chapter v.
A. A. Robb	Theory of Space and Time.
A. A. Robb	Absolute Relations of Time and Space.
M. Schlick	Space and Time in Contemporary Physics.
J. T. Shotwell	"The Discovery of Time", *J. of Phil.*, 1915.
L. Silberstein	Theory of Relativity.
Various	(1) Symposium of "Time, Space, and Material" (Whitehead, Lodge, Nicholson, Head, Stephen, Carr) in *Aris. Suppl., II*.

Various—contd.	(2) Symposium on "The Problem of Simultaneity" (Carr, Sampson, Whitehead) in *Aris. Supp., III*.
	(3) Symposium on "The Philosophical Aspect of the Theory of Relativity" (Eddington, Ross, Broad, and Lindemann), *Mind*, 1920.
	(4) Articles by McGilvary and Weyl in *Proceedings of Sixth International Congress of Philosophy*.
A. V. Vasiliev	Space, Time, Motion.
H. Weyl	Space, Time, and Matter.
A. N. Whitehead	The Principle of Relativity.
A. N. Whitehead	"Space, Time, and Relativity", *Proc. Arist. Soc.*, 1915–16.

III. GENERAL

E. A. Abbott	Flatland.
S. Alexander	Space, Time and Deity.
S. Alexander	"Space-Time", *Proc. Aris. Soc.*, 1917–18.
S. Alexander	Spinoza and Time.
Anon	An Adventure.
Aquinas	Summa Theologica (English Dominicans' Edition, I, pp. 97 ff.).
Aristotle	Physics, 217*b* ff.
Aristotle	Metaphysics.
Augustine	City of God, IX and X.
Augustine	Confessions, XI, 12–27.
J. L. Balmes	Fundamental Philosophy, Book VII.
G. Bénézé	"Note sur le Temps", *Rev. Phil.*, 1926.
H. L. Bergson	Time and Free Will.
H. L. Bergson	Matter and Memory.
H. L. Bergson	Introduction to Metaphysics.
H. L. Bergson	Creative Evolution.
H. L. Bergson	La Perception du Changement.
G. Berkeley	Principles of Human Knowledge (Secs. 97–8).
E. van Biéma	"L'Antinomie kantienne chez Leibniz", *Rev. de Mét. et de Morale*, 1908.
R. M. Blake	"On Mr. Broad's Theory of Time", *Mind*, 1925.
Boethius	Consolation of Philosophy.
J. E. Boodin	Time and Reality.

BIBLIOGRAPHY

J. E. Boodin	A Realistic Universe.
J. E. Boodin	"Pragmatic Realism", *Mind*, 1913.
J. E. Boodin	"The Concept of Time", *J. of Phil.*, 1905.
B. Bosanquet	Meeting of Extremes in Contemporary Philosophy.
B. Bosanquet	Value and Destiny of the Individual, chapter x.
E. Boutroux	De la Contingence des Lois de la Nature.
E. BOUTROUX	Natural Law in Science and Philosophy.
F. H. Bradley	Logic.
F. H. Bradley	Appearance and Reality, chapters iv, v, xviii.
R. B. Braithwaite	"Eddington's Gifford Lectures", *Mind*, 1929.
P. Breton	"Reversibilité de tout mouvement purement matériel", *Les Mondes*, 1875.
C. D. BROAD	Scientific Thought, especially chapter ii.
C. D. Broad	"Time", article in *Encycl. of Religion and Ethics*.
C. D. Broad	"Kant's First and Second Analogies", *Proc. Arist. Soc.*, 1925–26.
C. D. Broad	"Hallett's 'Aeternitas' ", *Mind*, 1933.
C. D. Broad	"Dunne's Theory of Time", *Philosophy*, 1935.
J. Buchan	The Gap in the Curtain (fiction).
E. A. Burtt	Metaphysical Foundations of Modern Science.
H. W. Carr	The Philosophy of Change.
H. W. Carr	"Time and History in Contemporary Philosophy", *Br. Acad.*, 1918.
R. G. Collingwood	"Some Perplexities about Time", *Proc. Aris. Soc.*, 1925–26.
B. Croce	Philosophy of the Practical.
G. W. Cunningham	The Philosophy of Bergson.
G. W. Cunningham	"Bergson's Conception of Durée", *Phil. Review*, 1914.
R. Descartes	Principles, I, 57.
E. T. Dixon	The Guidance of Conduct, chapter ii.
J. W. DUNNE	Experiment with Time.
J. W. DUNNE	The Serial Universe.
Eckhart	Works.
A. C. Ewing	Kant's Treatment of Causality.
A. C. Ewing	Idealism.
G. Fechner	Vier Paradoxa.
C. Flammarion	Lumen.
G. S. Fullerton	A System of Metaphysics, chapters xii, xiii and xxiv.

D. W. Gotshalk	"McTaggart on Time", *Mind*, 1930.
J. A. Gunn	Bergson and his Philosophy.
J. A. GUNN	The Problem of Time.
H. F. Hallett	Aeternitas.
J. Hilton	Lost Horizon (fiction).
S. Hodgson	Time and Space.
F. von Hügel	Eternal Life.
D. Hume	A Treatise on Human Nature.
W. R. Inge	Philosophy of Plotinus.
W. R. Inge	God and the Astronomers.
W. R. Inge	"Is the Time-Series Reversible?" *Proc. Aris. Soc.*, 1920–21.
F. M. Jaeger	Lectures on the Principle of Symmetry.
I. KANT	Critique of Pure Reason.
J. Laird	Study in Realism, chapter iii.
G. Lechalas	Etude sur l'Espace et le Temps.
G. W. LEIBNIZ	Works (*passim*, especially Correspondence with Clarke).
J. A. Leighton	"Time, Change, and Time-Transcendence" *J. of Philos.*, 1908.
P. W. Lewis	Time and Western Man.
A. D. Lindsay	"Kant's Account of Causation", *Proc. Aris. Soc.*, 1909–10.
J. Locke	Essay, II, 14 and 15.
H. Lotze	Metaphysics.
J. S. Mackenzie	"Notes on Problem of Time", *Mind*, 1912.
J. M. E. MCTAGGART	Nature of Existence, Vol. II.
J. M. E. McTaggart	Studies in Hegelian Dialectic.
J. M. E. McTaggart	Studies in Hegelian Cosmology.
A. Maurois	Captains and Kings (First Dialogue).
E. MEYERSON	Identity and Reality.
E. Meyerson	De l'explication dans les Sciences.
C. Lloyd Morgan	Emergent Evolution.
H. Münsterberg	The Eternal Values.
A. E. Murphy	"Alexander's Theory of Space-Time", *Monist*, 1927.
H. D. Oakeley	History and the Self.
H. D. Oakeley	"The Status of the Past", *Proc. Aris. Soc.*, 1931–32.
PLATO	Dialogues.
Plotinus	Enneads (translated Guthrie, pp. 986 ff.).
E. A. Ramige	Contemporary Concepts of Time.

P. P. Royer-Collard	Fragments, chapter vii.
H. Ruja	"Alexander's Conception of Space-Time", *Philosophy of Science*, 1935.
B. A. W. Russell	Our Knowledge of the External World.
B. A. W. Russell	Philosophy of Leibniz.
B. A. W. Russell	"The Experience of Time", *Monist*, 1915.
B. A. W. Russell	"Is Position in Time and Space Absolute or Relative?" *Mind*, 1901.
A. Schopenhauer	The World as Will and Idea.
A. Schopenhauer	On the Fourfold Root of the Principle of Sufficient Reason.
C. Sigwart	Logic.
M. Sinclair	A Defence of Idealism.
J. A. Smith	"Alexander's Doctrine of Space-Time," *Proc. Arist. Soc.*, 1924–25.
N. K. Smith	Commentary to Kant's Critique.
N. K. Smith	Prolegomena to an Idealist Theory of Knowledge.
H. Spencer	Principles of Psychology.
B. Spinoza	Ethics.
C. A. Strong	L'Etre et le Devenir.
C. A. Strong	"Continuity of Space and Time", *Mind*, 1928.
G. Tarde	"L'Action des Faits Futurs", *Rev. de Mét. et de Morale*, 1901.
A. E. Taylor	Elements of Metaphysics, I, 5, and III, 4.
B. Tschitscherin	"Raum und Zeit", *Arch. für Syst. Phil.*, 1899.
E. Underhill	Mysticism.
Various	(1) Essays in Critical Realism.
	(2) Symposium on "The Status of the Future" (Bosanquet, Hodgson, Moore), *Mind*, 1897.
	(3) Symposium on "Time and Change" (Macmurray, Braithwaite, and Broad), *Aris. Suppl.*, VIII.
	(4) Symposium on "The Time Difficulty in Realist Theories of Perception" (Carr, Jevons, Brown and Dawes-Hicks), in *Proc. Aris. Soc.*, 1911–12.
	(5) Articles on "Physics and Metaphysics, with Special Reference to the Problem of Time" (by McGilvary, Weyl, Whitehead, Vassilieff, Mead), in *Proceedings of the Sixth International Congress of Philosophy*

L. J. Walker	"Time, Eternity, and God", *Hibbert J.*, 1920.
J. Ward	"Sense-Knowledge (ii, Time)", *Mind*, 1920.
C. O. WEBER	"The Reality of Time and the Autonomy of History", *Monist*, 1927.
H. G. Wells	The Time-Machine (fiction).
A. N. Whitehead	Principles of Natural Knowledge.
A. N. Whitehead	Science and the Modern World, chapter vii.
A. N. WHITEHEAD	Concept of Nature.
A. N. Whitehead	Process and Reality.
A. N. Whitehead	The Organization of Thought, Essay VIII.
J. Wisdom	"Time, Fact, and Substance", *Proc. Aris. Soc.*, 1928–29.

INDEX

A-series, ch. vii *passim*, 236, 274
Abbott, 169
Absolute time, 8, 51, 75, 92, 102, 104, 177–8, 186, 287
Abstraction, 49–51, 227, 271, 273, 285
Accuracy of estimation, 27–35, 38, 42
Actualization, 208–9, 223, 241–2, 247–51, 256–9, 262–6, 273, 288, 291–3
Alexander, 6, 71, 109, 114, ch. vi, 237, 274, 275–6, 278, 280, 286, 291
  space-time, 128–40
  perspectives, 136–7
  relation of space and time, 130, 132–4, 137–40
  emergence, 130, 140–7
  identity and difference, 132–3, 138
Alogical, 124, 145, 263–6, 269, 279, 280–3, 288
Appearance—and reality, 11, 54, 93, 134, 156, 276, 281
Applicability of mathematics, 207–9
Aquinas, 79
Aristotle, 76, 109, 156, 231, 274
Asymmetry, 199, 220–2, 231, 236–7, 279–81
Atomism, 141–4
Augustine, 5, 277–8, 287

B-series (before-and-after), 46, 59–61, 74, ch. vii *passim*, 186, 197, 231, 236
'Balance-sheet' theories, 235–7, 265
Balmes, 45
Beaunis, 34
Becoming, 6, 120, 185–6, ch. xi, 263, 282, 285–8, 290–3
  time and change, 231–3

Becoming (*contd.*)
  irreducibility of becoming, 233–8
  Broad's view, 238–45
  time and logic, 241–2
  possibilities and future, 244–51
  possibilities and actuality, 247–9
  future and present, 250–1
Beginning of world, 93, 287
Being, 6, 120, 282, 285–8, 290–3
Benedicks, 52, 63
Bergson, 6, 28, 29, 34, 35, 50, 57–9, 61, 64, 66, 70, 78, 88, 93, 99, 107, ch. v, 137, 140, 146, 185, 226, 233, 237, 244, 276, 280, 285, 287
  view of space, 110–13, 117
  interpenetration, 112–15
  passing and passed, 116–19
  memory, 116, 119
  creativeness, 116, 119–21, 124
  reversibility, 116, 122, 124, 127
  freedom, 118–19
  élan vital, 121
  intuition, 121–3, 126
  general criticisms, 125–7
Berkeley, 2, 10
Berthoud, 44
Black, 49
Blake, 243
Boethius, 79, 291
Bolton, 44
Boodin, 10, 269, 272, 279, 281
Bosanquet, 6, 244, 276–7
Boutroux, 269–72
Bradley, 7, 9, 131, 148, 156, 175, 206, 243, 260, 261, 274
Braithwaite, 265
Bramwell, 34
Breton, 64–5, 227

Bridgman, 47, 63, 71
Broad, 55, 57, 75–6, 84–5, 101, 111, 121, 166, 167, 175–6, 178–9, 197, 233, 238–45, 247, 250, 251, 278
Burke, 145
Burnet, 26
Burtt, 7, 24
Butler, 21, 291

Calendar, 43
Campbell, 39
Carr, 17–19, 108, 113
Cassirer, 52, 70
Cause, 59, 64–6, 89, 91, 184–5, 196–8, 201–4, 222, 224, 226–8, 250, 262, 267, 279
Certainty, 194–6, 206–9, 268–70, 272
Chance, 142, 229, 264–6, 279, 281
Change, 7, 8, 17, 18, 75–6, 91–3, 98, 102, 109, 124, 140, 153–6, 231–3, 239, 261–3, 267, 272, 279, 281, 287, 292–3
Cisar, 47
Clarke, 287
Clifford, 232
Collingwood, 77
Common-sense views, 2–5, 10, 48, 58, 60, 66, 68, 96, 148, 178, 186, 213–15, 259, 279, 289
Compossible, 257, 259
Comte, 270, 272
Concepts, and percepts, 73–5
of physics, 54
Connectivity of experience, 16, 103–4, 108, 202, 250
Conservation, 263–6
Container view of time, 3
Contingency, 207, ch. xii, 279
distinctions and definitions, 252–6, 258–9
possible and actual, 256–9
logical and non-logical, 259–62
contingency and time, 262–6
hierarchy of sciences, 266–73
Continuity, 7, 18, 46, 92, 132, 250
Contradi tions, 9, 279

Convention, in physics, 40, 67
Creative, 109, 114, 119–21, 124, 127, 141, 146, 237, 276, 280, 288, 293
Critical velocity of light, 8, 55, 56, 61–6, 211–13
Croce, 275
Cunningham, 45, 52, 71, 123
Cunynghame, 44
Cycles of events, 8, 109, 124, 225–6

Date, and content, 192–4, 198–200, 201–2, 218–26, 227
'Déjà vu,' 34, 180
Delboeuf, 34
Democritus, 76
De Quincey, 31, 32, 181
Descartes, 10, 160, 278
Determining correspondence, 159, 161
Determinism, 218–19, 250, 254–5, 261, 262, 270, 271
Development, 235
Differential Calculus, 282
Difficulties connected with Time, 6–9
Dimensions, 67–70
and axes, 68–9
Diminution of Extent, 228, 266–70
Dreams, 166, 179–85, 193–8
Dunne, 78, ch. viii, 191, 194–7, 200, 229, 243, 251
regress, 166–79
criticisms, 171–9
observer, 170, 176–8
view of the future, 179–88
Duration, 26–35, 45–51, 91, 111–12, 122, 291
Durée, 78, 99, 109–13, 115–16

Eckhart, 79, 293
Eddington, 35, 43, 46, 52, 55, 58, 60, 65, 68, 71, 147, 212, 264–5
Edgell, 28
Einstein, 52–71, 79, 128, 293
Élan vital, 121, 244, 276
'Empty' time, 27–9, 193
Entailment, 204–5, 253–4
Entropy, 147, 217, 228, 264–5, 279

INDEX

Eriksen, 25
Estel, 30
Eternity, 8, 25–6, 79–80, 120, 157, 162–3, 210–11, 274, 285, 287, 289–90, 292, 293
Events—and time, 4, 9, 74–5, 130, 193, 201–4, 207, 209, 220, 223–6, 230, 233, 273, 287
Evolution, 120–1, 276, 287
Ewing, 103, 107
Experience, and time, 10, 278–9, 283, 286
Explanation—common sense, 2

Fact, 259, 271
Fawcett, 234
Fechner, 64, 227
'Filled' time, 7, 27–9
Flammarion, 34, 50, 64–5
Flux, 109, 114, 265, 290
Foresight, intellectual, 183–4, 208
Fouillée, 18, 30, 87
Freewill, 5, 118–19, 194, 272
Friction, 144, 263–6, 262
Future, 21–2, 170, 171, 178, 179, 185–8, 197, ch. ix *passim*, ch. xi *passim*, 276

Galileo, 43
Gentile, 275
Gilbert, 248
Gotshalk, 150, 154
Gould, 44
Growth, 234–5
Gunn, 26, 53, 58–9, 74, 77, 78, 100–1, 104–7, 272, 283
Gunther, 249
Gurney, 34
Guyau, 17, 25, 33

Hallett, 277
Happenings, 117, 174–5, 202–3, 207, 213, 217, 218, 220–1, 223–4, 230, 251, 263, 279, 281, 285, 288, 291, 293
Hegel, 7, 9, 148
Heisenberg, 171

Heraclitus, 6, 109
Hierarchy of sciences, 266, 270–3
Hinton, 168–9, 172, 174, 178
Hodgson, 18
Housman, 218
Hume, 89, 92, 93, 95, 102, 108
Hypostatization of time, 51, 104, 126, 155, 220, 221, 223, 226, 247–8, 257–8, 260, 278, 283, 287, 290

Idealists, 10, 275, 284
Ideas, succession of, 32
Identity and difference, 132–3, 138, 198–200, 286
Immortality, 170
Implication, 80–2
Importance of time, 6, 110
Impossibility—logical, 252–4, 257, 261
    practical, 252–4
Induction, 201, 204, 207, 216, 243, 253, 267, 282
Infinite regress, 9, 149, 155, 156, 166–79, 188, 232, 239, 243, 253
Inge, 235, 275, 283
Interdependence of space and time, 130, 134, 137
Interference and predictions, 170, 184–5
Interpenetration, 112–16
Intuition, 115–16, 121–3, 126, 280
Irrational, 121, 277–8, 283
Irreducible, 256–7, 269, 270–3, 279, 281–2
Irreversibility, 9, 24–5, 49–51, 64–6, 93, 122, 124, 127, 171, ch. x
    and irreparability, 214–19, 226–9
    'timelessness' of truths, 215–19
    date and content, 218–23
    asymmetry and irreversibility, 220–2
    and unreversedness, 222–3
    cycles of events, 224–6

Jaeger, 280
James, 15–20, 28, 31, 33, 34, 77, 78
Janet, Paul, 33–4

Janet, Pierre, 20, 33, 34
Jeans, 274

Kant, ch. iv, 73, 109, 121, 126, 148, 233, 250, 274, 277
  development of views in Critique, 86–94
  empirically real, 86–7
  form of intuition, 87–9, 98
  relation to space, 88–92, 93, 102, 104
  modes of time, 91, 103, 105
  causality, 89, 91, 93, 99, 103–8
  search for criterion, 92, 95–101, 104–5
  subjective and objective succession, 92, 94–104, 106–7
  simultaneity, 97, 105, 108
  unity of apperception, 101–4
  necessary connections, 104–7
Kemp-Smith, 87, 91, 105, 107
Kollert, 30

Laird, 83, 204
Langevin, 52
Law, 103, 227, 271
Leibniz, 145, 148, 177, 248, 256–9, 270, 273, 274, 287
Lewis, 109
Life, and time, 127, 280–1
Light signals, 57, 63
Linear inference, 205
Lived time, ch. ii, 76
Lloyd Morgan, 181
Locke, 27
Logic, ch. iii
  definitions and distinctions, 73–80
  temporal and non-temporal expressions, 80–5
  time irreducible to, 7, 241–2, 280–3
Lorentz, 52
Lorentz-Fitzgerald Contraction, 53–5
Lotze, 225, 235, 237

Macmurray, 121, 245

McTaggart, 9, 10, 25, 82, 131, ch. vii, 167, 232, 239, 240–1, 243, 247, 251, 274, 281, 291, 293
  proof of unreality of time, 149–52
  misperception and error, 148, 157–61
  non-temporal language, 153–6
  conditions of C-series, 158
  futurity of whole, 157, 162-3
Maritain, 52, 57–9, 213, 233
Maurois, 250
Measurement, 38–47, 54, 63, 69
Mehner, 30
Memory, 4, 19–21, 42, 77–8, 119, 291
Meredith, 29
Merrill, 47
Meyerson, 64, 76, 143, 227, 229
Michelson–Morley experiment, 52–4
Milne, 265
Mind, analogous to time, 114, 138–40, 280
Minkowski, 52, 55, 66–7, 70–1, 128, 129, 131
Mitchell, 34
Moore, 155, 283–4
Motion, 8, 76, 98, 129, 178–9, 212, 228, 231–2
  relative and absolute, 55, 63, 93
Mozart, 20, 31
Münsterberg, 30
Murphy, 131

Necessity, 81, 268, 272, 281, 282
  logical, 252–4, 256–9, 261, 266, 270, 289
  practical, 252–4
Newton, 8, 51, 75, 104, 107, 293
Nilsson, 43
Nisus, 146–7, 291, 292
Non-temporal uses of language, 80–5, 153–6, 217–19, 239, 249, 258
Nordmann, 43, 57–8, 62, 64
du Noüy, 32, 33, 271
Novelty, 140–6, 229, 244, 279
'Now', movement of, 152, 167, 171, 172–6, 185, 188, 243

INDEX

Oakeley, 111, 278
Observer, 170, 176–8, 188
Ontological argument, 83, 236, 239
Ontological — and cognitive, 9, 131–2, 134
Optimum time, 30, 42
Organic unities, 143
Osty, 34, 78

Parmenides, 6, 7, 9, 26, 148
Passage, 8, 151, 152, 154, 231
Passing and passed, 114, 116–19, 235
Past, 19–21, 77–8, 215–19, ch. x *passim*
Pearson, 50, 64, 227
Perception, 15, 40–5
Physics, ch. ii, 211–13
  and metaphysics, 61, 64, 71
  measurement, 38–47
  't' and time, 45–51
  relativity, 51–71
  simultaneity and temporal relations, 56–61
  critical velocity of light, 61–6
  hyphenation of space and time, 66–71
Physiological rhythms, 30, 42
Pilate, 289
Planning, 183, 194, 198–9, 200, 251
Plato, 9, 26, 148, 274, 280, 289, 291, 293
Plotinus, 231
Poincaré, 42, 62, 63
Possibility, 208, 245–51, 259, 260, 273
  logical, 246–7, 252–6, 257
  practical, 252–4
  subjective, 246, 254–6, 259, 261
Postulates of measurement, 39–41
Prediction, ch. ix, 242, 268
  and Dunne, 170, 179, 182–5
  content and date, 192–4
  relation between prediction and event, 192, 196–200
  scientific forecasts, 200–7
Present, 16, 22, 76–7, 172–3, 174–6, 187

Present, as durationless point, 18
  the 'given' and the 'now', 22–4
Probability, 182
Progress, 292, 293
Propositional functions, 80–2, 155
Protagoras, 290
Psychology, ch. i
  experiential basis of temporal notions, 16–26
  specious present, 16–19
  the 'given' and the 'now', 22–4
  estimates of duration, 26–35
  insufficiency of psychology, 35–7

Rate, and time, 44–5
Real, 9, 10, 109, 148, 161, 164–5, 213, ch. xiii
  reality as rational, 274–83
  reality and value, 283–93
  time and eternity, 285–8
Reichenbach, 57
Relations, external and internal, 154, 155
'Relational' view of time, 8
Relativity, 8, 51–71
'Repetition', 46
Rice, 67
Richards, 288
Ritchie, 39
Robb, 60
Roberts, 31
Römer, 61
Romanes, 33
Ross, 57
Russell, 107, 156, 237, 257, 275, 281

Schopenhauer, 107, 262, 281
Schumann, 30
Selection, 268–70
Sequence, logical and temporal, 204–5, 227
Shakespeare, 7, 27, 288, 293
Shotwell, 43
Shuffling, 141–2
Sigwart, 44–5, 106
Silberstein, 52, 67

Simultaneity, 55–61, 78–9, 92, 97, 105, 108, 212–13
Space, 130, 132–4, 137–40, 169, 280, 286
Space-time, 55, 66–71, 128–40
Spatialization of time, 50, 110–13, 171–4, 188, 249, 250, 281
Specious present, 17–20, 31, 76–7, 96–7, 286
Spencer, 33, 225–6
Spinoza, 9, 128, 148, 255, 259
Standard, 42–5
Stebbing, 39, 153
Stern, 28, 30, 31
Stevens, 30
Stout, 17, 21, 24, 26
Strong, 18, 30
Sturt, 21, 28, 31–4
Subjectivity of time, 7, 125–6
Swift, 184

't' of physics, 46–51, 59, 61, 71, 78, 124, 207, 265
Tarde, 250
Tautologies, 205
Taylor, 74, 261
Telepathy, 184
Tempo, 32–5
Tennyson, 283, 290
Tenseless language, 80–5
Thermodynamics, Second Law of, 144, 264–5
Thinghood, 95–7
Time-traveller, paradox, 211–13

Transience, 1, 41, 218, 237, 280, 288, 290–3
True, and false, 260–2

Ultimacy of time, 283, 284, 293
Unconscious, 182–3
Unidirectional, 25, 229, 236
Universal and particular, 290, 292
Universe of Discourse, 193
Unreversedness, 222–3, 236, 263
Urban, 283

Value, 275–7, 283–5, 288–93
Van Biema, 93
Verne, 206
Vierordt, 30, 34
Von Baer, 33
Von Cyon, 34
Von Hügel, 79, 283, 292

Ward, 21, 23, 24
Weber, 38, 46, 207, 217
Wells, 226
Westaway, 39
Weyl, 46
Whitehead, 54, 55, 57, 75, 104, 228, 269, 277
Wilcox, 288
Wisdom, 152
Wohlgemuth, 34
Wordsworth, 181
Wundt, 30

Zeno, 7

For Product Safety Concerns and Information please contact our EU representative GPSR@taylorandfrancis.com
Taylor & Francis Verlag GmbH, Kaufingerstraße 24, 80331 München, Germany

www.ingramcontent.com/pod-product-compliance
Lightning Source LLC
Chambersburg PA
CBHW052031300426
44116CB00024B/1179